WOMEN IN PERFORMANCE

Women in Performance: *Repurposing Failure* charts the renewed popularity of intersectional feminism, gender, race and identity politics in contemporary Western
experimental theatre, comedy and performance through the featured artists' ability
to strategically repurpose failure.

Failure has provided a popular frame through which to theorise recent avant-
garde performance, even though the work rarely acknowledges stakes tend to be
higher for women than men. This book analyses the imperative work of a number
of female, non-binary and trans★ practitioners who resist the postmodern doctrine
of 'post-identity' and attempt to foster a sense of agency on stage. By using feminism as a critical lens, Gorman interrogates received ideas about performance failure and negotiates contradictions between contemporary white feminism,
intersectional feminism, gender and sexuality.

Women in Performance: *Repurposing Failure* reveals how performance has the power to
both observe and reject contemporary feminist and postmodern theory, rendering this
text an invaluable resource for theatre and performance studies students and those
grappling with the disciplinary tensions between feminism, gender, queer and trans★
studies.

Sarah Gorman is a Reader in Drama, Theatre & Performance at the University of
Roehampton, London, UK.

WOMEN IN PERFORMANCE

Repurposing Failure

Sarah Gorman

Routledge
Taylor & Francis Group

LONDON AND NEW YORK

First published 2021
by Routledge
2 Park Square, Milton Park, Abingdon, Oxon OX14 4RN

and by Routledge
52 Vanderbilt Avenue, New York, NY 10017

Routledge is an imprint of the Taylor & Francis Group, an informa business

British Library Cataloguing-in-Publication Data
A catalogue record for this book is available from the British Library

Library of Congress Cataloging-in-Publication Data
Names: Gorman, Sarah, 1969- author.
Title: Women in performance : repurposing failure / Sarah Gorman.
Description: London ; New York : Routledge, 2020. |
Includes bibliographical references and index.
Identifiers: LCCN 2020010840 (print) | LCCN 2020010841 (ebook) |
ISBN 9781138223356 (paperback) | ISBN 9781138223332 (hardback) |
ISBN 9781315404905 (ebook)
Subjects: LCSH: Women in the theater. | Women in the performing arts. |
Failure (Psychology) | Performance--Psychological aspects. |
Theater--Psychological aspects. | Feminism and theater.
Classification: LCC PN1590.W64 G67 2020 (print) |
LCC PN1590.W64 (ebook) |
DDC 792.082--dc23
LC record available at https://lccn.loc.gov/2020010840
LC ebook record available at https://lccn.loc.gov/2020010841

ISBN: 978-1-138-22333-2 (hbk)
ISBN: 978-1-138-22335-6 (pbk)
ISBN: 978-1-315-40490-5 (ebk)

Typeset in Bembo
by Taylor & Francis Books

For Marjorie, Emily, Paul, and my father Jeff who passed away two days after I submitted the first draft of the manuscript. Thanks for your patience, Dad!

CONTENTS

FIGURES

ACKNOWLEDGEMENTS

I am grateful to all at Taylor and Francis and Routledge who have supported and encouraged the development of this project. I would like to thank my colleagues and students at Roehampton University, past and present, particularly those in the Department of Drama, Theatre & Performance. I would like to thank Carrie Hamilton and Caroline Bainbridge for their inter-departmental friendship and support. Thanks to Roehampton University's Research Office for supporting the final stages of writing and Eve and Ravenscroft for subsidising my *Performance Dialogues* project. Thanks to colleagues who have agreed to act as readers and mentors for funding applications: Lib Taylor, Roberta Mock, Emma Brodzinski and Trish Reid – particular thanks to Roberta for the brilliant Angry Wonder Woman gif she sent when we found out I had not been successful. A big thanks to colleagues who came to support the Congruence and Contestation Event at Roehampton University in 2015, in particular Lynette Leni Goddard, Jen Harvie, Annalaura Alifuoco, Johanna Linsley and Gerry Harris. Especial thanks to Jen and Gerry for collaborating on the special edition of *Contemporary Theatre Review,* published September 2018. Thanks to colleagues in the IFTR Feminism Working Group for valuable feedback on work in progress, in particular to Sarah Balkin, Aoife Monks, Elaine Aston and Paul Rae. Thanks to colleagues who have supported other recent talks and publications including: Bryce Lease, Dominic Johnson, Helen Nicholson, Maggie Gale, Clio Unger, Richard Gough, Caoimhe Mader McGuinness, Fintan Walsh, Graham Saunders, Nadine Holdsworth, Jesús Sanjurjo, Lisa Watts, Gianna Bouchard, Eleanor Roberts and Graham White. Thanks to Alissa Clarke, Rob Brannen and Ramsay Burt for inviting me to present my paper on Selina Thompson's *salt.* at DMU's *Borderlines VIII* event and to Jacki Willson, Jenny Lawson and Anna Fenemore for organising the wonderful *Lived Body in Performance* Symposium in Leeds. Thanks to colleagues who have taken time to talk over ideas: Sara Jane Bailes, Karen Juers-Munby, Alex Mermikides,

Lena Simic, Louise Owen, Dee Heddon and Sophie Nield. Thanks to Rachael Young, Lauren Barri Holstein, Lois Weaver, Karen Christopher, Selina Thompson and GETINTHEBACKOFTHEVAN who agreed to be interviewed as part of *Performance Dialogues*. Thank you to the artists, producers and promoters who have read over material and helped find photographs: Rachael Young, Anna Smith, Lucy McCormick, Bryony Kimmings, Phillipa Barr, Lucy Hutson, Annie Siddons, Charlotte Boden, Hester Chillingworth, Emma Beverley, Selina Thompson, Amanda Emery, Bridget Christie and Andrea Watson. Thanks to Adriana Nicolau Jiménez for her useful and timely review of Anglophone feminist theory and to George Easterbrook for recommending Annie Siddons' piece for this project. On the home front I would like to thank Marjorie, Jeff, Emily and Paul and the rest of the mighty Boult/Wilding/Gorman/Lansley clan. Thanks to all our friends who keep us optimistic and especial thanks to 360HC Homecare who have provided outstanding care for my Dad in the last months of this life and to Clare Battle and Liz Meenan for helping keep Mum sane. Thanks finally to the many friends and colleagues who, over the years, have shared the occasionally harrowing, always challenging experience of theatre-going.

1

INTRODUCTION: FEMALE AGENCY, ESSENTIALISM, NEGATIVITY AND THE REBIRTH OF IDENTITY POLITICS

It is a warm May evening in 2016, I find myself being ushered into a small studio upstairs at Battersea Arts Centre, London. The solo performer greets me at the door; she takes time to make eye contact and smiles warmly at each person as they enter. Seats are arranged in two blocks, each row level with the stage and small floor lights demarcate the performance area. The stage is set with: a heap of compost; a stretch of fake grass; a gold painted vase; a heap of gold fabric; a paper projection screen; a microphone; and brightly coloured potted plants. Rachael Young, the performer who welcomed me into the space, employs direct address to tell the audience of her experience coming to terms with her mother's death and visiting the grave for the first time in 11 years. She explains that after her loss she felt emotionally adrift and struggled to find a place in the world. The image on the front cover of the book is taken from this piece: *I, Myself and Me* by Rachael Young. She is shown reading from a list of internalised 'rules' she has gleaned from family and local community. At the outset the list appeared diminutive, it fitted neatly into her hand, but a comedic flick of the wrist revealed it to be significantly longer. With a deft sleight of hand Young let the remainder of the paper fall – it reamed from her hands and spooled copiously at her feet. Her list, or the 'black mantra' as she has called it, includes the directive to assimilate; to play down references to cultural difference; to 'settle down', 'get married' and have children. The list of rules includes contradictory information: to assimilate but concurrently become 'blacker;' to mimic stereotypes from popular culture: to have 'hard nipples' and a 'big ass' (Young 2016). *I, Myself and Me* is revelatory in that it actively critiques the multiple social directives aimed at young Black British women. It illustrates the social forces brought to bear upon a young woman by white supremacist culture and Afro-Caribbean culture. Young is one of a number of contemporary artists borrowing stylistic techniques from what Sara Jane Bailes has called a 'poetics of failure'. Until recently it was unusual to see these techniques used in an autobiographical context. Young performatively articulates her sense of self in relation to the hegemonic perception of 'failure'. She is *repurposing* failure because by performatively naming or 'calling out' the varying sources of oppression she garners a sense of agency and self-possession. Rather than experiencing failure as a disoriented, decentred 'failed' postmodern subject she recalibrates, or centres herself by ridiculing the manifold strictures she is required to observe.

Young is part of a new wave of female theatre makers and activists taking to the stage and streets to protest the resurgence of racist, misogynistic and homophobic values. A significant number of artists have chosen to return to the topic of 'identity politics' despite it having been denounced as anachronistic by postmodern cultural commentators such as Nicolas Bourriaud and Claire Bishop (Johnson 2013: 27). Artists such as Split Britches, Rachael Young, Selina Thompson and Bryony Kimmings have returned to the subject of identity in order to protest the rise of intolerant alt-right politics in a number of Western countries. This movement can be attributed in part to the global economic downturn of 2008. Conservative politicians such as Donald Trump, Boris Johnson and Nigel Farage have exploited the economic recession, using it as a means to promote a neoliberal capitalist agenda and argue that the increasing scarcity of resources is due to overpopulation and relaxed immigration policies rather than government decisions to scale back funding for public services. Opposition to neoliberalism has galvanised the concentration in feminist activity taking place across the globe. January 2017 saw protests against the inauguration of misogynistic US President Trump across Australia, Canada, Germany, the UK, the USA, China and India. The #MeToo movement met with global appeal with the social media hash tag adopted worldwide. *Bloomberg* reports that the day after Alyssa Milano asked Twitter followers to share their experiences of sexual harassment the #MeToo hashtag had been used 609,000 times (Griffin, Recht and Green 2018). Since 2012 numerous protests have taken place across India protesting against rape, with nuns recently speaking out against abuse in the Catholic Church. Mass protests have taken place in Poland against legislation to restrict women's access to abortion. In October 2018 women in Iceland staged a national walkout to protest against disparity in pay. The International Women's March in 2019 saw 80 events mounted across 31 different cities (Durkin and Busby 2019). In August 2019 in Mexico City women gathered to draw attention to the alleged rape of two teenage girls by police officers. The World Economic Forum reported that the Global Gender Pay Gap would take 202 years to close (Neate 2018).

The rise of social media has helped galvanise mass protest, with activists mobilising around issues such as Female Genital Mutilation, femicide, taxation on sanitary products and abortion legislation. Activist groups include One Billion Rising, Femen, Slutwalks, Daughters of Eve, Nuestras Hijas de Regreso a Casa (May our Daughters Return Home), Las Hijas de Violencia, West African Women's Rights Coalition, Project Alert on Violence Against Women, Pussy Riot, #BringBackOurGirls and many more. Although not all women feel included by the ideology of Western feminism, it is clear that women are mobilising to protest against growing levels of inequality.[1] The global economic downturn is customarily dated from 2008 and it is no coincidence that minoritarian groups began to convene around specific examples of social injustice around that time. Performances about subaltern categories relating to class, race, gender, disability and sexuality began to enjoy increased visibility on the UK stage from 2009 onwards. According to Stephen Farrier the postmodern turn towards queerness resulted in a 'tacit declaration of the death of identity politics' (Farrier 2013: 49). In spite of this artists increasingly marginalised by the economic downturn began to mobilise and create work around specific identity categories. Amelia Jones gave voice to the groundswell, announcing 'we are not "post" identity' (Jones 2012: xix). Whereas 'feminism' was regarded as anachronistic in the mid 1990s and early 2000s by 2010 it was enjoying a renewed sense of vigour (Hardy et al. 2014). *Harry Potter* star Emma Watson became UN Women's Goodwill Ambassador with *Paper Magazine* publishing her conversation with renowned feminist writer bell hooks as part of its 'Girl Crush' series (hooks and Watson 2016). Roxane Gay's *Bad Feminist* (2014), Chimamanda Ngozi Adichie's *We Should All Be Feminists* (2014) and Caitlin Moran's *How to Be a Woman* (2012) all became best sellers. Promotional copy for the 2019 *Calm Down Dear Festival* at Camden People's Theatre posed the question,

> [w]ho would have thought that when we took a punt in 2013 on programming our first ever festival of far-out feminist theatre – this was back when there was still some timidity around the word – that 'Calm Down, Dear' would one day be an unmissable feature of CPT's annual programme?[2]

I am aware that not all theatre makers have responded to the global economic downturn in the same way, but activists have felt the need to protest against the legislation of more conservative governments as they have been elected in countries such as Italy, Finland, Latvia, Sweden, Romania, Australia and the US. Sarah French has observed,

> [t]he growth in feminist independent performance during [2005–2015] can be viewed as a response to the increased presence of sexism in Australian society, in which feminist theatre-makers sought to critique public debates about gender roles and offer a counter-narrative to dominant discourses.
>
> *(French 2017: 5)*

After what Elaine Aston has described as 'feminism fatigue' in the 1990s and early 2000s, the late 2000s to 2010s has seen a wide range of artists mounting critically lauded productions exploring interlocking oppressions of gender, race, class, disability and sexuality (Aston 2013: 24).

This project is the culmination of research undertaken, over the last ten years, into the recalibration of identity politics, feminism and gender studies in Western performance. It responds to a perceived tension between the now established discourses of performing failure, postmodern and intersectional feminism. The praxis of performing failure has come to exemplify postmodern and postdramatic performance and as a result can be seen to replicate postmodern theories of human subjectivity and agency. Postmodern gender theorists, most notably Judith Butler, reject essentialising subject categories, such as 'man' and 'woman', and champion incomplete, queer subjectivities that remain fluid and indeterminate. In contrast, many contemporary identity theorists such as Kay Inckle and Rebecca Reilly-Cooper writing in the area of feminism, trans★ and disabled subjectivities find they are loath to renounced fixed identities and subject positions because, for better or worse, they inform the material experience of their day-to-day lives and provide a crucial concept around which to forge activist communities. The book is entitled *Women in Performance: Repurposing Failure* because it takes as its object of study the work of a number of female, trans★ and non-binary artists who borrow techniques from the praxis of performing failure and adapt them to foster a sense of agency on stage. The idea of a subject with agency is at odds with the 'post-humanist wave' that Rosi Braidotti suggests 'radicalises the premises of postmodernist feminism' (Braidotti 2010: 178). My chosen artists are trans★, non-binary or women in the inclusive sense and are *repurposing* failure because they borrow recognised stylistic techniques from postmodern practice whilst strategically occupying a clearly defined subject position. Featured artists include Rachael Young (see cover photograph); Young Jean Lee; Lauren Barri Holstein; GETINTHEBACK-OFTHEVAN; Selina Thompson; Bryony Kimmings; Project O; Lucy McCormick; Lucy Hutson; Kate Bornstein; Lois Weaver; Hester Chillingworth; Curious; Haranczak/Navarre; Bridget Christie; Lolly Adefope; Shazia Mirza; and Hannah Gadsby. Throughout the book I analyse challenging examples of work encouraging audiences to revisit hegemonic assumptions about identity and performance. Many of the performances, in so far as they push against notions of cultural propriety and behavioural constraint, may be regarded as controversial. Several examples are explicit and feature nudity, sex acts and swearing. If you are of a delicate disposition and likely to be offended by profanity and nudity then it may be a good idea to return this book to the shelf. The performances include moments of comedy and conversely critique *and* celebrate elements of Western popular culture. Some performances took place more recently than others and all provide the opportunity to engage imaginatively with gender politics and contemplate the tensions between those who theorise gender and those who interrogate it through performance. There have been crucial challenges to white feminism over the past 20 years and this project has given me the opportunity to consider how more recent strains of feminism have taken on board theories relating to race, queerness, intersectionality and trans★ theory.[3] The book draws from a wide range of disciplines: postmodernism; poststructuralism; intersectional feminism, white feminism, performance studies, Black feminism; scenography; queer studies; trans★ studies; sociology; disability studies; and comedy studies. My aim has been to gather examples of performance demonstrating a preoccupation with gendered, racial, class and ethnic identity, although I recognise there are a great many artists whose work I have not been able to include and many subject positions unaddressed. The majority of artists identify as feminist, although some, such as Rachael Young, explicitly state that they choose not to because they consider feminism to refer to an exclusionary white feminism. Some of the artists, such as GETINTHEBACKOFTHEVAN and Selina Thompson, distance themselves from conventional models of feminism whilst acknowledging that it remains important and relevant. I perform discrete readings of the performances, but within each chapter I also work to identify overlapping themes and ideas. For example, in one chapter I analyse how three different artists transform theatre spaces into club-like environments; in another I analyse the different relationships four comedians have to anger and comedy personae. Many of the performances work to challenge a white supremacist, patriarchal hegemony and although many artists identify as subaltern or minoritarian, they often resist processes associated with labelling and objectification. The featured artists detail the manifold ways in which they are shaped by oppressive discourses and push back against racist, sexist, colour and gender blind practice.

For the last 25 years my research interests have been situated in the field of gender studies, feminism, feminist performance, postmodern performance and a poetics of failure. A tension exists between subjects and I have become increasingly fascinated by the contradictions implied by mapping identity politics on to the recently established discourse of performing failure. As intimated above, mapping identity on to postmodern theory and performance is problematic because the discourse of feminism relies on the sovereign concept of 'woman', considered by some problematically reductive, essentialist and fixed. Sara Ahmed has observed, 'the model of feminism as humanist in practice and postmodern in theory is inadequate … feminist practice questions the humanist conception of the subject as self-identity' (Ahmed 1996: 71). Andy Lavender has written of his sense that contemporary artists demonstrate 'a new fascination with authenticity', suggesting a move 'beyond' postmodernism into post-postmodernism (Lavender 2016: 23). In relation to centred or sovereign subjects he writes:

> After decentring, we found ourselves diversely centred. To address a tense present: we are amid interdisciplinary cultural formations, interested in meaning, representation, utterance and content, but also mindful of display, surfaces, presentation. […] After the clarion calls of modernism, and the absences and ironies of postmodernism, come the nuanced and differential negotiations, participations and interventions of an age of engagement.
>
> *(21)*

Working along similar lines to Lavender and Ahmed, I aim to interrogate the work of artists who engage with humanist notions of subjectivity and 'authenticity' whilst incorporating elements of postmodern performance praxis.

In 2013 I articulated my sense that feminism and identity politics had taken a leave of absence from the UK stage and championed Nic Green's 2009 production of *Trilogy* as a 'return' of feminism (Gorman 2013). Around the same time I saw

Bridget Christie perform her award-winning comedy set *A Bic for Her* and was surprised by how refreshing and unusual it felt to hear the word 'feminist' used in a public arena. Prior to 2008 the UK alternative performance scene had become preoccupied by a tone of irony and self-reflexivity, features associated with post-modern performance, and, as part of this, had come to see identity politics as out-moded, irrelevant or anachronistic. I recognise that my sense of 'loss' or 'absence' is culture-specific, and realise that this pattern has not necessarily been replicated in other countries. Being located in the UK, and London in particular, I will inevi-tably be responding to a specific socio-cultural climate. It is possible to think about the influence of the postmodern aesthetic as fairly wide-reaching across mainland Europe and many Anglophone countries. In selecting my examples I have taken the decision to move away from a geographical 'survey' format because no authentic survey can ever truly be accomplished and even the bravest attempt would entail a truly disastrous carbon footprint. *Women in Performance: Repurposing Failure* sets out to capture the energy and techniques of cutting edge performance whilst situating the work in an intersectional feminist context. The book includes a number of examples of underexposed artists from the UK and US and documents an explosion in cultural activity at a particular historical juncture. Ten years on from Green's *Trilogy* I am struggling to keep up with the volume of performances by artists of colour, trans★ artists, female artists, non-binary artists, all interrogating gender and identity construction in myriad ways. Despite the perceived shift towards the right in government politics, in the UK, at least, there has been a substantial shift in the willingness of arts organisations to fund and promote per-formances about subjectivity, race, disability, class and gender.[4]

Over the course of my research – reading, interviewing, watching, reviewing, attending symposia, presenting papers – it emerged that for some feminism was and is exclusionary. Some artists of colour, such as Rachael Young, choose not to identify as feminist, not because they are unsympathetic to its cause, but because they see the movement, as it has been informed to date, to stand for *white* femin-ism. Historically white feminism has marginalised the experience of non-white middle-class women and at times been explicitly racist. Hazel Carby wrote 'White Women Listen!' in 1982 asserting, 'Black women do not want to be grafted on to "feminism" in a tokenistic manner as colourful diversions to "real" problems. Feminism has to be transformed if it is to address us' (Carby 1982: 128). That is not to say that all artists or writers of colour reject the term, many, such as Reni Eddo-Lodge and Selina Thompson, analyse their relationship to the term and state that despite its flawed history, it can still offer a useful way of identifying and naming different strands of structural inequality (Eddo-Lodge 2018a; Thompson 2018). In addition to registering the need to revise my own practice and understanding of feminism, I have become fascinated by the way the figure of 'woman' has come to metaphorically stand for the decentred, 'failing' subject of postmodernism. Like Braidotti I am disconcerted that the preferred way of signifying the modernist subject in crisis is to construct it as 'feminine' or 'feminised' and consequently denuded of rationality, fragmented and incomplete. Under postmodernism theories of subjectivity were radically reconceived whilst values associated with femininity and womanhood often went unchallenged. Braidotti described Gilles Deleuze's theory of 'becoming-woman' as 'a privileged position for the minority-consciousness of all' (Braidotti 2011: loc.4742). Similarly, Laura Cull Ó Maoilearca has observed that Deleuze's theories of 'becoming-woman' initially appear sympathetic to feminism but the denial of full subjectivity can be problematic. She writes,

> at a point when the gender gap in wages for UK workers appears to be widening rather than diminishing [...] many feminists are unwilling to abandon the struggle for equality, albeit that this struggle seems to require a strategic identification of oneself as some thing called a 'woman'.
>
> *(Cull Ó Maoilearca 2009)*

Throughout the process of mapping identity politics on to postmodern theory and performance I encountered similarly problematic metaphors relating to mental illness and disability. Frederic Jameson, in his seminal essay 'Postmodernism and Consumer Society', describes the postmodern experience of time as 'schizophrenic', borrowing the term as a way to illustrate the disorienting experience of trying to use linear linguistic syntax to describe the experience of postmodern time and space (Jameson 1985: 118). Lennard J. Davis has developed a theory of 'dismodern' subjectivity, arguing for 'disability as *the* postmodern subject position' (Davis 2013: 265 my emphasis) and Stephanie Jensen-Moulton conjectures that postmodern theatre maker Robert Wilson collaborated with disabled teenagers because 'disability itself represents the postmodern state' (Jensen-Moulton 2012). This exercise in mapping revealed that 'identity politics' had been supplanted by a postmodern theory of queer indeterminacy and flux, which, in turn, resulted in affective values being appropriated.[5] Fixed subaltern or minoritarian identity categories were deemed reductive and assimilative and useful only to the extent that they could stand in for the decentred, chaotic postmodern subject. Braidotti articulates her frustration with the gender blindness of poststructuralist and postmodern theory and is critical of Deleuze's drive to erase the difference between men and women. She writes:

> As far as the project of feminism goes, this fantasy can lead to the homologation of women into a masculine model. In a cultural order that, for centuries, has been governed by the male homosocial bond, the elimination of sexual difference can only be a one-way street toward the appropriation, elimination, or homologation of the feminine in/of women; it is a toy for the boys.
>
> *(Braidotti 1994: 185)*

Bailes acknowledges the artists described in *Performance Theatre and the Poetics of Failure* 'occupy what is generally described as the postmodern period' and their practice is congruent with much of Hans-Thies Lehmann's theory of the 'post-dramatic' (Bailes 2011: 3). Bailes has analysed the work of Samuel Beckett,

Elevator Repair Service, Forced Entertainment, Goat Island and mentions Richard Maxwell and the New York City Players, Kim Noble and Richard Dedomenici in addition to other artists. Contemporaries can be seen to include: Reckless Sleepers, Nature Theatre Oklahoma, Radiohole, Dood Pard, Sleepwalk Collective, Dead Centre and Jérôme Bel (prior to his work with Theater HORA). Failure, risk and indeterminacy are also crucial to much Live Art and Performance Art, with artists such as Marina Abramovic, Ron Athey, Franko B, Nao Bustamante, Vaginal Davis, Jack Smith, La Chica Boom working with contingency to maximise a risk of failure. Interestingly Johnson has observed that within the 'broad church' of Live Art, 'examinations of identity politics … have persisted amid the trend towards participatory, relational, applied or socially engaged' work (Johnson 2013: 25). The performance artists listed above regularly draw attention to the postmodern sense that it is impossible for the artist to be fully 'present' and the project of representation is forever beyond our reach. The work is self-reflexive and draws attention to the performative apparatus supporting work in either the modernist art gallery, proscenium arch theatre or modernist dance studio. Although these artists employ a variety of methods the figures on stage are often louche, uncertain and inept whilst manifesting nostalgia for a time when the authority of the artist was undisputed. The more theatrical work in this field, produced by companies such as Forced Entertainment, Goat Island and New York City Players, tends to be post-Brechtian in form and borrows techniques of distanciation whilst holding back from presenting a coherent image or theory of the world. Figures on stage are marked by a sense of amateurism or the failure to successfully realise the task in hand. The task might be to communicate effectively, to execute a piece of complex choreography or explain the purpose of their endeavour. Markus Wessendorf identifies the 'failure' within Richard Maxwell's work in his depiction of inarticulate characters who turn out to be 'losers in a society that reveres self-exposure' (Wessendorf 2001: 455). It is questionable whether any of the practitioners listed above deliberately set out to create a piece of 'postmodern' art or performance *about* failure, however their collective scepticism about the project of representation and the portrayal of fallible, insecure subjects is congruent with postmodern and poststructuralist theory and has been well documented by a range of established scholars (Ridout 2006; Bailes 2011; Power 2010; Muñoz 2009; Tomlin 2013; Bottoms 2007; O'Gorman and Werry 2012; Cerrato 1993; Gorman 2011). Within the praxis of performing failure figures on stage tend to be robbed of agency and unable to celebrate the 'solace' Lyotard attributes to realist narratives (Lyotard 1979: 81).

When considered through an intersectional lens the more theatrical of the artists listed above, such as Goat Island and Forced Entertainment, can be seen to operate according to an ideology of equivalence, or sameness, as if gender, ability and race are not factors mitigating the likelihood of failure.[6] In Braidotti's terms the 'fantasy' of sexual equivalence runs the risk of assimilating women into a masculine model. She writes that erasing the ontological difference between men and women is a 'one-way street toward the appropriation, elimination, or homologation of the feminine in/of women' (Braidotti 1994: 185). Applying intersectional theory to the unmarked indicators of race, gender and ability in postmodern theatre demonstrates how the fantasy of sameness risks assimilating the experiences of minoritarian subjects into a white, cis-gendered, able-bodied, masculine model of subjectivity. The tension between postmodernism and feminism has been widely documented and I will go on to explore this in more detail. Feminism and postmodernism are celebrated by Seyla Benhabib as being 'two leading currents of our time' and possessing, 'affinities in the struggle against the grand narratives of the Western Enlightenment and modernity' (Benhabib 1995: 17). However she warns,

> [p]ostmodernism can teach us the theoretical and political traps of why utopias and foundational thinking can go wrong, but it should not lead to a retreat from utopia altogether. For we, as women, have much to lose by giving up the utopian hope in the wholly other.
>
> *(30)*

Dissonance between identity politics and a postmodern praxis of failure can be identified in the work of Jérôme Bel and Kim Noble, although this tension occurs between issues of disability, class and postmodern praxis rather than feminism. In 2017 I wrote of Bel's work with Swiss company Theater HORA. His work has been widely celebrated by performance theorists, with André Lepecki arguing that Bel's oeuvre celebrates a poststructuralist critique of representation due in particular to its focus upon the 'still' and the 'slow'. According to Lepecki it demonstrates 'paranomasia', the 'interrogation of choreography's political ontology' (Lepecki 2006: 45). Theater HORA is a company of disabled actors who invited Bel to work with them in 2013. *Disabled Theater* was the resulting piece, which toured internationally for several years to great acclaim. Bel has described his work as 'political', asserting that 'it is political in the bodies of the performers I choose. It is difficult for example, for me to work with somebody very strong and beautiful! I have clearly decided to represent weak bodies' (Bauer 2008: 48). *Disabled Theater* represents an example of performing failure that puts questions of identity and *ability* centre stage. This piece played with the notion that disabled bodies could 'disable' the representational apparatus of theatre (Umathum and Wihstutz 2015: 7). I found this idea unnerving because, if this were the case, it meant that the performers' bodies were being actively co-opted, by an able-bodied choreographer, as metaphors for a rhetorical conceit. However, despite my reservations I came to the conclusion that Bel was borrowing the metaphorical weight of 'disability' in good faith and his intention was to deconstruct values associated with modernist dance while productively foregrounding the unmarked able-ism of those who employ the praxis of performing failure. Prior to Bel's collaboration with Theater HORA the able-ism of work in this area had gone unmarked. Able-bodied performers may be failing in their attempts to *represent*, but their relative privilege ensures that they are inured from the majority of social and cultural indignities.

I was similarly unsettled by Kim Noble's *You're Not Alone* (2015) another highly celebrated piece of work about failure. In this piece Noble constructs himself as sexually undesirable, lonely, vulnerable and deeply insecure. As part of the performance Noble dresses as his female alter ego Sarah and shares footage of his elderly father in a residential care home. Part of the performance revolves around the story of Noble befriending a male cashier named Keith at a local branch of Morrisons supermarket. He went on to follow Keith, incorporating undercover material and footage from their encounters into the show. *You're Not Alone* amassed a collection of sad, lonely, dysfunctional figures in a way that was deeply affecting, however I came away with the uncomfortable sense that Noble was in a position to recuperate a sense of dignity and self-worth from the enthusiastic reviews he garnered, whereas his 'friend', Keith, the cashier from Morrisons, remained an object of ridicule. The depiction of lonely, 'failed' characters ironically elevated Noble's status, he received four-star reviews and the piece was recognised as a notable success (Caird 2015; Hitchings 2015). It was clear that no matter how debased or inferior Noble proclaimed himself to be, he considered himself superior to the checkout worker and felt entitled to exploit intimate details of Keith's life for the sake of a potentially lucrative work of art. I share these examples of Bel and Noble's work in order to articulate my hesitancy about artists employing a praxis and poetics of failure without acknowledging that social status associated with race, social class and education play a key factor in facilitating social mobility and success. With the exception of the performance artists listed above, key practitioners are almost all white, cis-gendered, middle-class and able-bodied and these aspects of their identity customarily go unmarked. Failure to factor social mobility, access and physical ability on to the discourse of failure represents a key oversight and one that I will seek to address. The irony of my writing about failure as a white, middle-class, able-bodied academic is not lost on me and represents an issue to which I will return when I discuss Crenshaw's theory of intersectionality.

Within recognised examples of performing failure by companies such as Forced Entertainment, Goat Island and the New York City Players male and female performers work alongside each other as if equals, there is little sense that gender, class or race inflects the likelihood of failure because even gender as a mark of difference largely goes unmarked. This idealistic portrayal of gender parity should be seen to offer optimism and hope with regards to the feminist project, however it seems ultimately disingenuous to construct an illusion of parity when dramatising or interrogating failure. For scholars such as Braidotti and Luce Irigaray gender blind practice repeats assumptions found in Western philosophy about the sovereignty of the white male subject. Irigaray considers the drive to eradicate difference deeply problematic:

> this domination of the philosophic logos stems in large part from its power to *reduce all others to the economy of the same*. The teleologically constructed project it takes on is always also a project of diversion, deflection, reduction of the other in the same. And, in its greatest generality perhaps, from its power to

eradicate the difference between the sexes in systems that are self-representative of a 'masculine subject'.

(Irigaray 1985: 74, original emphasis)

Braidotti champions Irigaray's insistence upon sexual identity as a key ontological difference. She observes that for Irigaray, 'the difference between the sexes is radical, and it is constitutive of the human experience; it should be listed along-side mortality as the ineluctable frame of reference of the human being' (Braidotti 1994: 131). The praxis and poetics of performing failure can be seen to adopt a philosophical approach to representation and ontology and in attempting, in Irigaray's words, to 'reduce all others to the economy of the same' repeats differential blindness found in Western philosophical discourse. Braidotti sees Irigaray's insistence upon marking sexual difference as part of a 'political strategy aimed at stating the specificity of female subjectivity, sexuality and experience while also denouncing the logic of sexual indifferentiation of phallogocentric discourse' (131). I intend to adopt Irigaray's political strategy in reading examples of contemporary women's performance through the lens of ontological difference.

The artists repurposing failure within this book deliberately identify as 'other' or 'marginal' and actively choose to align themselves with at least one subaltern category. Theoretically this represents a return to essentialism, a position castigated by postmodernists and materialist feminists in the 1990s and 2000s (hooks 2015a; Braidotti 1994; Johnson 2013; Heddon 2012; Waugh 1998). However, the artists I discuss are liberated by a departure from the pressure to ascribe to particular feminist or gender theories and take to the stage in order to actively claim a position of agency. They can be seen to adopt an essentialist belief in ontological difference as political strategy and as a result their position is in keeping with that of Irigaray and Braidotti. The artists detail interlocking experiences of oppression, celebrate their cause and unapologetically rekindle an agenda for identity politics. For my chosen artists the current political climate is coercive and biased, they remain unconcerned that a fixed subject position might be seen to represent a linguistic mystification because there is work to be done drawing attention to systemic inequality. They are unfazed by Peggy Phelan's influential argument that visibility politics are 'compatible with capitalism's relentless appetite for new markets' and actively hone an illusion of self-possession (Phelan 1993: 11). They actively work to increase visibility by situating themselves centre stage and campaigning to make their voices heard.

Contemporary Western artists operate in a historical moment marked by neo-liberal 'precarity' and risk. The onus is on artists to support themselves financially and emotionally and find entrepreneurial ways to communicate a distinct world-view. Jen Harvie has defined neoliberalism as:

> [t]he revived form of liberalism which thrived first in Britain in the seven-teenth century and which recognizes and prioritizes the individual's right to seek self-fulfillment ... unrestricted by state-instituted regulations such as the

requirements to pay appropriate taxes, to heed trade restrictions or to observe employment laws ... In neoliberal capitalism, these principles of reduced state intervention and enhanced individual liberty to seek self-reward work in the service of maximizing private profit.

(Harvie 2013: 12)

For Rósín O'Gorman and Margaret Werry 'failure' has become 'trendy' and corporatised through neoliberal ideology. Risk and failure have been championed by business corporations, celebrated as a means of forging a pathway towards entrepreneurial discovery and financial success. They write:

Glossy feature articles everywhere from the *New York Times* to *Harvard Business Review* instruct us that we must fail in order to succeed ... Failure, in their eyes, is both the bed-partner of that neo-liberal fetish innovation and a necessity in a world without guarantees: in getting comfortable with failure, they imply, we can also get comfortable with neo-liberalism's other intimate, precarity.

(O'Gorman and Werry 2012: 1)

As O'Gorman and Werry imply, a number of business publications have appropriated the discourse of failure, some going so far as to borrow Samuel Beckett's celebrated quotation from *Worstward Ho* (1983): 'Ever tried. Ever failed. No matter. Try again. Fail again. Fail better' (Beckett 1999: 1). Publications such as *Open Culture* have announced, 'here in Silicon Valley, failure isn't always failure. At least according to the local mythology, it's something to be embraced, accepted, even celebrated. "Fail fast, fail often," they say. And eventually you'll learn enough to achieve real success' (Colman 2017). In *Slate.com* Mark O'Connell observes:

Fail Better, with its TEDishly counterintuitive feel, is the literary takeaway par excellence; it's usefully suggestive, too, of the corporate propaganda of productivity, with its appeal to 'think different' or 'work smarter' or 'just do it' ... Failure, in the #failbetter sense, is something to be embraced and celebrated, to be approached with a view to understanding how it might most effectively be transmuted into success.

(O'Connell 2014)

Mitch Sava and Jonathan Jewell point out that 'Penn State University even has a course for engineering students called Failure 101, encouraging experimentation and radical creativity' (Hilson 2011: loc. 132). Sava and Jewell regard failure apart from its potential to inform success. They argue that 'UK society has long been seen to be characterised by a pervasive fear of failure. But to shield ourselves from failure is to deny ourselves the fruits of our creative potential. It also makes our lives boring' (Loc. 3). In *Performance Theatre and the Poetics of Failure* Bailes sees the praxis of failure as part of a radical antiauthoritarian politics. She argues for its anticapitalist potential:

> The discourse of failure as reflected in western art and literature seems to counter the very ideas of progress and victory that simultaneously dominate historical narratives. It undermines the perceived stability of mainstream capitalist ideology's preferred aspiration to achieve, succeed, or win, and the accumulation of material wealth as proof and effect arranged by those aims.
>
> *(Bailes 2011: 2)*

Bailes argues for failure as an anti-capitalist aesthetic, and yet almost a decade after the publication of her seminal book, failure has been appropriated by the very discourse it sets out to critique. For Silicon Valley entrepreneurs the pedagogic value of failure is championed as an essential component of success, but it is unlikely to be entertained as part of a counter-cultural message. This more permissive attitude towards failure should be welcomed and yet the neoliberal attenuation orients the message strongly towards success and ultimately leaves the capitalist values celebrating success over failure in place.

Failure has found further popularity in popular discourses around self-help and self-care. For example, Elizabeth Day published *How to Fail: Everything I've Ever Learned From Things Going Wrong*, drawing upon the success of her podcast series *How to Fail with Elizabeth Day*. She includes thirteen chapters, each beginning 'How to Fail at …' with the relevant social imperative furnished to complete the phrase. Chapters include 'How to Fail at Fitting In'; 'How to Fail at Dating'; 'How to Fail at Babies' and 'How to Fail at Success' (Day 2019: contents page). She writes,

> I'm not actively advocating failure. It's that we will all experience it at some juncture in our lives, and that instead of fearing failure as a calamity from which it is impossible to recover, maybe we can build up the muscle of our emotional resilience by learning from others.
>
> *(Day 2019: 12)*

Day acknowledges her own privilege in writing the book, 'I'm acutely aware … I am a privileged, white, middle-class woman in a world pockmarked by racism, inequality and poverty' (13) and unsurprisingly the trials she describes, in particular her perception of success at work, are particular to a privately educated middle-class white woman. Aiming for a similarly popular market, J.K. Rowling published a commencement address given to Harvard graduates in 2008. It is entitled *Very Good Lives: The Fringe Benefits of Failure and the Importance of Imagination* and detailed her sense of failure as she found herself 'jobless, a lone-parent, and as poor as it is possible to be in modern Britain without being homeless' (Rowling 2008: 29). Rowling asserts, 'It is impossible to live without failing at something, unless you live so cautiously that you might as well not have lived at all – in which case, you fail by default' (34). Failure in these narratives is shown to be a levelling, humanising experience, and yet, as in the case of Kim Noble, an overall frame of substantial professional success legitimates these stories. Their marketability depends upon the qualification of success. Self-help and self-care discourses represent positive tools to inform a longer, healthier life, but the overarching message emanating from publications such as those by Rowling and Day is ultimately one of resilience. They function as a reminder that the citizen may struggle on the embattled pathway to success, but ultimately they will overcome obstacles in order to grow into a fit and capable worker with no need for state support or subsidy. Brené Brown has published widely on the topics of resilience and vulnerability. Her TED Talk in 2011 is regularly cited in relation to productivity and resilience. Her chief impetus is to eradicate shame and 'rehumanize work'. She writes, 'When shame becomes a management style, engagement dies. When failure is not an option we can forget about learning, creativity and innovation (Brown 2012: 15). Brown wants to 'debunk' the notion that vulnerability is a weakness:

> Our rejection of vulnerability often stems from our associating it with dark emotions like fear, shame, grief, sadness, and disappointment – emotions that we don't want to discuss, even when they profoundly affect the way we live, love, work, and even lead [...] It starts to make sense that we dismiss vulnerability as weakness only when we realize that we've confused feeling with failing and emotions with liabilities.
>
> *(33–35)*

Brown acknowledges that many invitations to talk come from business corporations asking her to focus on 'inspired leadership or creativity and innovation'. Although it is clear that her project is to rehumanise contemporary doctrines of life and work she is perhaps unknowingly promoting a neoliberal agenda by building failure into a narrative of resilience for the effective and creative entrepreneur (15). Learning to cope with a sense of shame, vulnerability and failure has become an important part of the neoliberal narrative of resilience. Sarah Bracke has observed that, 'the prevalence of resilience as a term knew a spectacular rise at a moment in time that is generally recognized as a shift in political economy and cultural hegemony, that is the 1980s or the beginning of the hegemony of neoliberalism' (Bracke 2016: 53). For Bracke, 'in a neoliberal political economy, resilience has become part of the "moral code": the "good subjects" of neoliberal times are the ones who are able to act, to exercise their agency, in resilient ways. Good subjects' (62). Brown and Bracke both figure vulnerability as an issue that needs to be resolved by the 'good subjects' of neoliberalism, which means that for all the attempts to introduce the topic of shame and vulnerability, the right to fail has been co-opted by an individualistic neoliberal ideology. Furthermore, the question of who has the 'right' to fail, as Bracke observes, is marked by ethnicity, class and race. When asked about performance and failure Selina Thompson articulated her sense that as a Black artist she always has to be seen to excel and produce work of an extraordinarily high standard. She describes her sense that:

lots of white people, especially men, especially middle class white men, make very mediocre work. And it's okay – it's all right. [...] I actually don't want to make exceptional work anymore. I want to make mediocre work, and for it to be okay.

(Gorman 2017)

The artists in this book provide a platform to interrogate the experience of subjects who may not feel they have the right to fail. Their work provides an opportunity to ask if it is possible to celebrate failure and resilience without those ideas being recuperated into neoliberal ideology.

The relationship between identity, vulnerability and failure Bracke and Thompson describe has informed significant activity in the field of queer studies with scholars such as Lee Edelman, Leo Bersani and Judith Jack Halberstam developing ideas around what has become known as the 'antisocial turn' in queer studies. In very simple terms, these writers identify a close relationship between queerness and failure and develop theories of queer negativity as a way of countering neoliberal, conservative, assimilation. Edelman's book *No Future: Queer Theory and the Death Drive* has been described as 'the most hotly debated text in queer theory published in the past decade' (Doyle 2009: 27). Edelman rejects the imperative to invest in a sense of the future and employs 'the Child' as symbol of a conservative, reproductive futurity. According to Doyle, Edelman sees work on queer utopias as assimilative, he associates them

FIGURE 1.1 Promotional photograph for *salt.* featuring Selina Thompson (2016) Photograph: The Other Richard

with: 'heteronormative/reproductive structures of thought and oppression. He queries the potential of this work to contest the normalising pressure of mainstream liberal gay politics and its investment in family, marriage and domesticity' (Doyle 2009: 28). Edelman's argument stems, in part, from a visceral response to the experience of seeing an anti-abortion advertisement enlarged on a roadside hoarding. He wrote,

> the Cambridge billboard thus seemed to announce what liberalism prefers to occlude: that the governing compulsion, the singular imperative, that affords us no meaningful choice is the compulsion to embrace our own futurity in the privileged form of the Child.
>
> *(Edelman 2004: 16)*

Halberstam has been part of the antisocial turn in queer studies, arguing for the idea of 'queer temporality'. They write: '"Queer time" is a term for those specific models of temporality that emerge within postmodernism once one leaves the temporal frames of bourgeois reproduction and family, longevity, risk/safety, and inheritance' (Halberstam 2005: 20). In *The Queer Art of Failure* Halberstam charts tensions between second-wave feminist 'mothers' and third wave feminist 'daughters'. They call for an 'anti-social feminism, a form of feminism preoccupied with negativity and negation' (Halberstam 2011: 129). Halberstam borrows Saidiya Hartman's directive to 'lose your mother' as a way of refusing a positivist, familial relationship to femininity and feminism (Halberstam 2011: 124). They state their intention to:

> trace broken mother-daughter bonds toward an anti-Oedipal feminism that is nonetheless not a Deleuzean body without organs. This feminism, a feminism grounded in negation, refusal, passivity, absence and silence, offers spaces and modes of unknowing, failing, and forgetting as part of an alternative feminist project, a shadow feminism which has nestled in more positivist accounts and unraveled their logics from within. This shadow feminism speaks in the language of self-destruction, masochism, an antisocial femininity and a refusal of the essential bond of mother and daughter that ensures that the daughter inhabits the legacy of the mother and in doing so reproduces her relationship to patriarchal forms of power.
>
> *(124)*

Halberstam's theory shares Edelman's scepticism of reproductive futurity, they ask feminists to:

> refuse the choices offered – freedom in liberal terms or death – in order to think about a shadow archive of resistance, one that does not speak the language of action and momentum but instead articulates itself in terms of evacuation, refusal, passivity, unbecoming, unbeing.
>
> *(129)*

Failure here is used as a counter-cultural, anti-positivist tool, with little sense that it might be recuperated by neoliberal ideology. It is pertinent to note that much writing around failure (Edelman 2004; Muñoz 2009; Halberstam 2011; Bailes 2011) took place in the mid 2000s to early 2010s, and as early as the late 2010s its oppositional value had been recuperated into mainstream neoliberal ideology. Interestingly a recent publication on the topic, *Beyond Failure: New Essays on the Cultural History of Failure in Theatre and Performance* states its intention to leave failure behind and consider, as the title suggests, what might lie beyond, or *after* failure (Fisher and Katsouraki 2019, my emphasis).

José Muñoz, who has written in detail about performance and queer politics, has pushed back against the negative turn to argue for the importance of queer failure, queer virtuosity and queer utopia. Muñoz has described Edelman's work as representative of a 'certain romance of negativity', he explains:

> The dominant academic climate into which this book is attempting to intervene is dominated by a dismissal of political idealism. Shouting down utopia is an easy move. … The antiutopian critic of today has a well-worn war chest of post-structuralist pieties at his or her disposal to shut down lines of thought that delineate the concept of critical utopianism.
>
> *(Muñoz 2009: 12)*

In *Cruising Utopia: The Then and There of Queer Futurity* Muñoz articulates the need for queer subjects to find 'a principle of hope' because they have been 'cast as hopeless in a world without utopia' (97). He describes artists such as Jack Smith as extolling 'a queer utopian practice' of both failure and virtuosity (169) and argues for 'a generative politics' that 'can be potentially distilled from the aesthetics of queer failure' (173). He sets out to interrogate the way his chosen artists 'thematize failure as being something like the always already status of queers and other minoritarian subjects in the dominant social order within which they toil' (173). Both Muñoz and the antisocial theorists construct queerness in opposition to conservative or normative ideology however their difference lies in the investment in futurity as it is associated with familial structures and as it lends an illusion of agency. Muñoz's theory of a 'generative politics' will be important to this project as a way of conceptualising agency in a way that continues to push against a conservative, individualistic sense of selfhood. Many of the artists featured in this book set themselves impossible tasks or exhaust themselves through the repetition of strenuous activity and it is in the attempts to make their voices heard and their determination to engage wholeheartedly with the task that marks this type of queer amateurism or failure as 'generative'.

Within the field of theatre and performance studies the topic of failure has been influenced by Bailes' publication with other scholars actively contributing to what has become an established field. *Beyond Failure*, the publication mentioned above, acknowledges that, 'debates around what Sara Jane Bailes has termed the "poetics of failure" are now well and truly established in theatre and performance scholarship' (Fisher and Katsouraki 2019: 3). Fisher and Katsouraki open their collection with 'two radically different responses to the problem of failure':

> On the one hand, failure leads to an almost messianic faith in the power of futurity – to the knowledge that present failures will be redeemed in a time yet to come; on the other hand, with the arrival of nihilism, we have a drastic disavowal of futurity, where the knowledge of failure produces a bleak assessment of the impossibility of salvation or redemption, and with it the very refusal of the future.
>
> *(2)*

This faith in, or disavowal of, futurity can be seen to usefully describe the ways in which failure has been co-opted by neoliberal ideology as a way of investing in the future and concomitantly rejected by queer artists who reject positivist 'careerist' imperatives to 'reproduce and be productive' (Muñoz 2009: 172). The two responses echo some of the tensions between postmodernism and feminism. Feminists such as Irigaray would argue for an ontological difference between the sexes in order to be able to invest in the utopia of a better future for women, postmodernists would disavow futurity and its reliance upon teleological narratives. Radical differences of opinion between seemingly affiliated disciplines will continue to emerge as I refer to tensions between queer and trans★ activists, who differ in attitudes towards essentialism; Black feminists, who contest the erasure of People of Colour from traditional feminist histories; and postmodern feminists, who eschew a fixed position in order to occupy a realm of undecidability and indeterminacy.

Constructing her argument for the relevance of failure, Bailes begins with Beckett's prescient observation that failure is 'intrinsically bound up with artistic production' along with Phelan's observation that 'representation cannot reproduce the Real' (Bailes 2011: 12). She introduces Marxist theory to develop Beckett's interweaving of form and content. She is drawn to a particular aspect of Marxian thought:

> [his] understanding of form and content as *enfolded*, form as 'the form of its content' in order to identify theatre as a praxis that can expand our understanding of revolutionary potential. [...] the materiality of thought is a precondition to the realization of change of any kind, the status of the image is therefore of critical importance, for the image externalizes thought itself, indexing its presence at a different place and its manifestation through a visual or rhetorical mapping.
>
> *(35)*

Cultural and political shifts are charted through an interrogation of the ways in which Forced Entertainment and Goat Island's work in particular resist the conservative ideologies of Thatcher, Regan and the Bush-Blair alliance. Bailes makes an argument for a poetics of failure having the potential to be both anti-capitalist and counter-hegemonic. Muñoz's influence can be seen in Bailes' use of Ernst Bloch; she writes, 'the aspect of "hope" underpins my argument with its implications for the futurity of performance – performance's promise, its potentiality and its present continuous ambition' (12). Bailes argues that,

> we cannot 'do' without failure, in both senses of that expression (we cannot make, not can we manage without). Its practicable potentiality enables us to go on, and we go on because failure is a driver in the attempt to continue, even when interruption or disorientation or inoperativeness are constituent features of continuation.
>
> *(12)*

Although Bailes acknowledges her chosen companies occupy the 'postmodern period' she does not necessarily hold them to formal expectations associated with postmodern or postmodern theatre, as outlined by Lehmann in *Postdramatic Theatre*. An investment in 'futurity', for example, would certainly be at odds with a postmodern rejection of teleological narratives.

Liz Tomlin has made an important contribution to the topic of failure within theatre and performance practice. She observes that there has been a 'proliferation' of performance in the UK, which is 'marked to some degree by signifiers of the aesthetic outlined above (failure), but not necessarily by the philosophical discourse' (Tomlin 2008: 361). For Tomlin, in order to be progressive, companies employing a postmodern aesthetic of failure need to 'apply the sceptical imperative' in order to '"shake" its own narrative and deconstruct the recurring motifs which have begun to establish themselves as conventions, if not clichés …' (365). Tomlin is critical of what she regards as the false binary created between theatre and performance, writing:

> this binary opposition is played out in various calibrations, the most familiar of which include performance against theatre (when theatre is understood as dramatic theatre), performance theatre against dramatic theatre, devised theatre against text-based theatre, and Postdramatic theatre against dramatic theatre. In each opposition the first term is commonly aligned with a radical, oppositional narrative of deconstruction, the second with reactionary, traditional narrative of logocentrism, whilst the binary itself is underpinned by a poststructuralist scepticism of representations of the real.
>
> *(Tomlin 2013: 8)*

For Tomlin some aspects of failure have come to represent a 'common citational aesthetic' (14). She warns there is a potential for 'the aesthetic of failure, through repeated use of the convention, to become the new mark of artistic sophistication and success' (48). She quotes James Frieze who has observed, '[f]ailure may not exactly be the new success, but … in some respects it is the new power' (Frieze in Tomlin 2013: 49). Nicholas Ridout has written that failure is a fundamental element of theatrical activity; indeed, failure is 'constitutive' of theatre (Ridout 2006: 3). Interestingly he repeats the binary Tomlin warns of in his distinction between theatre and performance:

> It is in the imperfections [...] of its miming of the ideological structures of a given social organisation that the theatre, perhaps almost inadvertently, or with coy slyness, discloses the weaknesses and blind spots in its own structures. Theatre is guilty while performance still makes some claim to innocence.
>
> *(4)*

Performance, when it is used to distinguish an event or activity from theatre, is customarily interpreted to mean a mode of activity that resembles theatre, to a certain extent, however it may take place in a theatrical space, an art gallery or the street and make no attempt to employ mimesis. Performance, as distinct from conventional theatre practice, tends to eschew denegation, it does not ask the viewer to suspend disbelief or suppress its nature as an attempt to represent the world. Marvin Carlson has identified a 'theoretical coziness' between performance and postmodernism, calling upon Nick Kaye's suggestion that 'performance may be thought of as the primary postmodern mode' and Charles Caramello's observation that 'performance is the unifying mode of the postmodern' (Carlson 1996: 123). Performance has often come to stand alongside 'experimental theatre' or 'postmodern theatre' as a description for the more self-reflexive and citational form. Lavender observes that contemporary theatre and performance work in a way that is 'beyond postmodernism', they occupy a 'changed cultural paradigm, albeit one attuned to continuing postmodern tactics and techniques' (Lavender 2016: 4). The performance examples I analyse cover a range of forms and, as outlined above, fit largely within a postmodern praxis of failure. However, in terms of being identified as theatre *or* performance most examples fit more comfortably into the latter. The work tends to be self-reflexive; the artists acknowledge the audience and many make reference to the act of performing or writing. In my discussion of queer heterotopias in Chapter four I make a distinction between 'conventional' theatre spaces and smaller black-box studios, but it is not my intention to reify Tomlin's binary between theatre and performance. Neither do I want to suggest that mainstream theatre is inadequately resistant, radical or deconstructive. I consider meaning to be context specific and plural, so that no one genre of performance or theatre should be identified as essentially radical or subversive. For me, all performances deploy signs that cumulatively contribute towards a preferred meaning, but it is fundamentally up to the reader to forge their own path. I position myself as an individual reader of each performance and while I gather evidence to support my readings, I accept that my interpretation may be at odds with the preferred meaning of the artists and other audience members.

FIGURE 1.2 Close up of Rachael Young reading from her extensive list of rules for young, Black women. From *I, Myself and Me* by Rachael Young (2016)
Photograph: Scott Johnston

For some theorists failure is always already constitutive of the theatre or performance form, for example, Ridout, O'Gorman and Werry call failure the 'hallmark' of performance. For others, such as Jordan Tannahill, failure is only attributable to a very particular type of performance or theatre practice, one that deliberately fosters mistakes or sets out to represent the story of a 'loser' or 'loner' (Tannahill 2015). Bailes develops a list of techniques, 'stylistic modes' and strategies that might be found within a poetics of failure:

> a consideration of (false) amateurism, interruption and stalling, incorporating inept or inadequate means to achieve a different end, the repetitive structure of the attempt, examining impossibility as a generative mechanism, the use of mis-comprehension and disorientation as compositional strategies, and awkwardness as performance concept.
>
> *(Bailes 2011: 30)*

The work I include here draws upon some of these tropes and creates other strategies anew. My chosen artists do not necessarily set out to create performance *about* failure, or even recognise they are employing a 'citational aesthetic', however their work can be seen to respond to an experience of social and cultural exclusion and they borrow recognisable performance techniques associated with a praxis of failure. The theoretical ideas I carry forward stem from Bailes, Tomlin and Muñoz but inevitably there will be many other relevant sources whose work lies outside of the scope of this immediate project. I employ Tomlin's idea of the sceptical imperative in relation to my discussion of ironic feminist performance in Chapter one and throughout the book I draw upon Bailes and Muñoz's celebration of failure as 'generative'. As Muñoz argues, 'a generative politics can be potentially distilled from the aesthetics of queer failure. Within failure we can locate a kernel of potentiality' (Muñoz 2009: 173). Like Bailes my project is marked by optimism and like Braidotti and Irigaray I see the strategic importance of using a defined (inclusive) concept of womanhood in order to chart new directions for feminist practice and theory.

The resurgence of interest in women and identity politics on the UK stage in the 2010s can be seen to dovetail with narratives announcing the beginning of a 'fourth' wave of feminism. Kira Cochrane identifies the fourth wave as emerging around 2013 and characterised by the use of intersectional feminism, humour and social media. She identifies 'waves' as a useful way to 'define the contours of a specific movement at a specific moment' while recognising the metaphor to be controversial. For example, social and cultural 'waves' identified in the UK and US do not necessarily map on to movements in other parts of the world (Cochrane 2013: loc.55). As Sarah French has pointed out, 'feminist writers have increasingly contested the metaphor of generational "waves," arguing that the notion of a linear development obscures the heterogeneity of feminism' (French 2017: 19). Elaine Aston and Geraldine Harris identify the 'third' wave of feminism beginning around 1990, at a time when the term 'post-feminism' came into use. Aston and Harris write: 'Whatever their "currency", both "third wave" and postfeminism tend to be identified as starting somewhere around 1990 [and] are defined "against" or in "generational" terms' (Aston and Harris 2013: 6). Jacki Willson describes 'third' wave tension between the 'Matriarchs' and the 'exciting, brave new "young" world' (Willson 2008: 9). Waves are helpful to my project in so far as they suggest that tensions between feminism and postmodernism preoccupied the 'third' wave and the emergence of intersectionality came to the fore in the 'fourth'. The resurgence of interest in intersectionality (Crenshaw published her influential essay in 1989) has led to a revision of what Claire Hemmings has referred to as the 'vilified "radical feminist"' and a decision to reconsider the strategic value of essentialism (Hemmings 2011: 61). Indeed, the third and fourth waves of Western feminism are preoccupied by essentialist and anti-essentialist debates. Aston cites Angela McRobbie's useful designation, the 'Es and anti-Es' to characterise 'debates that arose as feminists struggled with the issues fuelled by trying to move beyond identity-based politics into a more deconstructive postmodern feminist mode of theorizing' (Aston 2007: 115).

Willson provides a useful way of differentiating between the popular post-feminist backlash and the movement that adopted the designation 'post' to indicate it was working with cognisance of poststructuralist and postmodern theories of identity. She writes:

> Post-feminism … correlates with postmodernism in its consideration of many identities and different narratives as opposed to one master narrative, one fixed patriarchal – matriarchal viewing of the world. The use of the hyphen here, therefore implies both a link and a division. […] For the second form, postfeminism, there is no linking hyphen, for the postfeminist generation disregard and disrespect the work achieved by the second wave feminism; it means nothing to them, it is old hat … an irrelevance.
>
> *(Willson 2008: 9)*

As indicated above, the 'correlation' between feminism and postmodernism suggests something of an 'alliance'. Indeed, Patricia Waugh states, 'feminism has, to some extent, always been "postmodern"' (Waugh 1998: 179). Both movements set out to destabilise phallocentric paradigms of representation and identity and yet the postmodern insistence on flux, process and 'becoming' and the drive to celebrate femininity as a metaphor for the decentred postmodern subject present inevitable problems. As Harris has pointed out:

> For some, feminism cannot operate without the notion of a stable 'female subject', and the de-centring of the subject in postmodernism is seen as an attempt to prevent women's access to the privileges of a position hitherto denied to them […] In these terms, postmodernism takes on the aspect of a backlash against feminism if not a straightforward patriarchal conspiracy which, as Craig Owens puts it, 'may yet be another masculine invention engineered to exclude women'. This can also lead to the perception that postmodernism and poststructuralism have shown feminism the error of its postmodern ways.
>
> *(Harris 1999: 13)*

For many feminist theorists postmodernism represented a call to renounce any sense of investment in the concept of womanhood (Di Stefano 1990; Nicholson 1990; Waugh 1998). Those nostalgic for the term were accused of being reductive and 'essentialist, ' however, as Waugh points out, given that women have yet to achieve full subjecthood, they still remain 'other' to the generic white, male subject, any rejection of an essential womanhood may be 'premature' (Waugh 1998: 180). She writes,

> at the risk of sounding essentialist, I would still argue that, never having experienced the kind of sovereign subjectivity and political security of the average white, Western, male postmodernist, it would seem that feminists may have more to lose in a premature renunciation of the goals and methods of Enlightenment thought.
>
> *(180)*

Thinking along similar lines, bell hooks writes: 'it never surprises me when black folks respond to the critique of essentialism, especially when it denies the validity of identity politics by saying, "Yeah, It's easy to give up identity, when you got one"' (hooks 2015b: 58). In stating 'after decentring, we find ourselves diversely centred' Lavender provides a useful way of navigating both postmodernism and feminism. Subjects become 'diversely centred' according to their investment in the notion of a secure, unitary subject position. The artists featured in this book centre themselves in a number of idiosyncratic ways. Some, such as GETINTHEBACK-OFTHEVAN use opaque language and retain a sense of ambiguity, whilst others, such as Selina Thompson and Rachael Young, choose to deliberately identify with a recognisable social and cultural group in order to draw attention to the material conditions of their lives.

Postmodern theory has proved enormously useful for queer theorists; indeed the work of Judith Butler has been transformative in creating a liberating theory of gender performativity. However, queer theory has also contributed to the dissolution of identity politics as fixed subject positions came to appear assimilative. As Johnson has written, 'Butler is front and centre among feminists in her challenges to female essentialism … [she] wrenches the body away from a discrete ontology of substance' (Johnson 2013: 169–171). Butler is influenced by the work of Michel Foucault. She wrote, 'Foucault points out that juridical systems of power *produce* the subjects they subsequently come to represent' (Butler 1990: 2). She is anti-essentialist in that she rejects the notion that male or female bodies have a 'signifiable existence prior to the mark of their gender' and claims that gendered subjects come into being '*through* the mark(s) of gender' (8, my emphasis). For Butler gender 'attributes' are 'not expressive but performative' (180). This results in a theory of gender performativity whereby a sense of identity is 'performatively constituted by the very "expressions" that are said to be its results' (25). She writes, '[g]ender is the repeated stylization of the body, a set of repeated acts within a highly rigid regulatory frame that congeal over time to produce the appearance of substance, of a natural sort of being' (33). Butler's theory has played a large part in the rejection of essentialism within feminist theory, it is fundamental to queer studies' celebration of a fluid, indeterminate gender, but has been criticised by some trans★ theorists who feel it does not take into account the lived experience of trans★ people who want and need to identify as either male *or* female. The common misperception that performative equates to performance has also led to disagreement. Susan Stryker observes:

> Butler […] has been criticized in some transgender scholarship and community discourse for suggesting that gender is a 'mere' performance, on the model of drag, and therefore somehow not 'real'. She is criticized, somewhat misguidedly, for supposedly believing that gender can be changed or rescripted at will, put on or taken off like a costume, according to one's pleasures or whim. At stake in these critical engagements is the self-understanding of many transgender people, who consider their gendered sense of self as ontologically

inescapable and inalienable – and to suggest otherwise to them is to risk a profound misrecognition of their personhood, of their specific mode of being.
(Stryker and Whittle 2006: 10)

I will consider these tensions in more detail in Chapter four, however for now I want to focus upon the potential of performativity and the possibility of creating an illusion of agency. Harvie has argued that social materialist theories of subjectivity tend to represent a pessimistic and negative way of theorising the subject. As Butler, after Foucault, would have it, subjects are produced through 'juridical' power, a phenomenon over which they have no control. Harvie states that a performative analysis differs from a social materialist analysis because it 'concentrates overwhelmingly on the ways people can and do act with freedom to self-author, exercising agency, control and power through everyday acts of self-articulation and self-creation' (Harvie 2009: 43). Butler's theory has been appropriated in a number of ways; some emphasise the potential for performative agency more than others. For example, French draws attention to Butler's assertion that:

'performativity' is neither free play nor theatrical self-presentation; nor can it be equated with performance […] performativity is not a voluntary 'performance' done by a subject, but an involuntary repetition and embodiment of norms that produce the 'formative precondition' for the subject.
(French 2017: 23)

The insistence on the involuntary suggests that subjects are without agency, however in her revised preface to the 1999 edition of *Gender Trouble*, Butler wrote, 'the idea that sexual practice has the power to destabilize gender emerged from my reading of Gayle Rubin's "The Traffic in Women" and sought to establish that normative sexuality fortifies normative gender' (Butler 1999: xi). This reference to 'power' and the act of 'destabilizing' gender suggests that Butler creates potential for resistant or oppositional sexual practice to challenge the process of subject formation. Considered in these terms Butler's theory represents a postmodern theory of gender which rejects fixed gender boundaries and celebrates fluidity, whilst concomitantly offering agency for the subject to, as Harvie, calls it, 'self-author' or 'self-create'.

Harvie's reading of performativity as positive and empowering represents one of the more optimistic reappraisals of postmodernism and identity politics. bell hooks presents a more negative reading when she argues, 'the overall impact of postmodernism is that many other groups now share with black folks a sense of deep alienation, despair, uncertainty, loss of a sense of grounding even if it is not informed by shared circumstance' (hooks 2015b: 57). hooks finds the challenge to essentialism useful in so far as it helps 'African-Americans concerned with reformulating outmoded notions of identity' and it 'allows us to affirm multiple black identities, [a] varied black experience' (59). However, hooks has been critical of the failure of the white academy to recognise 'a critical black presence in the culture' and articulates her sense that, 'if radical postmodernist thinking is to have transformative impact, then a critical break with the notion of "authority" as "mastery over" must not simply be a rhetorical device' (54). hooks warns that, 'given a pervasive politic of white supremacy which seeks to prevent the formation of radical black subjectivity, we cannot cavalierly dismiss a concern with identity politics' (56). She asserts, 'any critic exploring the radical potential of postmodernism as it relates to racial difference and racial domination would need to consider the implication of a critique of identity for oppressed groups' (56). For theorists such as Elizabeth Grosz it is important to think twice about dismissing a sense of ontological difference or 'essential' identity out of hand. Grosz is critical of 'essentialism, naturalism and biologism', which she argues allows 'misogynist thought [to] confin[e] women to biological requirements of reproduction on the assumption that because of particular biological, physiological, and endocrinological transformations, women are somehow *more* biological, *more* corporeal, and *more* natural than men' (Grosz 1994: 14 original emphasis). However, she qualifies her criticism with the warning that,

> the binary opposition between the cultural and the natural – needs careful reconsideration. It is not adequate to simply dismiss the category of nature outright, to completely transcribe it without residue in culture, this in itself is a monist, or logocentric gesture par excellence.
>
> *(21)*

Regardless of whether the West is experiencing the exhaustion of the third wave or the eruption of a new fourth wave of feminism the question of identity and subjectivity remains unresolved. Work by transfeminists such as Emi Koyama and Stryker illustrate that issues of ontology and essentialism continue to inform and preoccupy contemporary debates about feminism and gender (Koyama 2006; Stryker 2017). Lavender's notion of 'diverse' centring demonstrates cognisance of multiculturalism, gender diversity and the need to take into account the 'nuanced and differential negotiations' each subject makes in relation to dominant culture (Lavender 2016: 21).

In sketching out a fourth wave Cochrane implies that contemporary feminists demonstrate an awareness of the tyranny of colour blindness informing previous iterations of white feminism. Kimberlé Williams Crenshaw's theory of intersectionality has been transformational in drawing attention to the fact that many subjects are multiply disenfranchised. Lambasting the racist behaviour of a Slutwalk participant Flavia Dzodan famously asserted, 'my feminism will be intersectional or it will be bullshit!' (Dzodan 2011). Crenshaw published her influential essay 'Demarginalizing the Intersections of Race and Sex: A Black Feminist Critique of Antidiscrimination Doctrine, Feminist Theory and Antiracist Politics' in 1989. As a legal practitioner and scholar Crenshaw witnessed Black women being failed by the legal system because accusations of discrimination at multiple intersecting levels fell outside 'the narrow scope of antidiscrimination doctrine' (Crenshaw 1989: 144).

She documents a discrimination case against General Motors, brought by five Black women. The court found that because General Motors had promoted white women there was no clear evidence of discrimination on the grounds of gender and the particularity of race was not permitted alongside gender as a mitigating factor. Crenshaw identified a tendency to treat race and gender as mutually exclusive categories, an approach supported by a 'single-axis' framework. For her the experience of Black women is 'multi-dimensional' (139) and the 'focus on the most privileged group members marginalizes those who are multiply-burdened and obscures claims that cannot be understood as resulting from discrete sources of discrimination' (140). Crenshaw employs an affective allegory to illustrate her perception of the multi-dimensional nature of discrimination and oppression, which is worth quoting at length:

> Imagine a basement which contains all people who are disadvantaged on the basis of race, sex, class, sexual preference, age and/or physical ability. These people are stacked – feet standing on shoulders – with those on the bottom being disadvantaged by the full array of factors, up to the very top, where the heads of all those disadvantaged by a singular factor brush up against the ceiling. Their ceiling is actually the floor above which only those who are not disadvantaged in any way reside. In efforts to correct some aspects of domination, those above the ceiling admit from the basement only those who can say that 'but for' the ceiling, they too would be in the upper room. A hatch is developed through which those placed immediately below can crawl. Yet this hatch is generally available only to those who – due to the singularity of their burden and their otherwise privileged position relative to those below – are in the position to crawl through. Those who are multiply-burdened are generally left below unless they can somehow pull themselves into the groups that are permitted to squeeze through the hatch.
>
> *(151–152)*

Crenshaw's allegory offers a sobering corrective to the illusion of social mobility or meritocracy fostered by Western politicians. Her model draws attention to the 'top-down approach to discrimination' and the need to consider the fact that some women experience discrimination in manifold ways. Reflecting back Crenshaw observes, 'some people look to intersectionality as a grand theory of everything, but that's not my intention' (Crenshaw 2017). Her aim is to create ideas for 'advocates and communities' to use and she is concerned that 'intersectionality can get used as a blanket term to mean, "Well, it's complicated."' She observes, 'sometimes "It's complicated" is an excuse not to do anything' (Crenshaw 2017). Patricia Hill Collins and Sirma Bilge see intersectionality as a way of repudiating the postmodern idea that 'identity politics disempowers oppressed people because it encourages them to cling to the status of victim' (Hill Collins and Bilge 2016: 99). They are aware of 'the postmodernist assumption that intersectionality is deeply flawed by essentialism' (99) and argue that those who consider it flawed 'typically rely on understandings of identity and intersectionality that neglect how inter-sectionality as a form of critical praxis operates across many different venues' (100). Hill Collins and Bilge argue against reading intersectionality as *just another theory* and insist it represents both theory and practice and should not be read in isolation from its resonance within campaigns for social justice. Hill Collins and Bilge share empirical evidence of studies that clearly demonstrate 'how disenfranchised people use identity politics for political empowerment' (99). Critics of intersectionality have argued it has been 'too easily appropriated by white-dominated feminist theory' and as a result has been 'cut off from its roots in Black and women of color feminism, and incorporated into a self-congratulatory progressivist narrative' (Car-astathis 2014: 59). For Jennifer C. Nash the mainstreaming of Crenshaw's theory has led to the identification of intersectionality as the *foremost* theory of Black female subjectivity and resulted in the erasure of 'the myriad political traditions that have long been part of black feminism, but that are often ignored because of the extent of intersectionality's institutionalization' (Nash 2013: 5). Jamie Utt has written a sobering blog post about white co-option. Working as a diversity and inclusion consultant within largely white organisations in the States he reports that he encounters phrases such as '"we really need to be more intersectional" or "intersectionality matters" or "let's make sure to bring in an intersectional analysis here"' and yet, 'when we are pressed to do work that might actually decenter whiteness or challenge systematic white supremacy in our spaces, we don't show up' (Utt 2017). The criticisms levelled against intersectionality emanate from a number of stables, the academic and more popular discourse about the theory demonstrates how widely assimilated it has become. The incorporation of theory into the mainstream should be considered positive because it means that it will attain a wider reach than more complex theories of societal oppression. Crenshaw's allegory of the basement serves as a crucial reminder of comparative privilege, a lesson I take on board as one fortunate enough to be able to say 'but for the ceil-ing' I would be in the upper room. The basement allegory represents a way of inviting people, myself included, to consider the danger of 'color blindness' and what Robin DiAngelo has identified as 'their own participation in racist systems' (Waldman 2018).

Given that I want to follow Irigaray and employ 'strategic essentialism' in order to re-imbue identity politics with the gravity it has lost, intersectionality presents itself as an invaluable tool. I use it in the knowledge that some, such as Nash, consider it to have been co-opted by white feminist scholarship. I do not intend it as an easy corrective to exclusionary models of white feminist theory and practice that have gone before and that endure today and certainly do not want to limit my engagement to 'it's complicated'. I want to perform an intersectional reading of my chosen performances because they describe experiences of being marginalised or 'othered' in many different ways and, as Crenshaw observes, a single-axis frame-work of analysis cannot do justice to what they have to say. The artists describe the experience of feeling othered by virtue of gender and sexuality, race, class, skin tone and ethnicity. Intersectionality is enjoying significant currency as part of a fourth wave of Western feminism because it provides a crucial way of articulating the importance of reinvesting in fixed notions of identity after their obsolescence under postmodernism.

As outlined above, the discourse of 'identity politics' was deemed anachronistic or passé in the era of postmodernism (Apter 1998; Johnson 2013). Figures such as Butler continued to interrogate theories of gender and feminism, but concepts of gender identity became subsumed under the potent influence of queer theory, which insisted upon fluidity and flux. Johnson illustrates the condemnatory insights of postmodern cultural commentators such as Nicolas Bourriaud and Claire Bishop. Bishop 'argues [for] the inadequacy of identity politics on account of its supposed apologia for neoliberalism' and Bourriaud condemns them as anachronistic because 'any stance that is "directly" critical of society is futile, if based on the illusion of a marginality that is nowadays impossible, not to say regressive' (Johnson 2013: 27). Presumably, marginality for Bourriaud is 'nowadays' impossible because he is pre-occupied with the decentred experience of the white, middle-class, straight male subject. Sue-Ellen Case registers her experience of coming to feel 'outside' of sexu-ality studies having once been central. She wrote: '[f]eeling that the materialist, class critique had disappeared with the lesbian/feminist voice, I could write nothing more in the field' (Case 2009: 11–12). Jill Dolan, in her revised introduction to *Feminist Spectator as Critic,* notes that scepticism around identity politics has meant that even the term 'lesbian' is contested and criticised by some for being 'assimilationist' and 'homonormative' (Dolan 2012: xxii). The work of Phelan has been influential, to a certain extent, in undermining discourses relating to identity politics. In 1993 she wrote, 'the current contradiction between "identity politics" with its accent on visi-bility, and the psychoanalytic/deconstructionist mistrust of visibility as the source of unity or wholeness needs to be refigured, if not resolved' (Phelan 1993: 6). She qualifies her hesitation by writing, '[v]isibility politics are compatible with capitalism's relentless appetite for new markets and with the most self-satisfying ideologies of the United States: you are welcome here as long as you are productive' (11). Stephen Farrier provides a sense of how postmodern queerness has destabilised the previous certainties. He observes 'definitions of queer that position us as "not quite here" or a "place holder" presented a problem for agency' (Farrier 2013: 49). Phelan's theory of 'active vanishing', of 'a deliberate and conscious refusal to take the payoff of visibility' can perhaps be seen to do the same (Phelan 1993: 19). Phelan champions what Shoshana Felman has identified as 'radical negativity' by arguing, 'I think radical negativity is valuable, in part because it resists reproduction […] As an act, the per-formance of negativity does not make a claim to truth or accuracy' (165).[7] Both Phelan and Felman work to contemplate ways in which a deliberate or radical negativity might challenge reactionary positivist logic. Muñoz uses Felman's theory to make a distinction between the use of negativity in antirelational queer critique and his use of a queer utopianism. He sees antirelational theorists using a generalised negativity as part of a 'binary logic of opposition', which dismisses 'political idealism' whereas he wants to adopt radical negativity to 'insist upon the essential need for an understanding of queerness as collectivity' (Muñoz 2009: 13).

Stephen Farrier has written about 'the problem' with queer collectivity, observing that the:

> tacit declaration of the death of identity politics that queer enacted, the extent to which change could be effected by groups of people who identify with particular modes of identity or who are marked by the culture in which they live with indelible social markers (of race, class, sex etc.) was eroded, or rejected by queer's impulse for the deferral of solidity in identity and, therefore, it also rejected collectivity, which served as a mode of organizing people with such solid identifications.
>
> *(Farrier 2013: 49)*

Farrier draws attention to the relationship between activist groups of like-minded subjects and change. As the markers of identity are undermined, so is the capacity for collective action. Intersectionality, as a form of praxis, provides the opportunity to re-engage with topics of visibility, agency, identity and collectivity. It is concerned with forging change in a white supremacist patriarchal society and is a measure of the potential to be found in allowing subjects to identify strategically as 'the same' or as part of a coalition. For some intersectionality represents a 'buzzword' or 'jargon' but the fact that it is being criticised in these terms means that it is enjoying a much wider circulation and readership than postmodern feminism (Eddo-Lodge 2018b). Given that I figure my chosen artists as enacting a version of 'performing failure' and failure is considered to represent a key feature of postmodern praxis it may seem anachronistic to use theories of identity to inform my analysis, however, I argue that the artists imaginatively engage with identity in order to interrogate their willingness to engage with, or reject, the subject positions on offer. Although they may claim outsider status as a position of radical alterity and experiment with forms of radical negativity they are ultimately asserting a right to be seen and heard and foster a sense of agency.

This project intends to find meaningful ways of reading the presence of failure and negativity in contemporary performance whilst acknowledging that practitioners do not necessarily identify as postmodern. As Tomlin has pointed out, tropes of failure have come to represent a 'common citational aesthetic' (Tomlin 2013: 14). Lavender similarly observes, 'We find ourselves in a cultural space that has the look and feel of one that is now definitely beyond the postmodern, even while it continues to trade in certain postmodern strategies' (Lavender 2016: 10). I intend to interrogate the work of a range of artists who draw upon a postmodern aesthetic of failure in order to articulate a sense of being ostracised, or set apart from, heteronormative, white, patriarchal culture. As part of my analysis I will read for signs of congruence and contestation and map the construction of subjectivity on to received ideas in order to discover how these artists are shaping queer, feminist and trans* discourses anew. I draw upon Crenshaw's theory of intersectionality in order to foreground the significance of unmarked privilege and ability, factors crucial to any discussion of failure. I acknowledge my own comparative privilege as one with comparatively few burdens and who, according to Crenshaw's allegory, enjoys close proximity to the 'hatch' (Crenshaw 1989: 151–152). I have been extremely privileged to talk with a number of the artists and witness the performances live, on at least one occasion.[8] Although I will forge connections between the materials across different chapters, they do not need to be read in chronological order and each has a discrete bibliography to aid further research. Chapter two, 'Taking Back Control: Invective, Irony and Inscrutability', interrogates three performances: *Number 1, The Plaza* by GETINTHEBACKOFTHEVAN (2013), *Straight White Men* by Young Jean Lee's Theatre Company (2014) and *Notorious* by The Famous Lauren Barri Holstein (2017). I argue that each practitioner employs irony as a tool to draw attention to the difficulty of speaking from a sincere or fixed subject position in a post-postmodern age. The artists adopt a metatheatrical approach and switch between registers in order to obfuscate the 'meaning' of the work. I analyse each example in turn and consider the relative efficacy of irony as a technique for distanciation. Each production constructs gender and sexuality differently and I draw upon Lydia Rainford's theory of irony as 'a form of internalized agency' and Tomlin's theory of the 'sceptical imperative' in order to demonstrate how the work is both located within, but navigates beyond, a postmodern aesthetic. Chapter three, 'Self-Care and Radical Softness: Refusing Neoliberal Resilience', features three pieces of work: *salt.* (2016) by Selina Thompson, *I'm a Phoenix, Bitch* by Bryony Kimmings (2018) and Annie Siddons' *How (Not) to Live in Suburbia* (2017). This chapter borrows Audre Lorde's idea of self-care as an 'act of warfare' and Lora Mathis' slogan 'RADICAL SOFTNESS AS A WEAPON' in order to demonstrate how each artist rejects an internalised sense of insufficiency and transforms the experience of shame and ostracism into a call for collective action.[9] Inna Michaeli's work on self-care as 'a neoliberal trap' has proved particularly useful here. In Chapter four, 'Nightclubbing: Queer Heterotopia and Club Culture', I draw parallels between the alternative construction of space in Rachael Young's *Nightclubbing* (2018), Project O's *Voodoo* (2016) and Lucy McCormick's *Triple Threat* (2016). Each practitioner draws upon a nightclub aesthetic in order to encourage a more permeable mode of interaction between artists and audience. Project O and Young include Afrofuturistic imagery and McCormick arrives with her (all male) 'Girl Squad' to invite audiences to participate in a visceral, interactive experience. Spectators are invited to connect through appreciation of music, visual spectacle, touch and dance. After Muñoz and Foucault I have designated these alternative theatre/club spaces 'queer heterotopias' and argue the drive to reconfigure space emanates from the experience of being 'othered'. Chapter five, 'Taking Pleasure: Binary Ambivalence and Transgression', reads the work of three queer artists in relation to recent theories of feminist, queer and trans* sexuality. I analyse Kate Bornstein's *Gender Outlaw: On Men, Women and the Rest of Us* (2016), Lucy Hutson's *If You Want Bigger Yorkshire Puddings You Need a Bigger Tin* (2013) and two pieces by Lois Weaver: *Faith and Dancing: Mapping Femininity and Other Natural Disasters* (1996) and *Miss*

Risqué (2001). Weaver, Hutson and Bornstein each articulate an idiosyncratic model of gender and sexuality, Weaver argues for the radical potential of the 'resistant femme', Bornstein charts their experience as 'gender outlaw' and Hutson foregrounds her ambivalence with the term 'queer' whilst revealing she enjoys 'jumping ship' between different gender identities. I use the work of Susan Stryker and Emi Koyama to underline disciplinary tensions between feminism, queer theory and trans★ theory and chart the ways in which artists push back against the heteronormative construction of gender. My final chapter, Chapter six is entitled 'Tempering Anger: Asserting the Right to Define as Comic *Without Further Caveat'*. It takes contemporary stand-up comedy as its object of study and uses Oliver Double's work on comedy personae along with Joanne Gilbert and Ellie Tomsett's work on self-deprecation to analyse the work of four contemporary comedians. I analyse Bridget Christie's *A Bic for Her* (2013), Lolly Adefope's *Lolly 1* and *2* (2015 and 2016), Hannah Gadsby's *Nanette* (2017) and Shazia Mirza's *Coconut* (2019). I argue each comedian has experienced a developmental journey, particularly in relation to anger: they have each transitioned from initial scepticism towards a drive to assert the efficacy of anger as countercultural critique. The book closes with a brief Afterword meditating upon the poignancy of three images from examples of work that could not be accommodated within the main structure.

My readings of these performances are not intended to be prescriptive but I do want to advocate for the chosen artists, in a similar manner to Jill Dolan in *The Feminist Spectator in Action* and impart a sense that they all deserve more focused critical attention (Dolan 2013: 15). I intend this publication to stand as an important resource to help navigate the increasingly complex relationship between performance and postmodernism, feminism, gender, queer and trans★ studies. Most significantly, I want to draw attention to what might have been lost for feminists by the 'poststructuralist turn' and argue for the relevance of Crenshaw's theory of intersectionality in emphasising the importance of factoring social mobility and privilege into each and every conversation about 'failure'. I will draw my Introduction to an end with a short intervention made by Deirdre Heddon at the Performance Studies International conference in 2012. Heddon expressed frustration with a question from a male colleague after an academic paper about female performers. She recalled, 'but Dee [he said], aren't you essentializing women?' Heddon went on to reflect:

> I've come to think of that accusation as a weapon or a gag, that's been turned back upon us. It's difficult to talk about women; it's difficult to focus research on women. Can I ask a question? We know, maybe what was gained by the poststructuralist turn in feminism but do we know what was lost? Is it controversial to say women do exist – in all their differences and across time and space? What would it mean to talk about different experiences as if they are real? As if they are matter, as if they do matter?
>
> *(Heddon 2012)*

Notes

1 Myriam François-Cerrah gave a presentation to the Oxford Union entitled 'Feminism has been hijacked by white middle class women' in February 2015. The piece was later published in the *New Statesman*, available here: https://www.newstatesman.com/politics/2015/02/fem inism-has-been-hijacked-white-middle-class-women (accessed 15 January 2020). This polemical piece, along with bell hooks' *Feminism is for Everybody* (2015a), Alice Walker's *In Search of Our Mother's Gardens: Womanist Prose* (1983), Carrie Hamilton's 'Enough middle-class feminism' (2010) and June Eric-Udorie's *Can We All Be Feminists?* (2018) draws attention to the emerging sense that feminism, as it is understood today, has unfairly and disproportionately prioritised experiences of white, middle class women.

2 'Calm Down, Dear 2019' Camden People's Theatre website https://www.cptheatre.co. uk/wp_theatre_season/calm-down-dear-2019/ (accessed 20 July 2019).

3 I am using trans★ to signal an intention to be inclusive in relation to transgender and transsexual people. I am following the example of Susan Stryker who states, 'using trans★ rather than transgender became a shorthand way of signalling that you were trying to be inclusive of many different experiences and identities rooted in acts of crossing, and not get hung up on fighting over labels or conflicts rooted in different ways of being different from gender norms' (Stryker 2017: 11).

4 See Arts Council Report- *Equality, Diversity and the Creative Case: A Data Report 2015–2016* http://www.artscouncil.org.uk/sites/default/files/download-file/Equality_diver sity_creativecase_2015_16_web_0.pdf and *Equality Action Plan Guidance* webpage at: https://www.artscouncil.org.uk/advice-and-guidance-library/equality-action-plan-gu idance (accessed 7 February 2020). https://www.artscouncil.org.uk/advice-and-guida nce-library/equality-action-plan-guidance

5 I use the term 'queer' in a number of different ways. It is predominantly used to refer to theories and ideas emanating from queer studies. I also use it to refer to performance practices associated with LGBTQIAA communities and to signal a generally 'anti-het-eronormative' value or imperative (Stryker 2017: 30) I use it, after Amelia Jones, to describe qualities of 'undecidability' and 'unknowability', which 'troubl[e] the idea that we can know what we see' (Jones 2012: 174). I am particularly influenced by the work of Jones and Jennifer Doyle who see similar deconstructive impulses in feminist and queer criticism. Jones outlines 'feminism's now two-centuries long rich and conflicted tendency to expose the circuits of meaning-making as inexorably productive of and supported by structures of power' (Jones 2012: 174). Doyle similarly states, 'queer/feminist art practices will hover over the thingness of the body as a way of exploring the weight and history of that body, as a way of exploring the politics of making bodies into things, and things into bodies' (Doyle and Getsy 2014).

6 See Gorman (2014).

7 Shoshana Felman's work *The Scandal of the Speaking Body: Don Juan with J.L Austin, or Seduction in Two Languages* (1980) has informed theories of radical negativity, performance and queer failure. Felman draws upon Don Juan's mythic seduction techniques, involving an insincere promise to marry, in order to interrogate Austin's theory of performative utterance. She writes, 'The theoretical collapse of the initial or general distinction between the performative and the constative is, seen so, not an intellectual failure but a signal success, showing the performative (namely, a form of utterance neither true nor false) to be fully as meaningful as the constative; it thus deprives positivism [...] of a place for the imagined distinction between what was called "emotive meaning" as opposed to ' cognitive (or scientific) meaning' (Felman 2003: xvi). Marvin Carlson explains, 'Felman sees a struggle between a force of playfulness, of transgression of established boundaries, and a force which seeks to police and defend those boundaries' (Carlson 1996: 65). For Muñoz, 'Radical negativity, like the negation of negation, offers us a mode of under-standing negativity that is starkly different from the version of the negative proposed by the queer antirelationist. Here the negative becomes the resource for a certain mode of queer utopianism' (Muñoz 2009: 13).

8 For edited transcripts of conversations with Lois Weaver, Rachael Young, Selina Thompson, Lauren Barri Holstein and GETINTHEBACKOFTHEVAN visit https://readingasawoman.wordpress.com/ (accessed 20 August 2019).
9 Lora Mathis website: https://www.loramathis.com (accessed 23 July 2019).

Bibliography

Ahmed, Sara (1996) 'Beyond Humanism and Postmodernism: Theorizing a Feminist Practice', *Hypatia*, 11(2), 71–93.

Apter, Emily (1998) 'Reflections on Gynophobia', in *Coming out of Feminism?* Oxford: Blackwells, pp. 102–116.

Aston, Elaine (2007) 'A Good Night Out for the Girls', in *Cool Britannia? British Political Drama in the 1990s*, Rebecca D'Monte and Graham Saunders (eds.), Basingstoke: Palgrave Macmillan, pp. 114–132.

Aston, Elaine (2013) 'Feeling the Loss of Feminism: Sarah Kane's Blasted and an Experiential Genealogy of Contemporary Women's Playwriting', in *Contemporary Women Playwrights: into the Twenty-First Century*, Penny Farfan and Lesley Ferris (eds.), Basingstoke: Palgrave Macmillan, pp. 17–34.

Aston, Elaine and Geraldine Harris (2006) *Feminist Futures? Theatre, Performance, Theory*, Basingstoke: Palgrave Macmillan.

Aston, Elaine and Geraldine Harris (2013) *A Good Night Out for the Girls: Popular Feminisms in Contemporary Theatre and Performance*, Basingstoke: Palgrave Macmillan.

Bailes, Sara Jane (2011) *Performance Theatre and the Poetics of Failure: Forced Entertainment, Goat Island and Elevator Repair Service*, London and New York: Routledge.

Beckett, Samuel (1999) 'Worstward Ho', *Beckett Shorts No. 4*, London: John Calder Press.

Benamou, Michel and Charles Caramello (eds.) (1977) *Performance in Postmodern Culture*, Milwaukee: Coda Press.

Benhabib, Seyla (1995) 'Feminism and Postmodernism: An Uneasy Alliance', in *Feminist Contentions: A Philosophical Exchange*, Seyla Benhabib, Judith Butler, Drucilla Cornell and Nancy Fraser (eds.), New York: Routledge, pp. 1–16.

Bauer, Una (2008) 'Jerome Bel: An Interview with Una Bauer', *Performance Research*, 13(1), 42–48.

Bersani, Leo (1996) *Homos*, Cambridge: Harvard University Press.

Bottoms, Stephen (2007) *Small Acts of Repair: Performance Ecology and Goat Island*, London: Routledge.

Bracke, Sarah (2016) 'Bouncing Back: Vulnerability and Resistance in Times of Resilience', in *Vulnerability in Resistance*, Judith Butler, Zeynep Gambetti and Leticia Sabsay (eds.), Durham: Duke University Press, pp. 52–75.

Braidotti, Rosi (1994) *Nomadic Subjects: Embodiment and Sexual Difference in Contemporary Feminist Theory*, New York: Columbia University Press.

Braidotti, Rosi (2010) 'A Critical Cartography of Feminist Post-modernism', *Australian Feminist Studies*, 20(47), 169–180.

Braidotti, Rosi (2011) *Nomadic Subjects: Embodiment and Sexual Difference in Contemporary Feminist Theory*, [Kindle e-book] Second Edition. New York: Columbia University Press.

Braidotti, Rosi (2013) *The Posthuman*, Cambridge: Polity Press.

Brown, Brené (2012) *Daring Greatly: How the Courage to Be Vulnerable Transforms the Way We Live, Love, Parent, and Lead* [Kindle e-book], London: Penguin Books Ltd.

Butler, Judith (1990) *Gender Trouble: Feminism and the Subversion of Identity*, New York: Routledge.

Butler, Judith (1999) 'Preface (1999)', in *Gender Trouble: Feminism and the Subversion of Identity*, Revised Edition, New York: Routledge, pp. vii – xxvi.

Caird, Jo (2015) 'Kim Noble: You're Not Alone (Soho Theatre)', *What'sOnStage.com*, 11 December. Available at: https://www.whatsonstage.com/london-theatre/reviews/kim-noble-youre-not-alone-soho-theatre_39331.html (accessed 7 February 2020).

Carastathis, Anna (2014) 'The Concept of Intersectionality in Feminist Theory', *Philosophy Compass*, 9(5), 304–314.

Carlson, M. (1996) *Performance: A Critical Introduction*, London: Routledge.

Carby, Hazel V. (1982) '"White Women Listen!" Black Feminism and the Boundaries of Sisterhood', in *Empire Strikes Back: Race and Racism in Seventies Britain*, Centre for Contemporary Cultural Studies (ed.), London: Hutchinson & Co., pp. 212–235.

Case, Sue Ellen (2009) *Feminist and Queer Performance: Critical Strategies*, Basingstoke: Palgrave Macmillan.

Cerrato, Laura (1993) 'Postmodernism and Beckett's Aesthetics of Failure', *Samuel Beckett Today/Aujourd'hui* 2, 21–30.

Cochrane, Kira (2013) *All the Rebel Women: The Rise of the Fourth Wave of Feminism*, [Kindle e-book] London: Guardian Books.

Colman, Dan (2017) 'The Museum of Failure: A New Swedish Museum Showcases Harley-Davidson Perfume, Colgate Beef Lasagne, Google Class and Other Failed Products', *OpenCulture.com*, 4 May. Available at: http://www.openculture.com/2017/05/the-museum-of-failure.html (accessed 21 August 2019).

Crenshaw, Kimberlé (1989) 'Demarginalizing the Intersection of Race and Sex: A Black Feminist Critique of Antidiscrimination Doctrine, Feminist Theory and Antiracist Politics', *University of Chicago Legal Forum*, 1989(1), 139–167. Available at: https://chicagounbound.uchicago.edu/cgi/viewcontent.cgi?article=1052&context=uclf (accessed 21 August 2019).

Crenshaw, Kimberlé (2017) 'Kimberlé Crenshaw on Intersectionality, More than Two Decades Later', Columbia Law School website. Available at: https://www.law.columbia.edu/pt-br/news/2017/06/kimberle-crenshaw-intersectionality (accessed 8 August 2019).

Cull Ó Maoilearca, Laura (2009) '*The Politics of Becoming (-Woman): Deleuze, Sex and Gender*', presented at Performance Now and Then Symposium at Gallery North, Northumbria University, November 2009. Available at: https://www.academia.edu/199365/The_politics_of_becoming_-woman_Deleuze_sex_and_gender (accessed 21 August 2019).

Davis, Lennard J. (2013) 'The End of Identity Politics: On Disability as an Unstable Category', in *The Disability Studies Reader*, 4th Edition, Lennard J. Davis (ed.), New York and London: Routledge, pp. 263–277.

Day, Elizabeth (2018) *How To Fail with Elizabeth Day*. Podcast. Available at: https://podcasts.apple.com/gb/podcast/how-to-fail-with-elizabeth-day/id1407451189?mt=2 (accessed 22 January 2020).

Day, Elizabeth (2019) *How to Fail: Everything I've Ever Learned From Things Going Wrong*, London: 4th Estate.

Di Stefano, Christine (1990) 'Dilemmas of Difference: Feminism, Modernity and Postmodernism', in *Feminism/Postmodernism*, Linda J. Nicholson (ed.), New York: Routledge, pp. 63–82.

DiAngelo, Robin (2019) *White Fragility: Why It's So Hard for White People to Talk about Racism* [Kindle e-book]. London: Penguin.

Dolan, Jill (2012) *The Feminist Spectator as Critic*, Second Edition, Ann Arbor: University of Michigan Press.

Dolan, Jill (2013) *The Feminist Spectator in Action: Feminist Criticism for the Stage and Screen*, Basingstoke: Palgrave Macmillan.

Double, Oliver (2014) *Getting the Joke: The Inner Workings of Stand-up Comedy*, London: Bloomsbury Methuen.

Doyle, Jennifer (2009) 'Blind Spots and Failed Performance: Abortion, Feminist and Queer Theory', *Qui Parle*, 18, 25–52.

Doyle, Jennifer and David Getsy (2014) 'Queer Formalisms: Jennifer Doyle and David Getsy in Conversation', *Art Journal Open*, 31 March. Available at: http://artjournal.collegeart. org/?p=4468 (accessed 1 September 2019).

Durkin, Erin and Mattha Busby, (2019) 'Women's March 2019: Thousands Around the World March to Demand Gender Equality – As It Happened', *The Guardian*, 19 January. Available at: https://www.theguardian.com/world/live/2019/jan/19/womens-march-2019-london-new-york-berlin-washington-dc-live (accessed 13 August 2019).

Dzodan, Flavia (2011) 'My Feminism Will Be Intersectional or It Will Be Bullshit', *Tiger-beatdown.com*, 10 October. Available at: http://tigerbeatdown.com/2011/10/10/my-fem inism-will-be-intersectional-or-it-will-be-bullshit/ (accessed 8 August 2019).

Eddo-Lodge, Reni (2018a) *Why I'm No Longer Talking to White People About Race* [Kindle e-book] London: Bloomsbury.

Eddo-Lodge, Reni (2018b) 'CRASSH Impact: Reni Eddo-Lodge and Heidi Safia Mirza', Research Event, Cambridge University, 29 May. Available at: http://www.crassh.cam.ac. uk/events/27770 (accessed 2 September 2019).

Edelman, Lee (2004) *No Future: Queer Theory and the Death Drive*, Durham: Duke University Press Books.

Eric-Udorie, June (ed.) (2018) *Can We All Be Feminists? Seventeen Writers on Intersectionality, Identity and Finding The Right Way Forward*, London: Virago.

Farrier, Stephen (2013) 'It's about Time: Queer Utopias and Theater Performance', in *A Critical Enquiry into Queer Heterotopias*, Angela Jones (ed.) Basingstoke: Palgrave Macmil-lan, pp. 47–70.

Felman, Shoshana (2003) *The Scandal of the Speaking Body: Don Juan with Austin, or Seduction in Two Languages*, translated by Catherine Porter, Stanford, CA: Stanford University Press.

Fisher, Tony and Eve Katsouraki (eds.) (2019) *Beyond Failure: New Essays on the Cultural History of Failure in Theatre and Performance*, Abingdon: Routledge.

François-Cerrah, Myriam (2015) 'Feminism Has Been Hijacked By White Middle-Class Women', *New Statesman*, 13 February. Available at: https://www.newstatesman.com/politics/2015/02/feminism-has-been-hijacked-white-middle-class-women (accessed 15 January 2020).

French, Sarah (2017) *Staging Queer Feminisms: Sexuality and Gender in Australian Performance 2005–2015*, Basingstoke: Palgrave Macmillan.

Gay, Roxane (2014) *Bad Feminist: Essays*, New York: Corsair.

Gilbert, Joanne (1997) 'Performing Marginality: Comedy, Identity and Cultural Critique', *Text and Performance Quarterly*, 17, 317–330.

Gorman, Sarah (2011) *The Theatre of Richard Maxwell and the New York City Players*, New York: Routledge.

Gorman, Sarah (2013) 'Feminist Disavowal or Return to Immanence? The Problem of the Naked Female Form in Nic Green's Trilogy and Ursula Martinez' My Stories, Your Emails', *Feminist Review*, 105, 48–64.

Gorman, Sarah (2014) 'Do We Have a Show For You? Yes, We Have Got a Show For You!: Sexual Harassment, GETINTHEBACKOFTHEVAN and the (Re)Appraisal of Postmodern Irony', *Performance Research*, 19(2), 25–34.

Gorman, Sarah (2017) 'You Can Say Much More Interesting Things About a Scar Than You Can About a Wound: Interview with Selina Thompson', *readingasawoman.com*. Available at: https://readingasawoman.wordpress.com/2017/08/15/you-can-say-much-more-interesting-things-about-a-scar-than-you-can-about-a-wound-interview-with-selina-thompson/ (accessed 21 August 2019).

Griffin, Riley, Hannah Recht and Jeff Green (2018) '#MeToo: One Year Later', *Bloomberg.com*. Available at: https://www.bloomberg.com/graphics/2018-me-too-anniversary/ (accessed 13 August 2019).

Grosz, Elizabeth (1994) *Volatile Bodies, Towards a Corporeal Feminism*, Bloomington: Indiana University Press.

Halberstam, Judith Jack (2005) *In a Queer Time and Place: Transgender Bodies, Subcultural Lives*, New York: New York University Press.

Halberstam, Judith Jack (2011) *The Queer Art of Failure*, Durham: Duke University Press.

Hamilton, Carrie (2010) 'Enough Middle-Class Feminism', *The Guardian*, 24 March. Available at: https://www.theguardian.com/commentisfree/2010/mar/24/middle-class-feminism-pol itics (accessed 15 January 2020).

Hardy, Elle, Claire Lehmann, Trisha Jha and Paula Matthewson (2014) 'Am I A Feminist? Four Women Reply (And They're Not From The Left)', *The Guardian*, 14 April. Available at: https://www.theguardian.com/commentisfree/2014/apr/14/fem inism-liberal-women-australia (accessed 15 January 2020).

Harris, Geraldine (1999) *Staging Femininities: Performance and Performativity*, Manchester: Manchester University Press.

Harvie, Jen (2009) *Theatre & the City*, London: Macmillan.

Harvie, Jen (2013) *Fair Play: Art, Performance and Neoliberalism*, Basingstoke: Palgrave Macmillan.

Heddon, Dierdre (2012) 'Feminist Performance: Legacies and Futures', Opening Plenary presentation at Performance Studies International Conference, Leeds University, 25 to 28 June.

Hemmings, Clare (2011) *Why Stories Matter: The Political Grammar of Feminist Theory*, Durham: Duke University Press.

Hill Collins, Patricia and Sirma Bilge (2016) *Intersectionality*, Cambridge: Polity Press.

Hilson, David (ed.) (2011) *The Failure Files: Perspectives on Failure* [Kindle e-book]. Axminster: Triarchy Press.

Hitchings, Henry (2015) 'Kim Noble: You're Not Alone, Soho – Theatre Review', *The Evening Standard*, 12 February. Available at: https://www.standard.co.uk/go/london/theatre/kim-no ble-you-re-not-alone-soho-theatre-review-10041114.html (accessed 7 February 2020).

hooks, bell (2015a) *Feminism Is for Everybody: Passionate Politics*, New York: Routledge.

hooks, bell (2015b) *Yearning Race, Gender and Cultural Politics*, New York: Routledge.

hooks, bell and Emma Watson (2016) 'In Conversation with bell hooks and Emma Watson', *Papermag.com*, 18 February. Available at: https://www.papermag.com/emma-watson-bell-hooks-conversation-1609893784.html (accessed 13 August 2019).

Inckle, Kay (2015) 'Debilitating Times: Compulsory Ablebodiedness and White Privilege in Theory and Practice', *Feminist Review*, 111, 42–58.

Irigaray, Luce (1985) *This Sex Which Is Not One*, translated by Catherine Porter with Carolyn Burke, New York: Cornell University Press.

Jameson, Frederic (1985) 'Postmodernism and Consumer Society', in *Postmodern Culture*, Hal Foster (ed.), London: Pluto Press, pp. 111–125.

Jensen-Moulton, Stephanie (2012) '*Disability as Postmodernism: Christopher Knowles and Einstein on the Beach*', Society for American Music Annual Conference, Davidson College, Hilton Charlotte Center City, 14–18 March.

Johnson, Dominic (2013) 'Introduction: Live Art in the UK', in *Critical Live Art: Contemporary Histories of Performance in the UK*, Dominic Johnson (ed.), London: Routledge, pp. 5–12.

Jones, Amelia (2012) *Seeing Differently: A History and Theory of Identification and the Visual Arts*, Abingdon: Routledge.

Kaye, N. (1996) *Postmodernism and Performance*, London: Macmillan.

Koyama, Emi (2006) 'Whose Feminism Is it Anyway? The Unspoken Racism of the Trans Inclusion Debate' in *The Transgender Studies Reader*, Susan Stryker and Stephen Whittle (eds.), New York: Routledge, pp. 698–705.

Lavender, Andy (2016) *Performing in the 21st Century: Theatres of Engagement*, Abingdon: Routledge.

Lehmann, Hans-Thies (2006) *Postdramatic Theatre*, translated by Karen Juers-Munby, Abingdon: Routledge.

Lepecki, André (2006) 'Choreography's "Slower Ontology": Jerome Bel's Critique of Representation' in *Exhausting Dance: Performing and the Politics of Movement*, New York: Routledge, pp. 45–64.

Lorde, Audre (2009) 'A Burst of Light: Living with Cancer', in *A Burst of Light and Other Essays*, New York: Ixia Press.

Lyotard, Jean-François (1979) *The Postmodern Condition: A Report on Knowledge*, translated by G. Bennington and B. Massumi, Manchester: Manchester University Press.

Marshall, Colin (2017) 'Try Again. Fail Again. Fail Better': How Samuel Beckett Created the Unlikely Mantra That Inspires Entrepreneurs Today', *OpenCulture.com*, 7 December. Available at: http://www.openculture.com/2017/12/try-again-fail-again-fail-better-how-samuel-beckett-created-the-unlikely-mantra-that-inspires-entrepreneurs-today.html (accessed 23 July 2019).

McRobbie, Angela (2009) *The Aftermath of Feminism: Gender, Culture and Social Change*, London: Sage.

Michaeli, Inna (2017) 'Self-Care: An Act of Political Warfare or a Neoliberal Trap?', *Development*, 60, 50–56.

Moran, Caitlin (2012) *How to Be a Woman*, London: Ebury Press.

Muñoz, José (2009) *Cruising Utopia: The Then and There of Queer Futurity*, New York: New York University Press.

Nash, Jennifer C. (2013) 'Practicing Love: Black Feminism, Love-Politics, and Post-Intersectionality', *Meridians: Feminism, Race, Transnationalism*, 11(2), 1–24.

Nicholson, Linda J. (ed.) (1990) *Feminism/Postmodernism*, New York: Routledge.

Neate, Rupert (2018) 'Global Pay Gap Will Take 202 Years To Close, Says World Economic Forum', *The Guardian*, 18 December. Available at:https://www.theguardian.com/world/2018/dec/18/global-gender-pay-gap-will-take-202-years-to-close-says-world-economic-forum (accessed 13 August 2019).

Ngozi, Chimamanda Adichi (2014) *We Should All Be Feminists*, London: Fourth Estate.

O'Connell, Mark (2014) 'The Stunning Success Of "Fail Better": How Samuel Beckett Became Silcon Valley's Life Coach', *Slate.com*, 29 January. Available at: https://slate.com/culture/2014/01/samuel-becketts-quote-fail-better-becomes-the-mantra-of-silicon-valley.html (accessed 21 August 2019).

O'Gorman, Rósín and Margaret Werry (2012) 'On Failure (On Pedagogy): Editorial Introduction', *Performance Research*, 17(1), 1–8.

Phelan, Peggy (1993) *Unmarked: the Politics of Performance*, Routledge: London.

Power, Cormac (2010) 'Performing to Fail: Perspectives on Failure in Performance and Philosophy', in *Ethical Encounters: Boundaries of Theatre, Performance and Philosophy*, Daniel Meyer-Dinkgraffe and Daniel Witts (eds.) Newcastle: Cambridge Scholars Publishing, pp. 125–134.

Rainford, Lydia (2005) *She Changes by Intrigue: Irony, Femininity and Feminism*, Amsterdam: Rodopi.

Reilly-Cooper (2016) 'Gender Is Not A Spectrum', *Aeon*, 28 June. Available at: https://aeon.co/essays/the-idea-that-gender-is-a-spectrum-is-a-new-gender-prison (accessed 15 January 2020).

Ridout, Nicholas (2006) *Stage Fright, Animals and Other Theatrical Problems*, Cambridge: Cambridge University Press.

Rowling J.K. (2008) *Very Good Lives*, London: Sphere Books.

Stryker, Susan (2004) 'Transgender Studies: Queer Theory's Evil Twin', *GLQ: A Journal of Lesbian and Gay Studies*, 10, 212–215.

Stryker, Susan (2017) *Transgender History: the Roots of Today's Revolution*, New York: Seal Press.

Stryker, Susan and Stephen Whittle (eds.) (2006) *The Transgender Studies Reader*, New York: Routledge.

Tannahill, Jordan (2015) *Theatre of the Unimpressed: In Search of Vital Drama*, Toronto: Coach House Books.

Thompson Selina (2018) 'Fat Demands', in *Can We All be Feminists? Seventeen Writers on Intersectionality, Identity and Finding the Right Way Forward for Feminism*, June Eric-Udorie (ed.) [Kindle e-book], London: Virago, pp. 31–46.

Tomlin, Liz (2008) 'Beyond Cynicism: The Sceptical Imperative and (Future) Contemporary Performance', *Contemporary Theatre Review*, 18(3), 356–369.

Tomlin, Liz (2013) *Acts and Apparitions: Discourses on the Real in Performance, Practice and Theory 1990–2010*, Manchester: Manchester University Press.

Tomsett, Ellie (2018) 'Positives and Negatives: Reclaiming the Female Body and Self-Deprecation in Stand-up Comedy', *Comedy Studies*, 9(1), 6–18.

Umathum, Sandra and Benjamin Wihstutz (eds.) (2015) *Disabled Theater*, Zurich: diaphanes.

Utt, Jamie (2017) '"We're All Just Different!" How White People Are Co-opting Intersectionality', *Everyday Feminism.Com*, 30 May. Available at: https://everydayfeminism. com/2017/05/white-co-opting-intersectionality/ (accessed 8 August 2019).

Waldman, Katy (2018) 'A Sociologist Examines the "White Fragility" that Prevents White Americans from Confronting Racism', *newyorker.com*, 23 July. Available at: https://www.new yorker.com/books/page-turner/a-sociologist-examines-the-white-fragility-that-prevents-whi te-americans-from-confronting-racism (accessed 12 March 2019).

Walker, Alice (1983) *In Search of Our Mothers' Gardens: Womanist Prose*, New York: Harcourt Brace.

Waugh, Patricia (1998) 'Postmodernism and Feminism', in *Contemporary Feminist Theories*, Stevi Jackson and Jackie Jones (eds.), Edinburgh: Edinburgh University Press, pp. 177–193.

Wessendorf, Markus (2001) 'The (Un)settled Space of Richard Maxwell's House', *Modern Drama*, 44(4), 437–457.

Willson, Jacki (2008) *The Happy Stripper: Pleasures and Politics of the New Burlesque*, London and New York: I.B. Tauris.

Young, Rachael (2016) *I, Myself and Me*. Touring Production.

2

TAKING BACK CONTROL: INVECTIVE, IRONY AND INSCRUTABILITY

After postmodernism female artists have the opportunity to draw upon a wide range of genres and stylistic techniques. They have the facility to shift between different registers appropriate to a variety of forms: performance installations, socially engaged projects and theatrical performances. This chapter will analyse the work of three artists who create experimental work for the Western stage. Their work can be seen to straddle theatre and live art forms and employ the self-reflexive tendency associated with postmodern performance. On one level their work can be read as an attempt to demystify the representational apparatus of realist theatre and its Aristotelian legacy and on another to illustrate the discursive construction of selfhood and identity. I will analyse three examples: *Number 1, The Plaza* by GETINTHEBACKOFTHEVAN (2013); *Straight White Men* by Young Jean Lee's Theatre Company (2014) and *Notorious* by The Famous Lauren Barri Holstein (2017). I will argue that my chosen artists deliberately create a productive tension between the displayed body and the authorial voice. They frame normative images of male and female characters in an ironic manner whilst foregrounding a failure to match social expectation. I will argue that at least two of the productions adopt an ironic, self-reflexive attitude in keeping with what Liz Tomlin has called a 'healthy scepticism' appropriate to deconstructive theatre whilst demonstrating that their experience of female subjectivity is shaped by a multitude of competing social forces (Tomlin 2008: 357). I will draw upon Lydia Rainford's sense of irony as a mode of 'radical negativity;' according to Rainford irony 'refuses to be contained in discrete moments of speech or narrative' (Rainford 2005: 7).

When invoking irony I intend to describe a rhetorical practice in which what is *shown* is at odds with what is *meant*. The intended, or preferred, meaning is freighted with ambiguity inviting audiences 'in the know' to recognise that the author intends to impart a value judgement without explicitly having to name the terms of criticism. In *Irony (The New Critical Idiom)* Claire Colebrook cites Umberto

Eco and Ihab Hassan who 'argued that our entire epoch, as postmodern, is ironic' (Colebrook 2003: 18). In *Postdramatic Theatre* Hans-Thies Lehmann has identified an 'ironic, sarcastic distance' that he calls 'playing with coldness' (Lehmann 2006: 118). Irony has become such a recognisable part of postmodern culture that the term 'post-irony' has come into being to illustrate the moment when 'one's ironic appreciation of something becomes genuine, usually due to either prolonged exposure or the enjoyment derived from how amusingly terrible it is' (Urban Dictionary 2017). Ross Chambers' work on irony has illustrated the complex and unstable nature of irony's signifying process. He writes, 'I can intend irony as much as I like, but it has not worked unless and until it has been perceived – "read into" my discourse by another'. He avers the recognition of irony depends upon 'ideological complicity – an agreement based on shared understandings of "how the world is" – but an ideological complicity that recognizes another discourse itself as ideological' (Chambers 1990: 19). Linda Hutcheon issues a similar warning, writing that 'while irony can be used to reinforce authority, it can also be used to oppositional and subversive ends – and it can become suspect for that very reason' (Hutcheon 1995: 29).

Lydia Rainford sees a fortuitous relationship between feminism and irony. Contemplating the 'double' relation of women to the 'order of things' described in the work of Judith Butler and Luce Irigaray, Rainford asserts,

> the ironic mode is considered as a form of internalized agency for the feminist: as well as reflecting her double relation to the patriarchal structure, it turns her alterity to her advantage by using it to negate the terms of the prevailing hierarchy.
>
> *(Rainford 2005: 4)*

She asserts that 'irony operates from within the structure it interrogates, repeating the beliefs of the structure in such a way as to negate their value; thus implying that the real truth is another thing altogether' (3). These critical voices display the potential pitfalls and dangers of deploying irony as a deconstructive tool. To describe or cite an ideological position, even with the intention to critique it, is to bring it, once again, into being and risk further ideological sedimentation. This can be seen to represent risky territory. Some feminist writers believe that their conscious deployment of irony goes unnoticed and is invisible to non-receptive audiences because they are not credited with the wit or facility to communicate in such ambiguous terms. For example, comedian Bridget Christie has written of her experience of jokes failing to successfully 'land'. In an attempt to introduce more politically pertinent material into a 'serious' section of her routine (in which she lambasts Bic for creating pink biros for the female market), she invented a 'reverse-heckle' in which she pretended that a male audience member had heckled, 'demanding that [she] address more complex feminist issues in greater depth'. Despite the routine being well received by the audience one reviewer failed to recognise the reverse-heckle as a deliberate conceit and recorded that she was 'thrown by a heckler'. Christie writes, '[It's a] shame when your performance skills, hard won over years of genuine stage deaths, are *mistaken for genuine errors*, isn't it? (Christie 2015: 196, my emphasis). This is an example of overlooked irony on the part of the reviewer, who presumably underestimated Christie's experience in tackling hecklers. Working along similar lines, Laura Bates, founder of the *Everyday Sexism* Project, observed, 'anti-feminists don't get irony. One commentator said of me: "Sexism doesn't exist, she's just a bitch who needs some dick to shut up".' Bates sarcastically counters, 'I felt so silly, I wished someone had pointed this out sooner before I wasted so much time and energy campaigning' (Bates 2015). Bates' comeback draws attention to a misogynistic refusal to entertain the notion that her utterances might be freighted with irony and points to a now familiar drive to silence and contain women who dare to speak out on social media.

The artists I have chosen to discuss in this chapter all employ an ironic attitude towards their subject matter. They adopt the metatheatrical technique of self-consciously framing their main activity as 'representation' and demonstrate how heteronormative images of men and women normalise and mystify the logic of gender binaries. Lauren Barri Holstein, GETINTHEBACKOFTHEVAN and Young Jean Lee can all be seen to use what Tomlin has described as a 'common citational aesthetic that underpins contemporary notions of performer and character'. That is, they all deploy figures on stage that appear to be playing a version of themselves. This might include calling the onstage persona the same name as the performer and asking the performers to speak directly to the audience. Tomlin warns that the ethics of theatrical deconstruction become compromised when tropes of performance such as this are repeated too often and become 'the new mark of artistic sophistication and success'. Artists who borrow the techniques of deconstruction alone, without attending to the ideological imperative behind the project, risk 'consolidating a new totalizing narrative of their own' (Tomlin 2013: 6). For Tomlin, after Lyotard, 'such philosophical positions, on postmodernism's own terms, need to be "submitted to the counter-violence of solicitation" in order to reveal the contradiction at their own heart and thus rupture the illusion of totality they currently appear to offer' (Tomlin 2008: 358). In order to maintain its radical potential to destabilise, conservative ideology contemporary performance must observe, for Tomlin, a 'healthy scepticism', which should ensure that 'the very conclusions it has reached in its deconstruction of the Enlightenment project are thrown rigorously and continuously into question...' (357). For the most part, the artists in question do practise a healthy scepticism. They achieve this by ensuring that their attitude towards the content of the performance remains uncertain. They frame their work in a self-reflexive and metatheatrical manner while maintaining an ideological opacity. This disguising or muddying of intention represents a type of inscrutability, a way that problematises the illusion of agency whilst ultimately remaining in control.

I want to return to Rainford's notion that irony has the potential to offer agency. As I have outlined in the Introduction, feminists have found themselves negotiating tricky theoretical terrain when contemplating female subjectivity after poststructuralism. Poststructuralism reveals the coherent self-contained Humanist subject to be an illusory mystification of language and yet feminists need to invest in the coherent subject position of 'woman' in order to find common ground and assert their identity. This identity stands in relation to men and invokes phallocentric logic, and yet without this fundamental, what Braidotti has called 'ontological difference', woman does not exist. As Rainford explains:

> [t]here are those that insist that some category of 'essence', however nominal, is crucial in order for feminism to maintain the specificity of its political cause. Without a definition of sexual difference and sexually different subjectivity, there is no foundation on which to base feminism's critique of patriarchy and hope of liberation.
>
> *(Rainford 2005: 2)*

I want to argue that the artists in question deploy irony and inscrutability to draw attention to the contradictory representations of women within contemporary popular discourse whilst problematising their relationship to, and understanding of, the concept 'woman'. I will argue that they frame their performances in a way that allows them to draw upon and cite reductive images of both sexes whilst refusing to ultimately reify or condemn. Their intention in relation to the images they show is ambiguous and remains largely undecided at the close of each performance. This ambiguity complicates the ability of the reader to arrive at a totalising reading and ensures the content of the piece remains under question and scrutiny long after the audience has left the building.

According to Rainford irony can be effectively deployed as a tool of opposition because a woman can use her,

> secondariness as a form of 'negative freedom,' repeating it back to the patriarchal structure in order to undermine the authority of (sexed) subjectivity itself. Irony creates a way to unravel the prevailing 'truth' of gender positions without being obliged to step outside these positions.
>
> *(Rainford 2005: 4)*

The artists in question can be seen, to some extent, to observe normative gender codes at least at the outset of each performance. The male characters in *Straight White Men* mostly manifest hyper-masculine codes of behaviour, which, according to socio-linguist Jen Coates, can be seen to include 'emotional restraint, ambition, achievement and competitiveness' (Coates 2003: 65). The female figures onstage in *Notorious* and *Number 1, The Plaza* wear costumes designed to emphasise sexualised parts of their bodies and use self-deprecating and apologetic language. Although these artists cite normative gender codes, they create a tension between the signification of the performers' bodies and the words they utter. Within each performance I identify the erasure of, or the figuring of, the female body as grotesque, alongside a determination to assert and demonstrate control over the *mise en scène*.

The artists assert their authority over the images they present while demonstrating a knowing self-reflexivity about the veracity or value of what they show.

Jennifer Doyle's work is relevant here. In her discussion of Aliza Schvart's performative exploration of insemination and abortion at Yale University (*Untitled [Senior Thesis]*, 2008) she explores the construction of the female body within right-wing abortion discourse and left-wing queer scholarship. She states that 'subjective coherence is a discursive effect' and cites Jane Blocker's distinction between the 'figurative' and the 'literal'. For Blocker 'the female and the queer are both defined against and precluded from the figurative because they are not seen to be performing at all' (Blocker cited in Doyle 2009: 45). Blocker's assertion goes some way to explaining the failure of Christie and Bates' jokes to 'land' successfully with their audiences. To a misogynistic audience, women will be held to what they say in a literal manner because they are not deemed capable of deploying the metaphorical linguistic tropes that would render their utterances 'figurative'. The work I will discuss is driven by a desire to find an authoritative place from which to speak, whilst undermining conventional values associated with neoliberal and heteronormative authority. In these pieces authority is repeatedly thrown into doubt because it is deliberately unclear whether the characters are speaking literally or figuratively. This attention to the nature of the authority of the speakers who frame the onstage activity can be seen, after Tomlin, to be an effective example of 'healthy' postmodern scepticism and an example of what Rainford has posited as 'negative freedom'. I want to argue that for the most part these artists achieve a 'healthy scepticism' and take advantage of 'negative freedom' by oscillating between positions of authority and subjugation during the course of each show. The metatheatrical frame of each piece shows a female interlocutor to be in control of events and the language the women use is directorial and assertive. However, there are times in each production in which this sense of control is undermined by either removing the female director from the frame, taking recourse to infantile and/or sexualised behaviour or a compulsion to apologise. The moments of subjugation work to undermine the illusion of authority fostered elsewhere, resulting in a seeming position of ambivalence in relation to gender performativity on the part of the artists.

I will work through my examples in chronological order, which means *Number 1, The Plaza* by UK company GETINTHEBACKOFTHEVAN comes first, having been produced in 2013. GETINTHEBACKOFTHEVAN comprises three core artists, Lucy McCormick, Jennifer Pick and Hester Chillingworth. The company regularly works with other associated artists, but ordinarily Pick and McCormick perform with Chillingworth directing. The company has been working together since 2008 and *Number 1, The Plaza* represents their third performance for theatre spaces. Promotional material states that the company 'make[s] broken genre performance ... plays with glory, endurance, artifice and the banal' and that 'text does not always say what it says that it says it is saying' (GETINTHEBACKOFTHEVAN 2019). They have said their work is 'always very interested in the idea of the show, maybe more so than other companies that also deal with "performance about performance"' (Gorman 2017) and cite their work as straddling both live art and theatre. Chillingworth has said,

> we are very aware of and interested in the fact that, in terms of programming, for some places we are either 'too rough' or 'too soft' quite often. For some places audiences just won't be able to deal with us or other places that pro-gramme hardcore performance art works we are, 'well that is just a bit theatrical'.
>
> *(Gorman 2017)*

The shows are humorous and the company is interested in the interplay between comedy and seriousness. Pick and McCormick's partnership often follows the recognisable pattern of a comedy double-act. For them irony is 'super-super important now because it is not only such a great tool for getting to places but it is quite embedded in who we are and the kind of stupid conversations we have' (Gorman 2017). The company makes reference to popular culture by citing con-temporary show-tunes and ballads by female singers. Chillingworth has spoken of their use of pop culture and irony:

> It's the '4 EVER' relationship between pop and irony that's difficult. While we find irony useful, we have been wondering if it's ever possible to uncouple it from pop. For example, it seems to us that if you play/use/reference a famous pop song on stage, you are (usually intentionally) creating a moment which brings notions of aspiration, attempt and the pathetic into the room. And as soon as we have amateurism and aspiration in the room, we probably have irony quite close by.
>
> *(GETINTHEBACKOFTHEVAN 2012)*

In terms of Tomlin's 'citational aesthetic' the company can be seen to employ a mode of direct address used in much contemporary experimental theatre over the past 30 years, and now increasingly in mainstream theatre. Pick and McCormick refer to themselves as 'Jen' and 'Lucy' onstage and often incorporate references to real-time factors influencing the show, such as citing the name of the venue and town and discussing events that took place on the journey to the venue. The performers constantly discuss their intentions for 'the show' and play upon audi-ence expectation as they deliver, or fail to deliver, meaning, spectacle and figurative transportation.

The company play with references to popular culture and spectacle, using Leo-nard Cohen's *Hallelujah* during their 2012 show *Big Hits* and a range of well-known show-tunes such as *Defying Gravity* from the musical *Wicked* and *Tell Me It's Not True* from *Blood Brothers*.[1] The shows often employ a low-budget aesthetic with minimal props. *Big Hits* featured a pair of amplifiers and speakers along with a small rotating disco-ball that was manually plugged in onstage. For this piece Pick wore a furry rabbit costume whilst other performers wore conventional clothing.

Number 1, The Plaza saw the lighting and sound desks installed upstage along with two freestanding bar stools. The performers both wore long hairpieces, over the ear microphones and evening dresses – Pick's was bright red with a long slit up the side and McCormick's a bronze metallic mini-dress with a V-neck collar. The company has said that they play with 'cheap shock' and 'triteness', wanting 'the irony of triteness to be the problem' (Gorman 2013).

Number 1, The Plaza is an experimental theatre performance lasting 1 hour 20 minutes, which takes the form of 'an evening with' Jennifer Pick and Lucy McCormick. At the outset the performers announce triumphantly that they are back on stage. McCormick shouts, 'we're back in the theatre! We're going to give it another go!' and Pick, 'we're back in the theatre and there's nothing anyone can do about it!' The performers operate the lighting and sound from on stage and spend their time either sitting on the bar stools, fiddling with items on or near the lighting desks or walking around the stage space. They perform musical numbers, swaying in unison on the bar stools, miming the playing of instruments and occasionally interrupting one another to introduce a new lighting state or smoke effect. At other junctures they 'show' the audience around their notional 'flat', which they intimate they share together. They indicate where the different rooms can be found onstage and mime the opening of windows and doors. Towards the end of the show they mime throwing large objects such as an oven towards the audience. From the outset both performers appear smeared in a chocolate-brown substance.

FIGURE 2.1 Lucy McCormick makes adjustments to the sound in *Number 1, The Plaza* (2013), GETINTHEBACKOFTHEVAN

Photograph: Julia Bauer

It is daubed sporadically on faces, arms and legs. Much of the performance is spent chatting conversationally and aimlessly to the audience, as if filling time. The performers reprise their double-act routine from previous shows, and yet on this occasion there is a marked antipathy. Pick is openly hostile towards McCormick at several junctures in the performances and regularly undermines her. Pick and McCormick imply that they cohabit in the fictional flat and the intense nature of their interpersonal relationship and their prolonged licking of one another's bodies during one section works to query the nature of their relationship.

This performance uses irony and radical negativity by obscuring the intention and attitude of the onstage characters to what they are doing. It is difficult to ascertain *intention* because the characters are inconsistent in their attitude towards one another, towards their commitment to the performance and towards the audience. They switch between virtuosic singing and seemingly clumsy improvisation. At times they appear to be in control of the onstage activity, and deliver well-executed harmonies, at others they seem to have lost sight of their intention to share favourite show-tunes and provide a diverting 'evening with' Jen and Lucy. The characters demonstrate ownership and authority over the stage and their fictional apartment whilst making self-deprecating statements about their right to occupy those spaces. They are self-reflexive about their intention to 'entertain' and refer to their contract with the audience throughout. And yet, at times they voice their resentment at having to meet the audience's expectations. They even

FIGURE 2.2 Jennifer Pick and Lucy McCormick mime musical instruments, *Number 1, The Plaza* (2013), GETINTHEBACKOFTHEVAN
Photograph: Julia Bauer

acknowledge the 'problem' of ironic representation. Reflecting upon the difference between their last foray on to the stage in *Big Hits* (2012) and their 'current' experience (2013) they have the following exchange:

MCCORMICK: We have been doing this for a long time now ...
PICK: Five Years
MCCORMICK: Fifty Years. It was different in those days ... everything's changed. What were we wearing? And everyone's very young. Things were very different, you could sort of walk down the street, couldn't you without a barrage of irony coming at you? (they chink wine glasses).

(GETINTHEBACKOFTHEVAN 2013)

Much of what Pick and McCormick do on stage verges upon the ludicrous. They state an intention to stage a certain kind of performance, but introduce long delays between songs by arguing, taking time for lengthy reflections or discussing the invisible fictional apartment in which they pretend to reside. Rainford's conception of 'negative freedom' is relevant here because the characters switch between a kind of phallic, patriarchal, neo-liberal authority, which is associated with financial affluence and ownership of property and insights that, for some, they and their work signifies 'shit'. They cited what Rainford calls their 'secondariness' in a crude and explicit manner, seemingly enjoying the 'negative freedom' the stage gives them licence to occupy. Furthermore they performatively cite a type of repugnant phallic authority by repeating disproportionately assertive, bullying behaviour.

The most obvious example of the performers asserting their authority is their unapologetic occupation of the stage space. They celebrate their return to the stage and state, 'we've started as we mean to go on, because tonight is a kind of "evening with" vibe and we are doing our favourite show tunes. We've got quite a selection – I'm sure there's something for everyone' (GETINTHEBACK-OFTHEVAN 2013). The presence of the lighting and sound desk on stage bolsters the impression of control, as Pick and McCormick take it in turns to operate the lighting, cue backing tracks and operate the smoke machine. They demonstrate they are capable of singing to a high standard and, at least to begin with, perform with energy, focus and commitment. Their ownership of the stage space is carried over into repeated reference to the notional apartment, presumably the eponymous 'Number 1, The Plaza', which they stalk around whilst clutching and sipping from wine glasses. The title of the residence suggests an aspirational location associated with the many 'luxury apartments' continuing to be built in large quantities across London despite the global economic downturn. Pick and McCormick repeatedly point out the locations of certain rooms, although nothing on stage actually exists to delineate different rooms or spaces. Apart from the lighting and sound desk the company have only two bar stools. They tell the audience the bar stools accompany a 'breakfast bar', a redundant piece of furniture associated with financial affluence and an aspirational lifestyle.

The performers further demonstrate ownership of the space by controlling the audience's experience of the passage of time. As mentioned above, the first show-tune is delivered in an energetic and focused manner, but from then on the show loses focus as the performers bicker, discuss petty differences and pick fights with the audience. They take time to spin playfully on their bar stools, taking turns to twist one another around or finding different ways to propel themselves. They could be seen to be taking liberties with the audience's patience and time, refusing to deliver the show-tune medley promised at the outset. A further aspect of control is represented through Pick's unpleasant behaviour. From the start of the performance she makes comments to undermine McCormick. In response to McCormick's compliment 'I like your dress', Pick replies 'yours is disgusting'. McCormick makes light of Pick's behaviour exclaiming, as if in delight 'there she goes! Something we can all enjoy. The point is she doesn't mean it.' She later asserts 'she's got the voice for it – it's something about the accent, I think!' During an extended period of bickering, McCormick muddies the distinction between their onstage personae and their 'real' selves by saying, 'this kind of stuff is quite hard for us because we actually get on very well ...' to which Pick replies, 'no we don't ... you are a cunt' (GETINTHEBACKOFTHEVAN 2013). McCormick shrugs off Pick's insults as if her upper-middle-class British accent renders her immune to accusations of cruelty. She exhorts Pick to insult the audience, as if to demonstrate how 'harmless' her insults really are:

MCCORMICK: She's got the voice for it! Tell that woman she's a cunt.
PICK: You're a cunt
MCCORMICK: See! It's fine – we don't mind, do we? Tell that man he's a cunt.
PICK: You're a cunt, sir.
MCCORMICK: We can all enjoy it! She's got the voice for it – it's something about the accent, I think!

(GETINTHEBACKOFTHEVAN 2013)[2]

This exchange cites the authority associated with class in contemporary Britain. An upper-middle-class accent is commonly associated with wealth, affluence, social mobility and a sense of cultural superiority (Morrison 2014: 499). Her cultural entitlement manifests at times as outright contempt, she scorns McCormick's attempt to develop a moment of gravitas by insisting, 'you pissed on it – standing there, ankle deep in your bloody, pissy little message!' and to the audience, 'here you are! Here's your fucking message!' Pick repeatedly asserts her authority over McCormick who speaks with a slight Northern accent by insulting her and also by taking on a patrician role as her 'guardian' or 'owner' when she pretends to be a cat. McCormick repeatedly brushes off Pick's insults, as if to maintain a sense of professional composure, however during sections of the performance in which they appear to role play being 'at home' in their apartment, she takes on the role of a cat and Pick the cat's 'owner'. As they pretend to walk around the flat Pick invites McCormick to show the audience her 'balances'. McCormick walks along a length of rolled dance floor separating the technical area from the main stage area. 'Good Girl!' praises Pick. McCormick lapses into the role of cat as if in response to a sense of abjection conferred by Pick's bullying demeanour. She claims that she has 'hurt her claw' and 'done a poo' and either tries to cuddle up to Pick or shrink away as if anticipating punishment. The first instance of McCormick's feline transformation comes after Pick has told the audience 'you're all a bunch of cunts – all of you!' and to McCormick, 'why don't you get out of my face you little shit?' McCormick admonishes, 'you're sounding a bit like you mean it now …' signalling a shift in tone to one of unease. This transformation underscores the dysfunctional nature of the relationship. McCormick's reference to accents suggests the power disparity may be related to a class differential and Pick's sense of cultural entitlement.

Pick goes on to reinforce her sense of superiority and control by asserting repeatedly and aggressively 'this is my house'. Her claim refers simultaneously to the fictional apartment and theatre space. Transitioning out of an intimate and erotic moment in which the figures lick the 'shit' off one another Pick advances to the front of the stage and shouts, 'get out of my home! This is my house!' She goes on to insist, 'this is my kingdom – get out of my fucking home. I command you be gone! This is my land! Get out!' McCormick giggles in the background, punctuating her delivery of *Defying Gravity* with exclamations such as, 'as if we live together! It's not true – it's about something bigger!' Pick's exhortations to the audience to 'fuck off', 'get out of [her] house' and 'go home' last for an extended period of time, producing a scenario which was received by laughter in the production I witnessed at Toynbee Studios, but which manifested deeply unpleasant behaviour. Pick's sense of entitlement, ownership and control in this instance is bolstered by a neoliberal ideology of wealth accumulation and white upper-middle-class privilege. Although she is speaking through a female persona her characterisation is based on patriarchal and colonial values. She wins her sense of cultural superiority by appropriating phallic symbols and heteronormative hyper-masculine traits.

Number 1, The Plaza refers to an exclusionary and discriminatory social hierarchy, associating this with a sense of cultural entitlement and control. In Rainford's terms this can be seen to be representative of the 'patriarchal structure' and the authority of 'sexed subjectivity'. GETINTHEBACKOFTHEVAN query and undermine the validity of these values by subtly undermining them throughout the show. The illusion of control conferred by the performer's claim to the stage is undermined by assertions such as 'we're back in the theatre and there's nothing anyone can do about it!' as if this is an admission that reviews have been far from favourable in the past. Furthermore the performers are covered in a brown substance that has been manufactured to resemble human excrement and throughout they invoke 'shit' in relation to themselves and the performance. The performers debase themselves by bringing on to the stage samples of their own excrement, contained in plastic food containers, and dropping it on to their metaphorical doorstep. As they let the brown substance slop on to the stage before them McCormick says, 'OK, so this is a sort of comment on various things …' to which

Pick replies, 'it's *not* a comment, it's just a pile of shit'. The 'shit' then can be seen to encapsulate the performance itself, the audience's desire for a 'message' and the performers themselves, who are ostensibly smeared with the substance. This invocation could be seen to refer to the practice of theatre-making and theatre-going on a wider scale, or operate at a more local level to seemingly repeat assertions by critics that their work is 'shit'.

In addition, although the performance begins with clarity, focus and aplomb, the performers quickly lose sight of their aim and shift into a mode of listless bickering and prevarication. They fiddle and experiment with lighting effects, rather than execute pre-planned cues, and McCormick constantly interrupts her delivery of the songs to speak and deliver sarcastic asides. The company set up an atmosphere of bonhomie and joviality and yet the illusion of binary cohesion leant by the 'double-act' fractures as one of the performers repeatedly expresses her contempt for both her partner and the audience. The 'promise' of comedic entertainment and diversion made at the outset is breached as the discourse of selfishness and control makes an incursion into the stage space. At the start of the show the performers assert what they 'have', that is the capacity to entertain, to divert and to charm. In the fictional stage-world they hint that they may be in a sexual relationship and they 'own' a luxury apartment in London.[3] By the end of the show all of this has been revealed to be without substance or foundation. McCormick is divested of all but her bra; she stands naked on the stage, dripping from the white wine 'shower' she used to wash off the 'shit'. The apartment exists only in the imagination, the partnership, both onstage and off, is in pieces and the audience has been denied a climactic moment of 'meaning' or transcendence. Instead, the audience is being told, in no uncertain terms, to leave. Although the company have insisted that theirs is a 'metaphorical space' the unease caused by Jen's hostility and contempt ring frighteningly true and effectively destabilise the companionable atmosphere created at the outset. For me, these moments represent a deliberate attempt to undermine the assertions of ownership and control made earlier. Reading through a liberal feminist lens, the assertion of, and then retraction of, control could be seen to be confounding. However, when read through a postmodernist lens, and one which bears in mind Tomlin's warning to work with a 'healthy' rather than 'cynical' scepticism, this construction/refusal of control creates a sense of uncertainty and unknowing. The piece could be read as a critique of the kind of liberal feminist ideology that pushes for women to participate in neoliberal capitalist society by borrowing phallic symbolism and behaviour. Pick's phallic behaviour is shown to be execrable and its influence signified through the cake and chocolate spread mixture they concoct. The performers' tacit participation in that system marks and debases them with 'shit'. The idea of sincerely setting out to communicate something 'meaningful' via performance is ridiculed by Pick's description of 'the pissy bloody little message', which for the company stages 'the contradiction at [its] own heart' and 'rupture[s] the illusion of totality' (Tomlin 2008: 358). The performers, at the outset, stage a post-feminist utopia in which two female performers take possession of the stage and an audience's undivided attention for two hours, and yet the company undermines this by giving voice to an unspoken hesitation that they might be 'shit'. As the performance progresses the terms upon which they are expected to 'succeed' are shown to be ideologically corrupt. Pick insists upon a selfish model of ownership and authority won through subjugation. This ideology punctures the show's initial sense of warmth and philanthropy and causes the show to grind to a halt. The phallocentric drive 'breaks' the performance. For me, the effect of Pick's toxic behaviour points to a critique of what Sara Jane Bailes has referred to as 'exemplar individualistic achievers'. Writing about Margaret Thatcher's legacy she observes:

> Thatcher was intent upon producing citizens whom she considered to be [...] individually driven 'wealth-creators' and 'risk-takers,' capable of creating a culture of winners who, according to her ideology, would succeed in rising to the top regardless of class, education, or background. Everyone else – the losers one supposes – was destined to sink to the bottom.
>
> *(Bailes 2011: 81)*

The intention of the artists towards their material remains ambiguous until the very end of the show. The performers set up one proposition, of shared bonhomie and enjoyable diversion, only to spoil and retract that promise. They present the illusion of collective endeavour, only to have this refuted by one of the performers in an obviously 'staged' but troubling performance. The company's attitude towards theatre-making and meaning-making is confused and ambivalent. This failure to meet expectations is largely experienced as humorous, but the force of repetition of Pick's directive to 'leave' and 'fuck off' causes an atmosphere of unpleasantness to permeate the space. It is not until Pick brings the lights to black-out and quietly says 'not really' that the audience are given an indication of the company's position and even this, according to Chillingworth, is an attempt to 'obfuscate and complicate what's real and what's not'.[4] This can be seen, then, to render the performance *about* inscrutability on the topic of women centre stage and the means by which they attain the right to speak. The company has explained their reluctance to be aligned with one fixed ideological position over another. Chillingworth has stated that:

> [g]enerally we would do our best to complicate or ruffle or scribble over any of these phrases or any moment that we think could be perceived as sincere because we tend to think that as soon as something lands as sincere, it's shot itself in the head [...] we really feel that it is not our position to say outright, and to stop and go 'no, seriously now – this is what we think about this', because that is actually when you can position yourself against an audience. We never want there to have been a 'get-out' clause, or even a 'get-on' clause. It should always be, for us, that the audience either get out or get on or whatever, because of their own position that they have established with it, in all its move-ability.
>
> *(Gorman 2013)*

The repeated oscillation of attitudes towards control and submission throughout *Number 1, The Plaza* is part of a deliberate strategy to obscure the visibility of a fixed ideological position. The company aims for the audience to negotiate the performance and develop their own 'message'. Irony therefore represents an ideal tool to employ when constructing a scenario about what it means to stage a performance with 'a message' and what it means to win the right to have a voice in mainstream culture.

The second example I will draw upon is *Straight White Men* by Young Jean Lee. This piece was first staged in 2013 and was developed during a series of workshops at Brown University. Of all of Lee's plays, *Straight White Men* has enjoyed the widest commercial success benefiting from five different productions: the first at Leeds Theatre, Brown University in 2013; the second at the Public Theater New York in 2014 (which toured internationally); the third in 2017 with Steppenwolf Theater in Chicago (all directed by Lee); the fourth by Marin Theatre Company in Mill Valley California in July 2018 (directed by Morgan Gould); and the fifth on New York's Broadway at the Helen Hayes Theater (directed by Anna D. Shapiro) in June 2018. Lee identifies as Korean-American. After studying with Mac Wellman at Brooklyn College in 2002 Lee started writing plays and directing them at downtown New York venues. Her best known pieces include *Songs of the Dragons Flying to Heaven* (2006), *The Shipment* (2009) and *Untitled Feminist Show* (2011). Her work varies in form and tone, but customarily focuses upon the notion of 'outsider' identity (Stevens 2018). In 2008 Lee gave an insight into what drove her by revealing that, 'I try to think of the worst idea for a show I could possibly think of, like the last show in the world I would ever want to make. And then I force myself to make it' (Maxwell 2008). Furthermore she told Michele Steinwald in 2012 that *Straight White Men* would be her 'worst nightmare' because it would take the form of a three-act play (Steinwald 2012). By citing her antipathy to certain theatrical forms Lee can be seen to be distancing herself from her work. She describes a kind of dislocated artistry, as if she is 'compelled' to write about difficult subjects against her will. She has said, 'I've always had a good radar for the zeitgeist' suggesting that her compulsion to write is tempered by a need to articulate difficult ideas and values circulating in a particular sociocultural climate (Steinwald 2012). Her drive to name racial or feminist oppression is reminiscent of, what Sara Ahmed has termed, a kind of 'killjoy' compulsion (Ahmed 2017: 36). Ahmed recognises the ambivalence involved in 'giv[ing] the problem a name'. She writes, 'when we give problems their names, we can become a problem for those who do not want to talk about a problem even though they know there is a problem' (36).

Speaking in similar terms about *The Shipment* Lee reveals:

> I do kind of have a bee in my bonnet about race, and nobody wants to hear a person of color ranting about race and how unfair the world is to them. You know you don't want to hear people whine and accuse white people. All of these things are very unpopular. So to find a way to talk about the things that

bother me in a way that's not going to make everyone roll their eyes and dismiss it, that's the hardest thing for me.

(Maxwell 2008)

Lee is caught by the twin compulsion to articulate her sense of unease about racism and sexism in a supposedly 'post-racial' America and to observe learned behaviour and maintain a dignified silence. Patricia Ybarra and Karen Shimakawa have both invoked Sianne Ngai's 'ugly feelings' in relation to Lee's work. For Ngai 'ugly feelings' are 'ambivalent effects that reveal the ways in which seemingly negative emotions both challenge and drive capitalist accumulation' (Ngai cited in Ybarra 2014: 525). For Ngai there is:

> [a] special relationship between ugly feelings and irony, a rhetorical attitude with a decidedly affective dimension, if not feeling *per se*. For the morally degraded and seemingly unjustifiable status of these feelings tends to produce an unpleasant feeling about the feeling [...] that significantly parallels the doubleness on which irony, as an evaluative stance hinging on the relationship between the said and the unsaid, fundamentally depends.
>
> *(Ngai 2007: 10)*

Ngai's description of the relationship between ugly feelings and irony is highly relevant. In *Songs of the Dragons Flying to Heaven* and *Shipment*, Lee has her characters talk in reductive terms about race and racism. Her characters speak with a bluntness, which runs the risk of crossing a line into racism, however the meta-theatrical frame adopted in each production provides an indication that the lines are not intended to be delivered with sincerity. Lee has her character Korean-American in *Songs* wryly observe, 'the truth is, if you're a minority and you do super-racist stuff against yourself, then white people are all like "Oh, you're a cool minority" and they treat you like one of them' (Lee 2009: 66).

What Young Jean Lee and GETINTHEBACKOFTHEVAN can be seen to dramatise is a moment of realisation when those outside of the privileged sphere of affluent, able-bodied white masculinity recognise that in order to be taken seriously in a neoliberal capitalist landscape they must replicate the values of the aforementioned 'risk-takers' and the 'wealth-creators'. As Lee's characters cope with their unease they invite the audience to recognise the advantages that come to them from operating within the privileged system of middle-class white neoliberal values. *Straight White Men* is constructed around a key character, Matt, who feels guilty about his own white male privilege and refuses to use these attributes to his advantage. He asserts that his aim in life is to 'be useful' rather than to accumulate wealth or achieve his potential via a prestigious job. For Ybarra, Matt 'renounces' privilege and a,

> refusal of the self-making performance of human capital that is forced on a wider swathe of people every day [...] Matt responds by rejecting the very

terms in which the self is appreciated under neoliberal capital; self-expression, self-actualization, and being one's best self.

(Ybarra 2014: 522–523)

Lee's performances dwell on the pressure put upon the middle classes to achieve their optimum performance whilst drawing attention to the disparity of opportunities available for those who cannot pass as 'straight white men'.

As mentioned above *Straight White Men* takes the form of a naturalistic play. However, it is presented from within a metatheatrical frame. The three-act structure is introduced by a prologue delivered by the 'Stagehand-in-Charge' who, Lee states, should be played by a 'transgender or gender nonconforming person' who is 'preferably of color' (Lee 2015: 62). Lee's play script further states that 'loud hip-hop with sexually explicit lyrics by female rappers' should be played as the audience enter. She specifies, '[i] t should be loud enough that people have to shout over it to be heard'. The Stagehand-in-Charge is required to deliver a short speech before the naturalistic three-act play begins. The remainder of the performance continues, with the Stagehand-in-Charge entering the main playing area only in order to attend to set alterations. The action of the play, in keeping with naturalistic convention, unfolds predominantly through dialogue and activity appropriate to a family social space, such as a sitting room or lounge. The 'home' on display belongs to Ed 'the father' and the narrative takes place over a series of days in which Matt, 'the eldest', Jake, 'the middle' and Drew, 'the youngest' visit their father's house to celebrate Christmas. The audience learns that the boys' mother has died and Matt is living with Ed and acting as his carer.

The three-act play revolves around making preparations for Christmas and enjoying seasonal food and drink. The brothers revert to adolescent behaviour and patterns of speech, aggravating one another by dredging up anecdotes, reading from diaries and singing songs from the past. They wrestle physically and verbally, with Jake and Drew vying for their father's attention. Ed accepts their behaviour with a sense of benign indulgence. One evening Matt begins to cry as the family eats a Chinese takeaway. This acts as a primary catalyst because Matt's brothers are shocked and repulsed by Matt's tears. The remainder of the play sees them return again and again to Matt's 'problem' in order to identify the reason for his tears. Initially sympathetic, Ed eventually comes to side with his younger sons and at the end of the play he brutally orders Matt to leave his house telling him to 'go … find some other way to fail' (Lee 2015: 75).

Lee developed *Straight White Men* during a series of workshops held at Brown University while Playwright in Residence. She worked with 'a roomful of women, queer people and minorities' asking them 'what do you want straight men to do?' According to Lee, they responded that 'they wanted the straight white male character to sit down and shut up' (Ulaby 2014). However Lee revealed that when she shared her working version of the character they 'hated him'. She said:

I realized that the reason why they hated him was – despite all their commitment to social justice – what they believed in most was not being a loser.

[Matt] is exhibiting behaviour that gets attributed to people of color: not being assertive, not standing up for himself, always being in a service position.

(Ulaby 2014)

This response from the workshop participants had a significant impact upon Lee because, as Ybarra stated, the play comes to be *about* the failure to realise potential and the eruption of 'ugly feelings' that arise as a result. Despite emanating from research with people of colour the play has come to be about the failure of a white male to self-realise or take control of his life. As with my discussion of *Number 1, The Plaza* I will set out to assess instances of Lee claiming authority and control over the onstage activity and moments in which the play undermines any sense of authorial control.

Lee's main technique for framing the three-act play lies in the metatheatrical prologue presented by the Stagehand-in-Charge. The prologue attempts to orient the audience towards her preferred meaning for *Straight White Men*. Furthermore, the title, an extra-diegetic signifying element, performs an unusual function by referring to a recent Western sociocultural phenomenon whereby a customarily unmarked social group comes to be labelled and named as one sub-category amongst many. Lee has explained:

[s]o now [straight white men is] a category for the first time, everyone else had their ethnic identity and you were just the default and now all of a sudden 'straight white male' is a label getting slapped on people. It's being used in a derogatory way associated with negative stereotypes [...] and unsurprisingly, they don't like it.

(Lee 2017)

Social determinants such as this are customarily associated with sociocultural analysis or a more intellectual discourse explored by journalists, academics, activists and social commentators. As a play title, *Straight White Men* is rather blunt and contentious because it reduces a complex social phenomenon into just three words. The title is humorous because it gives the discourse of social mobility the kind of mainstream public visibility it would not customarily enjoy and hints at the paucity of language available to address the complex issues it invokes. The title is one of the first indicators that Lee's relationship to the content of the play is ironic and that she intends to distance herself from the ideology of neoliberal self-affirmation championed by the characters in the play. In Rainford's terms, Lee can be seen to be using her 'negative freedom' as a woman of colour to draw attention to the neoliberal, white, patriarchal discourse. She is 'repeating' the discourse of unmarked privilege 'back to the patriarchal structure in order to undermine the authority of (sexed) subjectivity' (Rainford 2005: 4).

Further framing devices include the choice of pre-set music and casting requirements for the Stagehand-in-Charge. As mentioned above, Lee stipulates this role be taken by 'a transgender or gender nonconforming' performer who is 'preferably a person of color'. Lee states that the figure should enter with:

an air of authority. They should be given a sense of agency and control over their role so that they feel genuinely empowered to speak on behalf of the show. To this end, the performer should have a voice in choosing – as well as veto power over – their costume and performance style. If audience members speak to them, they should feel free to ad-lib responses.

(Lee 2015: 62)

Lee draws attention to the hidden labour of stage managers, lighting and sound operators by having a member of the backstage team come forward to introduce the performance. She uses a post-Brechtian anti-illusory technique in order to remind the audience that the fictional world they are about to witness is mediated through a complex representational apparatus. As part of the production I saw at the Pompidou Centre, Paris in 2014, an Asian American played the Stagehand-in-Charge and wore jeans, braces and Dr Marten boots. They read their announcement from a script in a slightly self-conscious manner. As part of the 2018 Broadway production transgender performer Kate Bornstein took on the role, with the script altered to accommodate 'Person in Charge #1' and 'Person in Charge #2'. Person in Charge #2 is played by Ty Defoe, who identifies as a Native American trans man. Bornstein revealed that in the Broadway production the People in Charge were there to 'greet' and chat to the audience as they came into the auditorium. Bornstein explained,

we'll be ad-libbing for about half an hour before the show. Then we climb upon to the stage and have an introductory moment and [for that] we have a script. The way we wanted to talk about the show was more like docents.

(Raymond 2018)

The version of the role described by Bornstein suggests a slight departure from that described by Lee in the 2015 script, a 'docent' is conventionally recognised to be a guide and their presence for half an hour prior to the start of the show indicates they were there to help orient the audience towards a certain reading of the performance. The 2015 script states that the Stagehand-in-Charge should deliver the following speech after the pre-set music has come to an end and before lights are illuminated on the main stage:

Good [afternoon/evening], and welcome to [name of venue]. I'm [name of person]. On behalf of [name producing company], I'd like to thank you all for being here. Throughout this performance, the actors will stay in character and pretend not to see you, unless they hear your cell phone ring or see you taking photos or videos, in which case they may come into the audience and attack you. We hope you enjoy the show.

(Lee 2015: 62)

The welcome and request not to take photographs fall within the remit of most pre-show announcements for mainstream Western theatre. The behaviour of the stagehands during scene transitions is similarly unremarkable: they take some props away and set new ones in place. However, the move to explain the conceits of naturalistic theatre practice can be read as ironic and humorous because, for the vast majority of audience members, that information will be familiar and self-evident. The prologue by the Stagehand-in-Charge represents a key moment of 'control' for Lee because by denaturalising the conventions of realist theatre she emphasises that she is self-consciously appropriating it as a stylistic technique. The prologue demonstrates she finds the conventions of naturalistic theatre 'strange' and gives voice to her reservations about this particular form. The Stagehand-in-Charge's speech indicates that she will be co-opting the form in an ironic rather than sincere manner and as such can be seen to be in control of the representational apparatus.

The prologue follows the loud pre-set music, which Lee has stated should be 'hip-hop with sexually explicit lyrics by female rappers' (Lee 2015: 62). The volume of the music represents an interesting incursion into the customarily ambient time during which audience members, in larger-scale commercial theatres, will purchase souvenir programmes, order interval drinks and locate seats. The reception will inevitably depend upon the demographic make-up of the audience, the location and choice of venue. Lee has stated that her audiences tend to be 'demographically similar […] artsy, college educated' people, which suggests they might share her enjoyment of loud hip-hop, however she has revealed that audiences at New York's Public Theatre were upset by the music (Steinwald 2012). It had the effect of 'enraging [the] subscriber base because they saw it as an act of hostility towards them'. On reflection Lee observes, '[t]hat said something interesting about privilege. This space needs to be made for *my* privilege. My artistic vision is to always make the show *I* feel the most comfortable with' (Harbourfront Centre 2015, Lee's emphasis). Lee's statement about the 'alienating' or 'unwelcoming' music underscores the different conventions, practices and value-sets associated with diverse social and cultural groups. This means that, for her, as a Korean-American female director, she feels the need to put additional measures in place in order to exercise control over the way commercial venues frame and present her work.

The final framing device is ostensibly a marker of 'control' showing Lee to stand at one remove. It is more ambiguous and takes place at the close of the play. After Ed has banished Matt, Lee gives Matt the lines, 'What a gift. What a gift', along with directions to '*sit alone, staring out at the audience*' (Lee 2015: 75). This action can be interpreted both intra- and extra-diegetically. Because the actor does not speak as he looks out at the audience, the audience could read the gesture as remaining within the fictional world of the play – the character could be staring despondently at the internal wall of the house. Alternatively it could be read as a moment that has the potential to permeate the fourth wall and show the actor staring at, and seeing, the audience for the first time. Ybarra believes that Matt 'break[s] the fourth wall, looking straight ahead at the audience', arguing that it represents a post-Brechtian method of distanciation. For Ybarra this intervention into theatrical realism helps Lee 'denaturalize[s] the liberal hero as a dramaturgical norm while underscoring the violence of everyday capitalist subjectivation' (Ybarra 2014: 515). For me, however, this ending is too cautious and represents a loss of control for Lee. The problem lies in the ambiguity of the final moment, its timidity represents a lapse in conviction after the unequivocal intervention at the start of the play. Lee takes steps to defamiliarise the ideology of the white, neoliberal hegemony represented on stage but ultimately perpetuates the idea that the neoliberal subject *should* do their utmost to self-realise in the most productive way possible. The interventions she makes before the realist play begins are easily forgotten and her sense of opposition recuperated by the conservative message of the play. Here irony can be seen to work against the preferred meaning of the author and unintentionally bolster conservative dogma. It falls foul of the 'dangers' associated with deconstructive performances. As Marvin Carlson has observed, 'this [ironic] process may also, especially for a conventional audience, simply re-inscribe or reinforce those [conservative] structures' (Carlson 2003: 190).[5]

As in *Number 1, The Plaza*, there are instances in Lee's play in which the artist's attitude towards the content is ambiguous. As suggested above, it is unusual to hear the language of sociocultural critique in mainstream Western theatre. As a result, when Lee's characters cite warnings against racism and sexism their sarcastic tone runs the risk of recuperating the deconstructive effect the material would ideally have. For example, during Act one Drew discovers a homemade board game created by their mother called 'Privilege'. Lee writes, 'Drew holds up a Monopoly game box with a large homemade label on top that reads: "PRIVILEGE"'. Drew refers to it as 'the game where you have fun by not having fun!' and Ed calls it 'one of your mother's craftiest inventions' designed to teach them 'how not to be assholes' (63–64). The game is a doctored version of Monopoly with the iron and thimble winning an 'undervalued domestic labor bonus' (63). 'Excuses' cards replace 'Community Chest' cards. Jake shares an example: '[w]hat I said wasn't sexist/racist/homophobic because I was joking. Pay fifty dollars to The Lesbian and Gay Community Services Center' (63). Drew picks up a similar 'Denial' card, which reads, 'I don't have white privilege because it doesn't exist. Get stopped by the police for no reason and go directly to jail' (63). Lee's achievement in foregrounding white privilege on a commercial Western stage should not be underestimated but the gravitas of the homophobia and racism she invokes as part of PRIVILEGE risks being undermined by the sense of sarcasm and macho bonhomie fetishised within the world of the play. Despite, or perhaps because of, their insecurities and failures, the male characters' chief mode of interaction remains one of adolescent antagonism. As a result, despite what Ybarra sees as Matt's 'new kind' of heroism, the prevailing ideology is that of neoliberal self-actualisation (Ybarra 2014: 515).

Lee's control and distanciated irony is undermined by the repetition of the male characters' ebullience and bravado. Throughout the play Matt performs domestic chores such as cooking an apple pie, preparing eggnog and vacuuming the carpet. Jake, in particular, makes sarcastic comments each time Matt offers to provide for the family. In Act two Matt offers to 'pick up a movie' for the family to watch.

Jake responds to his offer by saying, 'Dad, you got your servant back. Must be nice having someone around the house again', implying that Matt is taking the place of Ed's deceased wife (Lee 2015: 68). When Matt brings in a bowl of eggnog, the stage directions state, 'Jake takes a cup smiling simperingly at Matt' and says, 'Why thank you!' (68). He is disquieted by Matt's servitude to the extent that he intervenes to perform roles that Matt has offered to do:

MATT: Do you want a bagel?
ED: No, I want a cranberry juice with ice!
MATT: (Getting up) Coming right up.
JAKE: No, I'll go.

(Lee 2015: 72)

The normalisation of adolescent play fighting, bickering and humiliation is difficult to censure if none of the characters from within the diegetic world disapprove. The scenes of sibling rivalry are funny and enjoyable to watch and I would argue that this fosters a desire to condone ignorant behaviour as 'harmless fun', or allowing 'boys to be boys'. The family unit thrives without their mother; the only reference to her is as an absent carer for their father and as a figure who encouraged her sons to be empathetic. Matt is the only character shown to heed her advice, and at the end of the play he is rejected from the family unit as a 'failure'. Furthermore the caring work he performs is undermined and feminised. Ultimately Matt, who is socially responsible and self-aware, is repeatedly undermined. Matt's most visible deviation into 'feminine' behaviour comes when he bursts into tears during a family meal. The remainder of the play sees the characters relentlessly interrogate Matt about the cause of his unhappiness. Although none of the characters explicitly describe the tears as 'feminine' they have caused significant disruption, even to the extent that the family repeatedly return to and speculate about the cause of the breakdown. One of the first questions Drew asks is, 'When's the last time that guy had a girlfriend?' (68) as if Matt's status as a normative heterosexual male may be in question. Later Drew asks, 'Matt, what the hell happened last night? Why did you cry?' (70) Although Jake's tendency is to leave Matt's behaviour unchallenged, Drew sees avoidance as 'cowardly macho bullshit' and suggests Matt goes to see a therapist (68). Drew surmises that Matt is unhappy because he is caring for his father when he should be living 'his own life'. Family members repeatedly return to his failure to fulfil his potential:

ED: He's so gifted.
DREW: I know! The guy's brilliant. What has he ever been doing since grad school?
ED: He's been working for his political groups.
DREW: Yeah, as like an admin assistant! I don't get it. He could be running those places.

(Lee 2015: : 69)

Drew suggests therapy, which provokes Jake to sarcastically invoke the credo of neoliberal 'risk-takers'. Jake asks, '[w]hy does he have to focus on his own happiness like a selfish self-actualizer?' and insists that 'Drew's trying to tell Matt that he's sad because he's not an ambitious self-actualizer hypocrite' (70). However, for all the sarcasm freighting Jake's words, *Straight White Men* can be seen to repeat the ideology of self-investment and self-actualisation by having Matt's father banish him. His family arrives at a consensus that his life needs to change, to take a more active, positive direction. Ed chastises Matt telling him that his lack of ambition makes him feel as if he has not 'done a good job as a father'. He comes to the extreme decision to ask him to leave, saying, 'I can't have you staying here anymore' (75). Refusing Matt's offer of care, Ed says, 'If I ever need a nurse, I can afford one … so take this check and go … *find some other way to fail*'. Stage directions state that, 'Matt cries. Ed sits there defeated' (75, my emphasis). The end of the play capitulates to Lee's workshop participants who were offended by the empath's status as 'loser'. At the end of the play the 'loser' is sent away from the homestead in a quasi-Shakespearean act of banishment. Matt's rejection signifies his deviance as a straight white man who, instead of pushing himself towards greater personal and financial capital gain, chooses to remain on the margins, trying not to 'not to make things worse' (74). To have this moment of rupture stand as the final image of the play, followed by Matt's ambiguous gaze towards the audience, suggests that for all its ironic intention, the neoliberal ideology of self-actualisation is the one that triumphs. I understand that Lee may well have felt an epilogue to be overly crude, but had the Stagehand-in-Charge reappeared at the close of the show the final image could have been very different. The diegetic world of the play would have been bookended by a reminder that the failure of a straight white man to take up his position of entitlement is not necessarily a tragic waste of potential.

Browsing reviews for the Broadway production of *Straight White Men* I discovered coverage about a spontaneous interaction between an audience member and Person in Charge#1. Press articles reveal that an audience member at one of the 2018 Broadway performances heckled Kate Bornstein. Press reports revealed that a woman in the audience booed Bornstein and shouted, 'you're not welcome here!' (Keeley 2018). Although this incident took place at the beginning, rather than end, of the show, the nature of the play, as a conventional piece of naturalism enjoyed by subscription members, serves as a warning that the ironic intention of the show and the show's title can be misconstrued as affirming the patriarchal white supremacist values it actually sets out to undermine. Regrettably, as indicated above, *Straight White Men* does not offer a way out of the double-bind of ironic representation but risks reiterating conservative values. In Rainford's terms this is perhaps because although the piece 'interrogates' and 'repeats' the beliefs of the patriarchal structure, it does not go far enough to criticise or negate (Rainford 2005: 3). Furthermore, Lee is hard placed to turn her 'alterity to her advantage' if the alterity is eclipsed by generic, normative ideology (4). Rather than maintaining an inscrutable authorial presence throughout, Lee's agency, or sense of control, over the preferred meaning of the piece recedes. As a result Lee could be seen to fall foul of what Tomlin would identify as a 'cynical' scepticism. The rhetoric that sets out to defamiliarise patriarchal ideology has 'little capacity' because it is delivered briefly at the outset. The diminutive act of resistance therefore struggles to 'move the discourse of postmodernism forward, or to offer any concept of "beyond" to the status quo' (Tomlin 2008: 363).

My third example, that of The Famous Lauren Barri Holstein, deliberately negotiates a range of attitudes towards femininity and sexuality throughout the performance. Holstein is a US artist currently based in London. She has been producing experimental performance since 2010. Holstein trained as a dancer and choreographer and, despite drawing upon a range of performance and live art practices, still considers her work to be largely 'choreographic' (Barbican 2017). Holstein has described her work as 'vagina-based' and deploying an aesthetics of radical negativity by using 'strategic ineptitude' that 'critically disrupt[s] the boundaries between "the show" and "not-the-show"' (Drew 2013; Holstein 2015: 178). Holstein puts herself centre stage in each production; presenting the persona of 'The Famous', whose relationship to Lauren Barri Holstein as woman and artist remains intentionally ambiguous (Gorman 2017). Holstein's work is highly visual. It regularly features her naked or half-dressed body smeared in ketchup, covered in fake hair, eggs, mango, feathers, toilet roll and, in *Notorious*, a dead octopus. She employs a live camera feed to project close-up images of her face and vagina and talks directly to the audience. She sings along to backing tracks of songs by popular female artists such as Katy Perry, Brittany Spears, Miley Cyrus and Nicki Minaj; uses hoists to suspend herself and colleagues from the lighting rig; and draws upon grotesque female archetypes from fairy tales, Disney and contemporary popular culture. Her performance work is 'vagina-based' because Holstein invents moments that draw prolonged focus on to her vagina. In *Splat!* (2013) she inserted the handle of a knife into her vagina and flung balloons filled with red paint against the knife, so that they exploded. This section lasted for the 3 minutes 46 seconds of *Get Ready for This* by 2 Unlimited.[6] In *How to Become a Cupcake* Holstein inserts an ice-lolly into her vagina, rolls backwards into a shoulderstand that tilts her pelvis aloft and sustains the pose for a prolonged period of time as an assistant melts the lolly with a hair dryer. As part of *Notorious* she inserts plastic test tubes filled with coins into her vagina and 'ejaculates' the contents on to the stage taking advantage of the forward thrust of the hoist to propel them as close to the audience as possible.

The movement work in Holstein's shows are related to task-based activities, for example, eating a mango whilst attempting to 'become' the mango or simulating sexualised poses from popular films (Holstein 2015). In *Splat!* Holstein performs an *en-pointe* dance as an interlude between other more chaotic moments of the show. She explains her transition away from this medium:

> I kept coming across two obstacles with 'dance': 1) it became difficult to
> escape the marriage of 'beauty' and 'women's bodies'; and 2) I felt like dance,

as a form, was somehow very descriptive, representational, expressive. I had to find my way through these obstacles.

(Barbican 2017)

In addition to using 'The Famous' as her main artistic persona Holstein appropriates a number of other female personae. In *Notorious* she takes on the persona of a 'witch-bitch' whose function is to '[be] the feminist killjoy in the room' and to perform acts of 'pleasurable repulsion … emotional delinquency … unapologetically creating problems' (Barbican 2017). She has revealed that the inspiration for *Notorious* lay in 'the way female artists are often pathologised'. She has said that '[i]t is much easier to see a woman as victim, as crazy, as tragic, than it is to accept her in all her complexity' (Moses 2017). For Kim Solga, the personae in Holstein's work,

> showcas[e] what happens to young female bodies torn physically as well as emotionally between a historical feminism that sought to empower them, and a contemporary 'post-feminist' popular culture in which empowerment is available only to female bodies made sexually attractive in depressingly conventional ways.
>
> *(Solga 2013: 67)*

Holstein's personae reveal themselves to be egotistical, emotionally vulnerable, exploitative, sexualised and exhibitionist. As one critic described it, 'persona piles upon persona – fame-hungry provocateur, shamed slut flayed with dead mollusc, sexy virgin, the diva performer ordering her crew' (Winter 2017). The lack of continuity of personae is key to Holstein's artistic vision and her critique of contemporary feminine subjectivity. She writes,

> [t]his 'coherent' model of subjectivity, though, rejects the admittance of mess, failure, humiliation, disgust etc. Once this 'complete' female subject falls, or fails to fulfil her self-determined 'success' (as is inevitable), that subject is at once regarded as a victim.
>
> *(Holstein 2014: 99)*

Holstein's words are redolent of Doyle who, as cited previously, avers that 'subjective coherence is a discursive effect' (Doyle 2009: 30). Holstein refuses to allow her personae to achieve coherence, a position that heightens the sense of ironic distanciation. Holstein's relationship to the flawed, tragic characters remains ambiguous as she tries them on and rejects them like articles of clothing.

Holstein is working in a similar context to GETINTHEBACKOFTHEVAN. Indeed, Lucy McCormick worked with Holstein, performing in *Splat!* Both companies present sexualised female bodies whilst constructing a varied range of subject positions. For me, Holstein's work obscures her attitude towards subject matter in a similar way to GETINTHEBACKOFTHEVAN, although her work draws upon visual spectacle and allegory to a greater degree. Like both GETINTHEBACK-OFTHEVAN and Young Jean Lee, Holstein exploits what Rainford has called the 'negative freedom' of her 'secondariness' by repeating exaggerated tropes of commercialised femininity back to the neoliberal white patriarchal structure (Rainford 2005: 4). Her sarcastic asides serve to undermine the act of inhabiting faux celebrity personae. The dictatorial control deployed by The Famous, whereby she tersely orders colleagues around, draws attention to customarily suppressed signs of theatrical labour and achieves a distanciating effect. Her sense of determination shifts between acute focus and careless dismissal, for example, at one moment The Famous will commit to singing a song with sincerity only to undermine its gravitas by asking for the track to be repeated over again. Similarly, she might position herself to deliver an important speech, but delay its delivery by talking to an operative about the timing of the cue or the readiness of the equipment. Holstein's stepping in and out of persona queers her relationship to the performance itself, creating a tension of ironic inscrutability. Because distanciation occurs throughout the show, her aesthetic can be seen to comply with what Tomlin has called a 'healthy scepticism', mobilising questions about the ethics and credence of art making throughout. Holstein's work does not work with fracture, mess and inscrutability to merely gesture towards or borrow tropes of postmodern performance, but rather her use of chaos embodies an ethical drive towards deconstruction in questioning female agency, language and subjectivity throughout.

As with *Number 1, The Plaza* and *Straight White Men* I will analyse *Notorious* in order to draw attention to instances when Holstein both appropriates and relinquishes agency and 'control' of the stage. *Notorious* runs for approximately two hours in length and features three female performers. The main playing area is both in front of and behind a large curtain made out of matted white wigs. Two easy chairs stand at either side of the playing area along with matching side tables and domestic lamps. Conversational activity takes place on the side chairs, with Holstein talking to the audience, and she dances and clips on the hoist centre stage. Holstein mounts a podium just left of centre to better frame the live-streamed close-up of her vagina. She addresses the audience directly throughout the show, often intimating that she is disappointed or 'hates' them.

The opening image features three back-lit female figures suspended on hoists from the lighting rig accompanied by the sound of a crackling fire, eerie sighing and hissing. The performers wear long, matted, grey-white wigs and garments designed to look as if hair is growing out of their skin. Holstein's companions are revealed to be 'Brogan' and 'Krista' – their names coinciding with their 'real' names as professional artists, Krista Vuori and Brogan Davison. They appear as Holstein's supporters, co-performers and technical assistants.

The remainder of onstage action alternates between: Holstein singing and gyrating to well-known tracks; cast members sitting stage right on and around the easy chair; Holstein climbing on to a piece of rostra to allow Vuori to get a close-up of her vagina; Holstein gyrating/thrusting on a hoist; Holstein speaking directly to camera; and Holstein sitting in the easy chair stage left speaking contemplatively to the audience. The performance does not unfold with any causal or linear logic; instead it is propelled according to The Famous' next whim. She asserts, 'OK I am ready' and asks, 'can I have my track?' as if to underscore the fact that she controls all onstage action. Davison and Vuori mostly work to support Holstein but during one section, Vuori gyrates in the hoist and delivers a deliberately un-sexy and ludicrous narrative about a lesbian sex fantasy. Holstein regularly orders Davison and Vuori around or speaks on their behalf.

The most obvious example of Holstein forging the illusion of agency and therefore 'control' can be witnessed via the persona of 'The Famous' who engineers and drives the show forward. She uses a live camera feed to enlarge her face and draw the audience's gaze. Furthermore, she monitors the behaviour of the audience, picking specific individuals out to feature in her stories or chastise for disrespectful behaviour. During one of the performances I saw at the Barbican, London in November 2017 The Famous enjoyed a prolonged exchange with an audience member who needed to go to the toilet. She gave permission, only to warn 'you had better fucking come back'. When she felt the audience to be unusually quiet, for example, during a section in which she was manipulating an edible eyeball between her labia, she railed, 'you guys are really fucking quiet … you've got to give me something. We've done this for five nights in a row!' an outburst which prompted a round of appreciative (and guilty) applause (Holstein 2017). The Famous is clearly constructed as the driving force. When her colleagues perform they 'fill' space so that she can prepare for another scene; they are constructed as assistants despite being similarly dressed as witches. Holstein further asserts control by urinating on stage. Urinating in *Splat!* she stated that she did it to 'mark her territory on stage' (Holstein 2015). Towards the end of *Notorious* she pours a large bag of popping candy on to the floor. She clips herself into a harness, rests her feet on Vuori and Davison's shoulders and urinates on to the pile below. The confectionary is designed to emit loud crackles and pops when moistened. In this instance it hissed, popped and cracked, sounds reminiscent of the fire crackling at the start of the show.

Holstein can be seen to retain a sense of agency over how she is 'read' or identified by appropriating a number of different personae. The fluctuation between roles prevents spectators from fixing her as a single, coherent subject. The performances are mounted and driven by 'The Famous' and yet the audience are presented with one superficial character after another and are hard placed to give a name to the character appearing before them. In *Notorious* the shift in personae is less obvious than in previous productions. To begin with she wears the long matted hair associated with a witch along with coloured contact lenses rendering her eyes disturbingly pale with tiny irises. Another persona wears a dead octopus over a white wig cap, bright contact lenses and a thong woven with knotted lengths of fabric, a heavy beaded necklace and an ornate breast-plate. Holstein reveals a third persona to be a 'sexy baby' for which she wears frilled shorts, made to resemble a nappy, and a white embroidered crop top. Sexy baby's hair is an enormous backcombed blonde wig, which shimmers when lit from the back. Sexy baby hula hoops and delivers a long confessional speech, in a squeaky voice, from the armchair stage left. Octopus woman begins by simpering and caressing the octopus legs as if they were plaits of hair only to rip the beast from her head and tear it apart. Holstein's witch persona bears a resemblance to 'The Famous' and yet dwells upon the mystical powers assigned to witches and wise-women. This flitting between personae shows a figure attempting to find a voice that 'fits' or rings true, and whilst Holstein does not settle for any one, fixed persona, the experimentation gives her licence to articulate and critique some of the more toxic, misogynistic values associated with post-feminist subjectivity.

Holstein displays control and authority in her manipulation of time. She dances feverishly to one song, only to ask for the song to be repeated. She insists the audience are patient with Krista when she is out of breath and they 'give her time' to recover; she fiercely retorts, 'this is not a democratic space!' when heckled by an audience member. Furthermore, she deliberately tries the patience of the audience. Twelve minutes before the end of one of the performances I witnessed, audience members began to applaud, assuming, because Holstein had been lying silent and still centre stage for a number of minutes, the show had come to an end. Holstein curtailed the applause with 'Uh no! You've got a way to go, you'll know when it's over believe me!' (Holstein 2017)

Other moments of heightened agency can be found in Holstein's celebration of the mystical power of witchcraft. She shows herself bringing ostensibly dead witches back to life, indeed, the performance begins with an image of inert, hanging bodies associated with the persecution of women believed to be witches in the 17th century. At Holstein's behest, those bodies come back to life and unshackle themselves. She celebrates a witch's power to rejuvenate during a long speech to camera. She whispers about the things 'some people say' she is capable of as a witch, describing her organic, erotic encounter with nature thus:

> sometimes at night I feel as if my body starts to disappear and disintegrate. I sink into the soil and rot like road kill. I think it attracts all the animals in the forest. Some people say I have sex with animals, like wild animals. [...] Sometimes there's a snake that comes and he crawls around my body. He goes around my neck and squeezes and he winds around my legs and thighs and he goes inside me and nibbles at the edges of my vagina. And while I'm decomposing I'm also orgasming. In the morning I am rejuvenated and satisfied.
>
> *(Holstein 2017)*

Holstein's witch articulates an uncompromising and active sexual desire that extends beyond normative sexual practice. She melts into organic matter by becoming one with the soil and communes with animals in a way she finds ultimately 'rejuvenating'. Further insights into the 'power' of the witches emerges as Holstein half-jokingly apologises, on behalf of herself, 'Krista' and 'Brogan', for atrocities committed against audience members' families. In one instance she confesses:

I know that I can be a whore sometimes and also I'm really sorry for being such a slut. I'm also really sorry for sucking all of those dicks and I'm also really sorry to this lady here (with the fur on your collar?) I knew you were coming to see the show and I collected all my drain hair and I stuck it to your head. Brogan's really sorry (person with red hair and tank top) she took you on a date in a rowboat at Tower Bridge. She fed you spaghetti hoops. Brogan had a massive line of anal beads in her bag – first she rammed them down your throat and then up your butt. You exploded on her and she dumped your bleeding body and ran off. She's really sorry about that.

(Holstein 2017)

Holstein's lacklustre apologies for ludicrous atrocities refers to a type of adolescent behaviour which, if anything, renders the witches all the more frightening for their insincerity and desultory moral relativism.

Holstein's adoption of personae, celebration of erotic perversity and control of the audience's gaze points to her negotiating a clear position of agency throughout *Notorious*. These features buoy The Famous/Holstein up and allow her to occupy a position of strength and autonomy for the duration of the show. However, she acknowledges that her power is contingent upon the audience's patience and indulgence. Holstein's personae negotiate ways of securing and retaining that power by shifting between subject positions of domination and subjugation. By apologising for being 'sluts' they make themselves vulnerable in a way that acknowledges female 'secondariness' but having done with the apologies shift the tone of the conversation to reassert authorial control. Holstein's guilty allowances show her to be interpellated into a conservative heteronormative ideology and repeat heteronormative values 'back to the patriarchal structure in order to undermine the authority of (sexed) subjectivity itself' (Rainford 2005: 4). However the repeated return to Holstein's assertive persona as The Famous creates an uneasy tension between a sexualised, autonomous being and an acerbic cultural commentator.

Holstein's control over the performance is rarely in question but moments when she introduces misogynistic language can be seen to threaten the balance. She appropriates terms such as 'slag, bitch, whore' to describe herself in a variety of roles. For me, the performative violence of these terms is such that it is difficult to recuperate them even when uttered in jest. Once uttered toxic misogyny infiltrates the stage and permeates the atmosphere of the performance. Holstein's control is further in question when she and her peers apologise for their deviant behaviour. An apology is an attempt to beg indulgence and suggests a resolution to make amends, again, a way of complying with patriarchal values. Although Holstein retains ultimate control until the end of the performance, the moments of apology pay lip service to a conservative sense of sexual propriety and mark her pro-sex stance as 'deviant'. Finally I would argue that Holstein's agency comes into question during moments when she polices the audience and when she confesses that she is 'angry'. These moments become uncomfortable because she employs a mode of rhetorical enquiry that suggests the relationship between the audience and the diva is reciprocal, they imply that she has an investment in their approval and support. For example, Holstein follows her story of decomposition and animal sex with an assertive dance to Miley Cyrus' *We Can't Stop*, a song about self-realisation and abandon.[7] As part of this dance she pulled gummy snakes from her vagina and eats them. Her movements were assertive and sexualised, she grunted with exertion as she repeatedly and violently jerked her body. Towards the end of the song Holstein gestured for the track to be stopped and took off her long wig. She switched to a squeaky high pitched voice and said, 'I'm really sorry for sucking all of those dicks'. She began a long list of apologies with, 'I know I can be a whore sometimes and I'm really sorry for being such a slut' (Holstein 2017). The shift in tone from sexual abandon to timid apology marks a confusing shift, although the apologies go on to become so ludicrous that they ultimately signify impudence rather than acquiescence. As I have argued above, apologising for having sex with multiple partners and referring to oneself as a slut and a whore invokes a conservative patriarchal ideology that sets out to contain and curb women's behaviour. As Rainford has pointed out, feminist critique 'acknowledges a peculiar double-bind' because it 'strives to challenge and break from the (unequal) sexual terms, relations and hierarchies of patriarchy, but [the] cultural forms and discourses at its disposal are themselves enmeshed in patriarchy' (Rainford 2005: 2). For me patriarchal condemnatory terms such as 'whore' and 'slut' are almost impossible to recuperate unless the artist is able to control the context in which they are spoken. This might happen, for example, in a queer space in which more liberal attitudes towards sexuality are championed. Holstein's tone is one of sarcasm and yet the performative effect of the sexual insults result in her being marked by the tyranny of misogyny despite ironic intention. Holstein creates an uneasy tension as she apologises, as if holding the audience to account for its complicity in sedimenting these values. The tone of censure attached to these terms serves as a reminder that they enjoy weight and credence for many constituents.

Inevitably, an artist cannot guarantee the spectator will take their preferred meaning from an artwork or performance. However, Holstein deliberately courts confusion by shifting between assertion and subjugation. Bridget Christie and Laura Bates' anecdotes in Chapter one have demonstrated the illegible nature of feminist irony for some, and I am fearful that the apologies here work to undermine the deconstructive effect of irony. Holstein has stated that she has received hate mail, and death-threats from those who have misconstrued her work as 'sincere'. They have written to express their offence. She revealed how, after *How to Become a Cupcake*:

> this one guy wrote me a really long Facebook message. He was saying that I'm desperate and attention-seeking, and that I must have been making better art at some point but have stooped to this level, and how badly crafted it all was. I just found it really interesting because he was conflating me with 'The Famous', and then both of us with the show itself, as if that show was an

expression of me and everything that I believe in the world, and that none of it was a theatrical *choice*. Which I think is hilarious/amazing, because once you're in a theatrical space, you're in a space of conflict between reality and pretence, and in my mind it should always be read that way – that's the exciting thing about that space, to play with that line.

(Gorman 2017)

The potential illegibility of irony is compounded by the nature of the theatre venue. *Notorious*, like *Straight White Men*, was programmed into a comparatively mainstream theatre venue rather than the 'dirty warehouse' Sexy Baby suggests would be more appropriate (Holstein 2017). The production I witnessed in November 2017 appeared in the Barbican's Pit venue, a smaller performance space with a reputation for showing experimental theatre work.[8] Holstein has noted that she is 'really overly passionate about bringing difficult work into mainstream spaces' (Gorman 2017) and as a result she can be seen to deliberately obfuscate her intention. She uses sexually condemnatory language to exacerbate the tension between 'reality and pretence'. The tension she creates acts as an uneasy reminder that these terms have real-world effects upon women's lives and bodies and occupies an uneasy space between legible irony and toxic misogyny.

Like GETINTHEBACKOFTHEVAN and Young Jean Lee, Holstein maintains an ambiguous attitude towards her material. Towards the end of *Notorious*, sitting in an armchair she confesses,

I've been on this journey of redemption – before this I was a baby ghost waiting for a body ... Ach, fuck me. Actually, this is all bullshit – this is theatre, so it's all pretend ... it's all just a big joke. [...] Deep down I'm just an angry bitch.

(Holstein 2017)

She questions the audience's motivation in coming to see the show and asks if audience members feel 'proud that you could elicit empathy ... you feel human?' She asks, did 'you want to see some radical feminist art ... so you could play your part in taking down the patriarchy?' (Holstein 2017). Holstein foregrounds her own insincerity by saying 'I just want to you know I didn't mean any of it ...' but simultaneously ridicules the idea of the audience wanting to foster some kind of allegiance in witnessing 'feminist art'. She repeatedly undermines what has gone before so the end of the performance is held by an uneasy tension as she lies on top of a pile of fizzing space dust. She lies in silence for a prolonged period of time, chastising those who pre-emptively applaud. Despite her vulnerable confession only minutes before and her assertion that she 'didn't mean' any of it, the closing section retains a sense of insistence and control. It undermines the effect of her previous vulnerability. As with the other artists her position is inscrutable and difficult to define. For Tomlin, Holstein's work can be seen to maintain a 'healthy' scepticism because she continues to use a metatheatrical frame throughout and experiments with 'reality and pretence' in a way that holds the apparatus of representation up for scrutiny. Her position in relation to the content of *Notorious* remains ambiguous but she holds the audience to account, questioning what they want from the performance. Although not quite as explicit as Pick's 'not really', Holstein signals the end of the audience's 'ordeal' by saying, '*now* it's fucking over!' (Holstein 2017: my italics).

GETINTHEBACKOFTHEVAN, Young Jean Lee and Lauren Barri Holstein each adopt an attitude of distance and ambiguity towards their material in order to articulate complex questions about female subjectivity, agency and control. I have identified this attitude as one of 'inscrutability' and argued that this approach enables the artists to interrogate topics of gender and sexuality whilst distancing themselves from the increasingly atomised discourse of white feminism. As part of each production GETINTHEBACKOFTHEVAN, Young Jean Lee and Lauren Barri Holstein stage a range of gendered archetypes and behaviours with the intention that they be received ironically. All three productions can be seen to be deconstructive in so far as they draw attention to the process of performance making and foreground audience expectation. GETINTHEBACKOFTHEVAN represent one particular character's ownership of the stage space as part of an unrestrained sense of middle-class entitlement; Lee attempts to demystify the heteronormative gender roles within her three-act play by having a transgender Stagehand-in-Charge read out a prologue; and Holstein confuses her audiences by alternately begging their indulgence and railing at them for passivity. As part of my analysis I have monitored how 'healthy' the artists' cynicism can be seen to be in relation to Tomlin's warning that much contemporary experimental performance borrows the tropes of deconstruction without drawing attention to ideological systems reinforced within the diegetic and extra-diegetic world of the show. *Number 1, The Plaza* and *Notorious* both maintained a healthy scepticism in so far as they retained an ironic distance from their subject matter and the process of performance making throughout, but *Straight White Men* proved problematic and possibly representative of a 'cynical' scepticism because the point of narrative closure in the diegetic work invisibly mapped on to the end of the performance itself, and as such failed to adequately mark the misogynistic and racist values espoused within the diegetic world of the play.

I have adopted Rainford's sense that irony has an 'affinity with feminism' due to its 'double relation with the prevailing order of things' and that feminism is caught within a double-bind because it is 'indebted to the structures it criticizes' (Rainford 2005: 4). This means that the staging of both normative and resistant gender roles sediments conservative ideology because they are informed by and grounded in phallocentric logic. Disruptive behaviour and images acknowledge the 'prevailing order of things' and reference phallocentric behaviour. In each production woman's 'secondariness' comes into play, specifically in the way performers compensate for the absence of phallic activity either by providing a supposedly ironic stand-in version, or by going to extreme lengths to assert their right to claim centre stage. As Rainford has observed,

[t]he structural and epistemological uncertainties provoked by the doubleness of irony means that its intervention is not simply a countering movement – a case of denying prevailing truths and asserting or implying new ones – but of (potentially) unraveling the whole structure in which the debate is being pursued.

(Rainford 2005: 8)

This attempt to 'unravel the whole structure' is what underlies much postmodern performance, and the metatheatrical nature of this work has much in common with a postmodern aesthetic. Given that the artists are, as Lehmann would have it, 'playing with [a distanciated] coolness' they cannot be seen to be aligning themselves with any one, fixed position, and so go to considerable lengths to obscure their relationship to what is said on stage (Lehmann 2006: 118). GETINTHE-BACKOFTHEVAN have spoken about this as 'ruffling' or 'scribbling over' moments that could be read as 'sincere' (Gorman 2013). This is particularly problematic for the question of 'agency' and the degree of control the artists can be seen to exercise over their work. It is significant that Rainford argues,

the ironic mode is considered as a form of internalized agency for the feminist: as well as reflecting her double relation to the patriarchal structure, it turns her alterity to her advantage by using it to negate the terms of the prevailing hierarchy.

(4)

In what Angela McRobbie has termed 'the aftermath' of feminism many female artists have chosen to obscure their relationship to their antecedents, finding themselves at odds with third-wave '"anti-porn" feminists or seeing the concept as a kind of deterrent' (Holstein 2015: 84; McRobbie 2009: 1). Rainford has pointed out that although Butler's theory of gender performativity and Irigaray's theory of gender as ontological difference might appear to be at odds, both thinkers fundamentally:

begin from a position which acknowledges the peculiar double-bind of feminist critique: that it strives to challenge and break from the (unequal) sexual terms, relations and hierarchies of patriarchy, but the cultural forms and discourses at its disposal are themselves enmeshed in patriarchy.

(Rainford 2005: 2)

Rainford and Tomlin provide an invaluable way of theorising female artists' forays into postmodern performance. The 'double-bind' of feminist critique means the artists must locate themselves both within a recognisable discourse and at a distance from it. The inscrutable irony deployed within *Number 1, The Plaza, Notorious* and *Straight White Men* represents a fascinating example of female artists setting out to use performance as a tool to critique white male privilege whilst simultaneously acknowledging the role artworks play in circulating and sedimenting and naturalising hegemonic discourse.

This chapter has explored the resistant potential of irony and inscrutability in the work of three female-led performance companies. These practitioners deploy irony as a tool of radical negativity; they replicate patriarchal dogma whilst undercutting the audience's ability to perceive intention. In the next chapter I will explore the work of three practitioners who depart from the potential of irony by adopting a register of sincerity. I will investigate examples of work by Bryony Kimmings, Annie Siddons and Selina Thompson, artists who have created solo autobiographical performance in order to translate the experience and memories of emotional upheaval. I will consider Kimmings' *I'm a Phoenix, Bitch*, Siddons' *How (Not) to Live in Suburbia* and Thompson's *salt.* as examples of performance as self-care. The artists cite the process of writing and performance as key elements of recovery. In relation to the shift away from irony, Lavender has observed a return to sincerity in the work of a number of contemporary practitioners. He suggests this work is a 'backwash from the tide of postmodern performance'. For him the sincere persona 'appears to signal a specific self, a being at the borderline between characteristic originality [...] and characterful fabrication' (Lavender 2016: 118). Nao Bustamante pre-empted this shift, implying as far back as 2007 that the self-reflexive ironic mode had exhausted itself. She wrote 'the new radicalism is sincerity [...] there's a way in which sincerity is the thing now for me' because 'my side hurts from making fun of everything' (Bustamante 2007). I will argue the work of Thompson et al. in my next chapter departs from an ironic postmodern mode in order to depict experiences of hegemonic castigation. Each artist employs performance making as a facet of self-care, whilst rejecting the popular neoliberal discourse, which functions to put responsibility for wellbeing on to the individual worker-citizen regardless of social or economic context. The artists apprehend the sense they have 'failed' in one way or another by failing to live up to exclusionary standards of white Western womanhood. They shape their narratives, not only to help make sense of their own experience of extreme alienation but also to raise awareness of racism, internalised misogyny and loneliness to provide solace to others.

Notes

1 *Hallelujah* by Leonard Cohen, 1984, Columbia Records; *Defying Gravity* by Idina Menzel and Kristen Chenoweth, from *Wicked* 2003, Decca Broadway; *Tell Me It's Not True* by Willy Russell, from *Blood Brothers*, 1983.
2 Chillingworth has revealed that, 'the focus on Jen's "posh" voice was never really for us about positioning her insults as "harmless" but rather as shining a light on a voice which sounds privileged and is therefore permitted space to fill as it pleases (however nasty) and goes unchallenged. We *allow* it because of how the voice sounds (middle class/posh/privileged) even if we don't like it and know what it's saying is not ok' (personal correspondence, July 2019).
3 Chillingworth has stated that, 'it's more complicated than Lucy and Jen being framed as being in a romantic relationship – the whole idea of relationship is being queered. We're peddling the "tabloid story" that maybe they're together (more sexual than romantic I'd say) but we're laughing at it (while refusing to confirm or deny). We're acknowledging the fetishisation of female intimacy for a male gaze, and playing with it' (personal correspondence, July 2019).
4 She clarifies that, 'our aim is for Jen to dodge a position or message, yet again, in the last moment' (Chillingworth, personal correspondence, July 2019).

5 *New Yorker* critic Hilton Als has been critical of the Broadway production of *Straight White Men* for similar reasons. Having lauded Lee's work in *The Shipment* and *Untitled Feminist Show*, Als was disappointed by this production. He felt that Lee had written 'a "straight" play' in order to 'hang out with the Broadway boys' and that in 'trying to lampoon whiteness, she's made a "white" play: shallow, soporific, and all about itself'. He acknowledges that the piece is 'winking at us about the asshole culture' that she 'takes down' but ultimately feels that it 'refutes' the 'humor, recklessness and passion' of her previous work (Als 2018). I share some of Als' reservations but would take issue with the suggestion that the play is shallow.

6 *Get Ready for This* by 2 Unlimited, by Phil Wilde, Jean-Paul de Coster and Ray Slijn-gaard, Byte, ZYX and PWL Label, 1991.

7 *We Can't Stop*, single by Miley Cyrus. Written by: Miley Cyrus, Mike L. Williams II, Pierre Ramon Slaughter, Timothy Thomas, Theron Thomas, Douglas Davis and Ricky Walters.

8 It should be noted, however that *Splat!* Holstein's 2013 piece was programmed into the main performance space of the Barbican Theatre, a venue long associated with The Royal Shakespeare Company and with a strong subscriber-base.

Bibliography

Ahmed, Sara (2017) *Living a Feminist Life*, Durham: Duke University Press.

Als, Hilton (2018) 'The Soullessness of "Straight White Men"', *The New Yorker*, 30 July. Available at: https://www.newyorker.com/magazine/2018/08/06/the-soullessness-of-straight-white-men (accessed 10 April 2020).

Bailes, Sara Jane (2011) *Performance Theatre and a Poetics of Failure*, London: Routledge.

Barbican (2017) 'Barbican Meets: The Famous Lauren Barri Holstein', *Barbican Blog*, 18 October. Available at:http://blog.barbican.org.uk/2017/10/barbican-meets-the-famous-lauren-barri-holstein/ (accessed 15 February 2019).

Bates, Laura (2015) 'Anti-feminists Don't Get Irony', *The Guardian*, 16 March. Available at: https://www.theguardian.com/lifeandstyle/2015/mar/16/laura-bates-anti-feminists-irony (accessed 27 August 2017).

Bustamante, Nao (2007) '9th Letter'. Available at: https://www.youtube.com/watch?v=Nu4ptXbWLsg (accessed 31 January 2020).

Carlson, Marvin (2003) *Performance: A Critical Introduction*, London: Routledge.

Chambers, Ross (1990) 'Irony and the Canon', *Profession*, 90(19), 18–24.

Christie, Bridget (2015) *A Book For Her*, London: Penguin.

Coates, Jennifer (2003) *Men Talk: Stories in the Making of Masculinities*, Oxford: Blackwell Publishing.

Colebrook, Claire (2003) *Irony (The New Critical Idiom)*, Abingdon: Routledge.

Doyle Jennifer (2009) 'Blind Spots and Failed Performance: Abortion, Feminist and Queer Theory', *Qui Parle*, 18, 25–52.

Drew, William (2013) '"Splat!" Disney and the Vagina', *Exeunt Magazine*, 6 April. Available at: http://exeuntmagazine.com/reviews/splat/ (accessed 22 August 2018).

GETINTHEBACKOFTHEVAN (2013) *Number 1, The Plaza*, Touring Production.

GETINTHEBACKOFTHEVAN (2012) 'Love/Hate' *Adjunct* Issue 1, Cambridge Junction. Available at: http://www.getinthebackofthevan.com/files/junction-zine-final_v2.pdf (accessed 23 August 2018)

GETINTHEBACKOFTHEVAN(2019) Website. Available at: http://www.getinthebackofthevan.com/ (accessed 8 August 2019).

Gorman, Sarah (2013) 'Interview with GETINTHEBACKOFTHEVAN', *readingasawoman*. Available at: https://readingasawoman.wordpress.com/2013/11/12/interview-with-getintheback-ofthevan/ (accessed 8 August 2019).

Gorman, Sarah (2017) 'Interview with Lauren Barri Holstein', *readingasawoman*. Available at: https://readingasawoman.wordpress.com/2017/11/09/interview-with-lauren-barri-holstein/ (accessed 8 August 2019).

Harbourfront Centre (2015) 'World Stage 2015 – Straight White Men Talkshow – Young Jean Lee Harbourfront Centre', 8 June. Available at: https://www.youtube.com/watch?v=vtqoAjrs7oY (accessed 11 August 2019).

Holstein, Lauren Barri (2014) 'Splat! Death, Mess, Failure and "Blue-Balling"', *Performance Research*, 19(2), 98–102.

Holstein, Lauren Barri (2015) 'The Agency of the Displayed Female Body: The Political Potential of the Negative Affects in Contemporary Feminism and Performance', PhD Thesis, Queen Mary University of London, London.

Holstein, Lauren Barri (2017) *Notorious*, Touring Production.

Hutcheon, Linda (1995) *Irony's Edge: The Theory and Politics of Irony*, London and New York: Routledge.

Keeley, Matt (2018) 'Armie Hammer Defended Legendary Trans Activist Kate Bornstein From a Broadway Heckler', *Hornet.com*, 9 August. Available at: https://hornet.com/stories/kate-bornstein-straight-white-men/ (accessed6 February 2018).

Lavender, Andy (2016) *Performing in the 21st Century: Theatres of Engagement*, Abingdon: Routledge.

Lee, Young Jean (2009) *Songs of the Dragon Flying to Heaven* in *Songs of the Dragon Flying to Heaven and Other Plays*, New York: Theatre Communications Group.

Lee, Young Jean (2015) *Straight White Men*, playscript published in *American Theatre*, April 2015, 62–75.

Lee, Young Jean (2017) 'Young Jean Lee Talks STRAIGHT WHITE MEN, Steppenwolf Theatre Company', 25 January. Available at: https://www.youtube.com/watch?v=MdQibq7gY6o (accessed 13 July 2017).

Lehmann, Hans Thies, (2006) *Postdramatic Theatre*, translated by and introduction by Karen Juers-Munby, Abingdon: Routledge,

Maxwell, Richard (2008) 'Young Jean Lee by Richard Maxwell', *Bomb Magazine*, 6 November. Available at: http://bombmagazine.org/article/3249/young-jean-lee (accessed 8 August 2019).

Morrison, Andrew (2014) 'A Class Act? Lecturer's Views of Undergraduates' Employability', *British Journal of Sociology of Education*, 35(4), 487–505.

Moses, Caro (2017) 'The Famous Lauren Barri Holstein: Notorious', *This Week London*, 2 November. Available at: http://thisweeklondon.com/article/the-famous-lauren-barri-holstein-notorious/ (accessed 22 August 2018).

Ngai, Sianne (2007) *Ugly Feelings*, Cambridge: Harvard University Press.

Rainford, Lydia (2005) *She Changes by Intrigue: Irony, Femininity and Feminism*, Amsterdam: Rodopi.

Raymond, Gerard, (2018) 'Interview: Kate Bornstein on Their Broadway Debut in Straight White Men', *Slant Magazine*, 11 July. Available at: https://www.slantmagazine.com/blog/pretty-damn-bowie-kate-bornstein-on-their-broadway-debut-in-straight-white-men/ (accessed 6 February 2018).

Shimakawa, Karen (2007) 'Young Jean Lee's Ugly Feelings about Race and Gender: Stuplime Animation in Songs of the Dragons Flying to Heaven', *Women and Performance*, 17 (1), 89–102.

Solga, Kim (2013) *Theatre & Feminism*, London: Palgrave Macmillan.

Steinwald, Michele (2012) 'Young Jean Lee in Conversation with Michele Steinwald at The Walker Arts Centre', 1 June. Available at: https://www.youtube.com/watch?v=cUZLv2aNfiM (accessed 8 August 2019).

Stevens, Beth (2018) 'Scribe Young Jean Lee talks STRAIGHT WHITE MEN', *The Broadway.com Show*, 13 August. Available at: https://www.youtube.com/watch?v=Ck6v9h3FSFY (accessed 6 February 2019).

Tomlin, Liz (2008) 'Beyond Cynicism: The Sceptical Imperative and (Future) Contemporary Performance', *Contemporary Theatre Review*, 18(3), 355–369.

Tomlin, Liz (2013) *Acts and Apparitions: Discourses on the Real in Performance, Practice and Theory, 1990–2010*, Manchester: Manchester University Press.

Ulaby, Neda (2014) 'In Straight White Men: A Play Explores The Reality of Privilege', *Code Switch: Race and Identity Remixed*, 17 November. Available at: http://www.npr.org/sections/codeswitch/2014/11/17/364760889/in-straight-white-men-a-play-explores-the-reality-of-privilege (accessed 13 July 2017).

Urban Dictionary (2017) Website. Available at: http://www.urbandictionary.com/define.php?term=post-ironic (accessed 27 August 2017).

Winter, Anna (2017) 'Notorious Review at the Barbican Pit, London – "Masturbation, Mastication and Micturition"', *The Stage*, 8 November. Available at: https://www.thestage.co.uk/reviews/2017/notorious-review-barbican-pit-london/ (accessed 22 August 2018).

Ybarra, Patricia (2014) 'Young Jean Lee's Cruel Dramaturgy', *Modern Drama*, 57(4), 513–532.

3

SELF-CARE AND RADICAL SOFTNESS: REFUSING NEOLIBERAL RESILIENCE

As part of its 2019 Spring season The Marlborough Theatre, Brighton advertised a 'Radical Softness Season'. The venue's promotional copy explained that this would take the form of a 'season of performance interrogating what it means for self-care to be an act of Radical Softness', featuring work by Willy Hudson, Louisa Robbin and FK Alexander. Around the same time South London Gallery advertised a Black Women's reading group. The reading group was to be organised around Audre Lorde's famous assertion, 'Self-Care [is] an Act of Warfare'. Self-care and the idea of 'radical softness' took on a newfound urgency in 2019 informing both academic and populist articles about the relationship between resilience, self-care and the neoliberal imperative for each citizen to take responsibility for their mental and physical wellbeing. The term 'radical *softness*' has been attributed to Californian queer trans poet Lore Mathis who created images featuring the words 'RADICAL SOFTNESS AS A WEAPON' on Instagram. The images themselves sparked controversy as Mathis has been accused of appropriating the work of Black feminist poet and commentator Audre Lorde without due accreditation. In an epilogue to *Burst of Light*, a collection of essays about the experience of living with liver cancer, Lorde wrote, 'caring for myself … is self-preservation, and that is an act of political warfare' (Lorde 1988: 130). Feminist writer Sara Ahmed has, in turn, translated Lorde's assertion into 'Selfcare as Warfare'. The notion of 'selfcare as warfare' or 'radical softness' represents a potent example of radical negativity because it invests in a customarily maligned or denigrated value and celebrates its potential as a counter-hegemonic tool. Within this chapter I want to argue that three different performances by artists Selina Thompson, Bryony Kimmings and Annie Siddons represent radical acts of 'self-care' whilst eschewing populist neoliberal formulations. I will interrogate Thompson's *salt.* (2017); Kimmings' *I'm a Phoenix, Bitch* (2018) and Siddons' *How (Not) to Live in Suburbia* (2017) from the perspective of artists using performance as part of a process of reconciliation after having experienced trauma and/or mental distress. These artists return to and excavate trauma in order to interrogate its effect on their notion of 'self'. The process of excavation helps each artist reconcile and come to terms with the transformational nature of the experience. They do not necessarily frame the performances as cathartic, there is little sense of wanting to purge the memory of trauma; instead they invite the audience to 'sit with' their experience in order to contemplate how it might affect them in turn. I will argue that these performances resist co-option into the neoliberal populist model of self-care and explore the types of alternative radical power structures proposed by Audre Lorde.

As stated above the theory and practice of 'self-care' is enjoying renewed attention in populist and academic circles. For some, such as *The Body is Not an Apology* website, this means a return to the work of Black feminists such as Alice Walker, Lorde and Nikki Giavanni. Indeed, for Black critical theory scholar Jennifer C. Nash self-care is a crucial part of second-wave Black feminism and its 'politics of claiming, embracing, and restoring the wounded black female self' (Nash 2013: 3). For others self-care is associated with the 'clean-living-hard-working' movement, as typified by Gwyneth Paltrow's 'goop' website (Goop 2019). Writing for *Flare. com* Adebe Derango-Adem argues:

> Practicing self-care has never felt more urgent than in these socially, politically and spiritually troubling times. Self-care is now part of everyone's vocabulary – you'll find more than 3.3 million instances of it on Instagram, although most involve skincare regimes … But if we look closely at the #selfcare hashtag, we'll see that the idea of self-care now seems miles from what civil rights activist, writer and feminist, Audre Lorde detailed nearly 20 years ago in her book of essays, *A Burst of Light*. Increasingly it feels like we are responsible for how good we feel, regardless of the position we are in.
>
> *(Flare 2017)*

Critical voices, such as that of Derango-Adem, are mobilising to articulate a sense of unease about the slippage between radical Black feminist thought, as exemplified by Lorde, and a version of self-care that puts the onus on the contemporary citizen to take full responsibility for their health and wellbeing regardless of social and cultural milieu. Ahmed describes the latter as a type of 'neoliberal feminism' whereby 'feminism is repackaged as being about upward mobility for some women, those who accept responsibilities for their "own wellbeing and self-care"' rendering feminism 'a white woman's upward mobility fantasy' (Ahmed 2014). However, Ahmed does agree that self-care can represent a potent tool for resistance because in caring for ourselves and others we are 'redirecting care away from its proper objects of capitalist labour and growth'. In 'Self-Care: An Act of Political Warfare or a Neoliberal Trap?' Inna Michaeli interrogates the neoliberal appropriation of self-care. She argues for the need to recognise and resist its depoliticising effects:

Critically, our vulnerability and the care we can (or cannot) expect from our families and societies, as well as our social movements, are influenced by our gender, race, ethnicity, class, sexuality, ability, and other identity markers of privilege. Long after Audre Lorde, Black feminists still take the lead in politicizing self-care as a radical act for Black women and women of color.

(Michaeli 2017: 53)

Judith Butler, Zeynep Gambetti and Leticia Sabsay have explored the contemporary drive to privatise self-care and resilience. They approach the sense of 'softness' associated with self-care in terms of 'vulnerability' and observe that 'vulnerability is the effect of social power' rather than being a personal, private experience. They argue that vulnerability 'emerges as part of social relations' (Butler, Gambetti and Sabsay 2016: 4). Working along similar lines, Sarah Bracke understands resilience as a counterpoint to vulnerability and describes how it belongs to 'a particular political economy':

the prevalence of resilience as a term knew a spectacular rise at a moment in time that is generally recognized as a shift in political economy and cultural hegemony, that is, the 1980s or the beginning of the hegemony of neoliberalism.

(Bracke 2016: 53)

Because neoliberal ideology champions individualisation and the drive to overcome all obstacles, self-care has become part of a discourse of resilience; the individual citizen needs to exercise self-care in order to demonstrate they are taking responsibility for their own wellbeing. For Bracke the ideal neoliberal subject is one who has internalised 'resilience as part of the "moral code"', and who is 'able to act, to exercise their agency, in resilient ways' (Bracke 2016: 62). Resilience serves as a useful insight into why neoliberal hegemony regards self-care to be the responsibility of the 'good' citizen. The ideal neoliberal citizen is one who takes personal responsibility for maintaining optimum physical and mental fitness so they can realise all work commitments with optimum efficiency and avoid seeking support from the welfare state. 'Self-care' has become popular as part of a neoliberal dogma of resilience and self-preservation. As André Spicer has observed,

while self-care may work for individuals, it doesn't come without dangers. This once radical idea is being stripped of its politics to make it more palatable to a mass market. As this happens, the central insights associated with self-care may well get lost.

(Spicer 2019)

In creating these autobiographical performances Thompson, Kimmings and Siddons render themselves vulnerable and ultimately they demonstrate resilience by recovering from trauma. However, the trials they describe empty the notion of neoliberal resilience of all meaning. By forging a meaningful connection with the audience and outreach groups beyond the theatre, they demonstrate how the sharing of an individual experience can raise awareness of oppressive social and economic forces and galvanise community action.

By weaponising self-care Lorde is actively resisting received theories of power and empowerment. Lorde's work pushes against individualism and calls for women to forge communities and alliances (Ahmed 2014). In her epilogue to *Burst of Light,* Lorde's famous statement 'Caring for myself is not self-indulgence, it is self-pre-servation, and that is an act of political warfare' comes towards the end of a section of writing in which she explains the difficulty she has in stepping away from work. She wrote, 'Overextending myself is not stretching myself, I had to accept how difficult it is to monitor the difference. Necessary for me as cutting down on sugar. Crucial, Physically, Psychically' (Lorde 1988: 130). In *Burst of Light* Lorde describes her attempts to maintain control over her body and refuse unnecessary surgical treatment. She resists her doctors' enthusiasm for surgical intervention, conducting her own research into the potential efficacy and ultimately takes the decision to choose holistic treatment abroad. She demonstrates that self-preservation is about checking the compulsion to put all her energies into writing and activist work (130). This must have been arduous given that her work was *about* care-giving, consciousness raising and fostering positive feminist communities. This 'slowing down' and movement *away from* the centrality of work is what most obviously differentiates a feminist model of self-care from what Michaeli has described as a 'populist neoliberal model'. Michaeli notes the 'profound differen[ce]' between the neoliberal model of 'self-care' and that of Black feminist 'radical feminism and activism' (Michaeli 2017: 52). She makes a point of identifying what is 'wrong' with self-care in 'its populistic neoliberal configuration'. Firstly she criticises it for 'privatizing' responsibility for health and wellbeing on to the individual rather than seeing it as the responsibility of a supportive and healthy society. Secondly she argues that the neoliberal model 'obscur[es] the social, economic and political sources of physical, emotional, and spiritual distress and exhaustion' and thirdly she insists that its effects are 'deeply depoliticizing. ' She reiterates the importance of factoring different support networks available, or not, to people of different 'gender [s], race, ethnicity, class, sexuality, ability and other identity markers of privilege' (53). I want to argue that the artists in question use performance as a *model for and method of* self-care. They do this partly as a way of coming to terms with obstacles and challenges presented by a white, patriarchal heteronormative culture and partly as a way of envisioning a more distributed sense of 'care'. I see their work as resisting what Michaeli has called the 'populist' model and working to draw attention to the ways in which female bodies continue to be rendered 'docile' at the hands of white, middle-class institutions of power.

Selina Thompson is a Black British artist and activist based in Birmingham. She identifies her oeuvre as performance art and works across a number of different art forms, including: art installations, durational performances, community arts initia-tives and live performance for theatre spaces. She has received particular attention for: *Chewing the Fat* (2013); *Dark and Lovely* (2015); *Race Cards* (2015); and *salt.* (2016) She has worked on projects with teenagers to increase awareness of voting rights and ideas of 'freedom' (*Sortition,* 2018, *The Missy Elliot Project,* 2017). Thompson is a prolific writer and her essay 'Fat Demands' has been published in June Eric-Udorie's (2018) collection *Can We All Be Feminists?* Her work is socially and politically engaged and focuses in particular upon the experience of being a young, working-class, Black artist in contemporary Britain. In a contribution to *The Outsider's Handbook* she advises readers to 'stay soft. Cry lots, demand and expect love and care and gentleness, and give all of those things to others, abundantly ... It will keep you alive, in the richest most beautiful way' (Thompson 2018). She states, 'I make work because it's the only way I can live. It's the only way I can bear how awful everything is and how powerless I feel about that a lot of the time' (Gorman 2017).

Thompson has been outspoken about the topic of cultural diversity in the arts, criticising venue programmers for including her work in a Black history programme without consultation and allocating funding in short-term 'piecemeal' portions. She explains:

> I feel like diversity in the industry creates two tiers of work. What's the phrase? 'Separate is never equal'. It always makes it hard to know whether your work is there because people want it there or whether it's there because you're black and they need you ... As Jamila Johnson-Small puts it, 'they need *this year's interesting negro*' That's a really difficult psychological space to occupy.
> (Gorman 2017)

Thompson's work has been significant for its unguarded criticism of racism and the widespread influence of white supremacist values circulating within the UK arts scene. As part of *Race Cards*, an installation containing one thousand hand-written cards about race and representation, Thompson asked, 'how do you go about exposing white supremacy in liberal arts spaces'; 'how do you feel when you hear the word "diverse"?'; 'whatever happened to multiculturalism?' Along with other artists and cultural commentators Thompson has identified white, liberal audiences and artists as responsible for creating and perpetuating white middle-class hegemony within the arts. Academics such as Lynette Leni Goddard have identified the UK theatre industry as 'white-led' and 'Eurocentric' (Goddard 2007: 10) but up until very recently it was highly unusual to hear or read the term 'white supremacy' used in relation to liberal arts organisations and leaders. This term would ordinarily be reserved to describe the activity of extreme right-wing organisations and in the UK, at least, arts organisations would be largely seen to embody a progressive leftist liberal spirit of 'inclusion'. Thompson has argued that this represents the illusion of inclusion, created to meet Arts Council quotas rather than representing an active interest in decolonising the arts. In *White Fragility* Robin DiAngelo argues that white people lack the 'radical stamina' to confront internalised racism and participate in meaningful conversation. She shares her sense that 'white progressives cause the most daily damage to people of color' (DiAngelo 2019, Waldman 2018). Season Butler has joined Thompson in criticising the notion of cultural 'diversity' arguing that 'there is a euphemistic vagueness around diversity – it keeps white supremacist logic intact. White supremacist logic would prefer that we think of ourselves as meritocratic' (Butler 2017).

In addition to marking the whiteness of the UK arts scene Thompson has been crucial in disturbing a widely held assumption that race is not really a 'problem' for the UK. In her introduction to *Seeing Differently* Amelia Jones writes of her experience of living in the UK, recalling that her British friends repeatedly asked her, 'Why … are Americans so obsessed with race?' She confessed that she wanted to reply, 'Why… do British people imagine race isn't a factor in British life? And why are they so obsessed with class?' (Jones 2012: xxv). Along with debbie tucker green, who in her 2018 production of *ear for eye* projected images of British families reading out examples of British white supremacist legislation, Thompson reminds audiences that racism is not confined to the US and white supremacist values are not just the preserve of right-wing extremists but colourblind British liberals as well.

Thompson's demeanour is one of friendliness and informality. Reviewing *Dark and Lovely* Lyn Gardner wrote that she found Thompson 'so personable you could eat her up', whilst also identifying 'glimmers of anger' as Thompson talked about 'cultural appropriation and the psychology of colonization' (Gardner 2015). She has confessed, 'my coping mechanism with the stereotype of "angry black woman" that is placed onto me, is to be quite effervescent and bubbly'. She has also observed that, as she gets older and more confident, she is less concerned with how audiences receive her anger (Gorman 2017). Speaking about the development of *salt.* Thompson reflects on the fact that she had made this piece primarily with audiences of colour in mind. In response to a question about audience she revealed:

> It's interesting because when you ask I realise how little I have thought about that audience. I've been much more concerned with, 'if I'm a black woman watching this … how is it not replicating that hurt?' And I actually feel great about that. There is a displacement of the white gaze, I hope.
>
> *(Harvie 2017)*

In *salt.* Thompson describes her experience of taking a voyage to trace the Transatlantic Slave route, starting in Antwerp, then on to Ghana, Jamaica and back to England via the US. Thompson has borrowed Saidiyah Hartman's term 'excavating a wound' as a way of explaining the motivation for undertaking the voyage. Influenced by Hartman's *Lose Your Mother,* in which Hartman spends four months in Ghana as part of her research into popular narratives about the slave trade, Thompson wants to honour those brutalised and murdered and invite audiences to 'sit with' both her experience on the voyage and the continuing legacy of slavery. In conversation with Jen Harvie, Thompson recalls that *salt.* 'takes a feeling I had already and makes it visible … that desire to die wasn't quite there when I came back – there was a quieting' (Harvie 2017).

The majority of Thompson's work to date has been autobiographical; the pieces tend to start from a subject of personal interest and are then developed through a process of research and consultation with artists, friends and collaborators. The quotation above reveals that Thompson experienced a period of mental distress prior to the creation of the show. She acknowledged a 'small' breakdown, which she had prior to going on her voyage and a 'massive breakdown' experienced at the end of the year after completing the show (Harvie 2017). She has described her compulsion to undertake the voyage as 'slightly fucked up' and something that, for a year, had been 'growing in my chest' (Harvie 2017). salt. was and is a project of self-care because it fulfils a profound psychological need and is driven by a desire to find a way of quieting her sense of unease about what it means to live as part of the African diaspora in contemporary Britain.

salt. uses direct address, with Thompson speaking to the audience as 'herself' throughout.[1] She is dressed in a plain, long white dress and moves confidently about the stage. The stage is furnished with a stretch of blue cloth; a workstation-cum-altar with shelves; an illuminated triangle; and a tall chair surrounded by long, green leafy plants. On the top of the altar/workstation stands a bottle of water and several large blocks of pink-white salt are stacked on the shelves below. The play script refers to the first section of the show as 'opening the ritual' and describes the bottle as holding '*libations… a long-necked bottle atop the altar with rosemary suspended in the water that is inside it, a glass of water, incense and a burner, and a pestle and mortar that contains some finely ground rock salt*' (Thompson 2017: 13). As part of the introduction Thompson explains:

> I am twenty-eight.
> I am Black.
> I am a woman.
> I grew up in Birmingham which is where all my family live.
> I am second generation and third.
> By which I mean
> I'm adopted. Both my birth parents, my mother and father, were Rastafarians from Jamaica, who moved to the UK when they were thirteen.
> The parents who adopted me, my mum and dad, were both born here, and their parents were from Jamaica and Montserrat.
> And we are all descended from enslaved people.
>
> *(Thompson 2017: 14)*

In practising a politics of self-care Thompson employs two main techniques. Firstly she identifies and names specific instances of sexist and racist oppression and attributes them to specific people and sociocultural entities. In intersectional terms, this entails demonstrating how 'oppression cannot be reduced to one fundamental type' and how the subject finds herself caught up in a 'matrix of domination' (Hill Collins 2000: 18). Thompson can be seen to be championing Nash's sense of self-love as a 'resistant ethic of self-care' that can 'transform love from the personal into a theory of justice' (Nash 2013: 2). Thompson insists upon the value of her sense of self and draws attention to the social forces that would have her believe otherwise. She practises a politics of self-care by excavating a long-standing sense of unease and embarking upon a literal and metaphorical journey to discover the fundamental cause of unhappiness. Furthermore, Thompson capitalises on what Lorde has described as the political use of the 'erotic', a strategy for adapting one's consciousness to resist the European-American tradition, that associates the 'erotic' with the pornographic and to attend instead to the capacity for, and sharing of 'joy' and the 'physical, emotional, and psychic expressions of what is deepest and strongest and richest within each of us, being shared: the passions of love, in its deepest meanings' (Lorde 2007: 56). Thompson invests in the idea of the erotic as a 'deeply female and spiritual place' and excavates her trauma in order to access 'the power of our unexpressed or unrecognized feeling' (Lorde 2007: 53). In her work the erotic takes the form of shared vignettes, which may, or may not, have been imaginary. She celebrates her experience in Jamaica by revelling in sensual imagery and describing her sense of psychological and physical relief at the onset of her menstrual period. By utilising these techniques she resists the trap of the populist neoliberal model of self-care. By naming racist behaviour and identifying structures of domination she draws attention to the specific 'social, economic and political sources of physical, emotional, and spiritual distress and exhaustion'. Furthermore she evades the 'privatization of responsibility' and the depoliticising effects of the neoliberal drive to take responsibility for self-care by clearly demonstrating that she has been rendered vulnerable by hostile forces (Michaeli 2017: 53). By asking her audience to 'sit with' her experience she extends an invitation for them to consider how they might identify with, or be implicated in, Eurocentric racism.

Thompson identifies racist behaviour from many constituencies, but most explicitly from the 'Master', the captain of the first cargo ship and from 'Europe' itself. The captain of the ship had been oppositional to Thompson and her filmmaker colleague joining the ship, going so far as to set off from both Harwich and Hamburg without them (Harvie 2017). He insisted upon being addressed as 'Master' and announced that whilst he did not mind women being on board as a welcome 'diversion', he would not permit them to film. Thompson described their first encounter:

> The Master
> blonde curly hair, bright blue eyes, and the sort of infantile, malice-laced bounce that I associate with men like Boris Johnson
> Says that he doesn't mind having women there, as a diversion, had he known what our work was about, he would never have agreed to our presence on board. That he doesn't want any trouble. That his ship is not a slave ship.
> I explain that we are not making a project about him or his ship, that we only want to film the sea itself, to document our experience.
> He tells us that our tickets will be released only if we promise not to film.
> Europe pushes against me

everything in me says 'no',
But I relent.
And we are leaving Europe
Or at least we thought we were
But the ship sails under an Italian flag, and even as we leave this point in the
triangle, something in me.

(Thompson 2017: 24)

In interview Thompson described her experience aboard the first cargo ship as
'horrible' and states that it was an 'incredibly triggering space' (Harvie 2017). The
three weeks she and her collaborator spent on board proved devastating; they
found themselves on the receiving end of sexist and racist behaviour from the Italian crew; the film maker was denied a creative outlet; and this exacerbated the
tension and led to estrangement between the two women. The filmmaker found
the environment so upsetting that on arrival in Ghana she made the decision to
return home. The Master's irrational ban on filming ultimately jeopardised the
project. In a section of the performance entitled 'The First Side: the Hold',
Thompson describes the strained relations on board:

The six white officers speak Italian.
The nineteen Asian crew members speak Filipino.
So the two Black women sit in silence.
There is no phone reception, no internet.
We eat with the officers.
And we notice that the word 'nigger' keeps coming up at dinner.
I try to tell myself that maybe it is an Italian seafaring word.
I hear the master say 'Chinaman'.
I give up.
The Master is a big man. He will look in my face at dinner as he refers to
Africans as niggers as loudly as I am speaking to you now.

(Thompson 2017: 26)

Throughout the piece Thompson alludes to survival strategies she employed, for
example, in the speech above she states that she 'give[s] up'; at others she says that
she 'shuts down'. She relates instances in which someone has made racist and/or
sexist comments but she withholds her instinctual response. For example, in
response to questions about where she might be 'from', she confessed to thinking
'suck your mom' and mentally 'flip[ping] over a table'. When people are racist she
is compelled to remain reserved and pragmatic, or else risk expulsion from the ship
or refused access into a country. She and her colleague are accused of being sex-
workers by customs officers; she is repeatedly searched and screened for 'infection'
at airports; and she has to tolerate the Master telling her that Africans are 'feral
children' who will 'hate [her] worst of all'. She has to endure him telling her that
'the continent will never progress' and that 'racism is ancient history' (26).

Thompson articulates her sense of the broader sociopolitical environment that has secured the sense of Eurocentric hegemony on board. She does so by undertaking a ritualistic set of actions. These actions are physically arduous and visually striking. Laying out chunks of rock in order of size she avers, 'this is imperialism and racism and capitalism and God knows what else' (31). She dons a pair of plastic safety goggles (asking the front row to do the same) and takes a large sledgehammer to the blocks of salt. Adopting rhythms akin to a nursery rhyme she lists the attributes of each block – associating each with one of the social groups on board the ship. She raises the hammer above her head and brings it down with violent force upon each block of salt. As each rock shatters and the verse comes to a close Thompson repeats, '[a]nd we're still at sea in the morning' (30). The smallest blocks represent Thompson and her artistic partner. Stage directions state, '*By the end, the rocks representing the two Black folk are finely ground dust, almost invisible. The final rock remains pretty much intact*' (29: original italics).

The rock smashing is visually stunning – Thompson raises the sledgehammer in order to smash the blocks of Himalayan rock salt into smaller pieces. The audience acts as witness to the ritual and senses the anger and devastation fuelling her energy. Thompson moves from 'lowest' ranked social entity to highest, starting with herself and her collaborator evoking an image of the miserable collective, each subject externalising frustration through the exchange of angry words. She moves on to the Filipino crew who are 'silenced, suspicious' with 'no solidarity for the artist'; to the Officers who '[call] us niggers, lurking about'. In turn they 'alienate the crew/ And terrorise the artists'. Interestingly Thompson does not end the rhyme with the Master. She observes that he controls 'by intimidation and aggression' and that he 'terrorise[s] the artists', but demonstrates that the Captain, in turn, is subject to oppressive forces. She goes on to list 'the Union'; 'the Company'; and the European 'States' who perpetuate the system of oppression in order to maintain a tyranny of colonial rule. She notes the 'corrupted' union, the 'capitalist' company and the European States:

> These are the States
> European
> States
> Feeding off 'the other' to stay in control
> That pressure the company
> That corrupts the union
> That grinds down the master
> He bullies the officers
> They alienate the crew
> And terrorise the artists
> Shouting at them
> And they're shouting at me
> And we're still at sea in the morning.
>
> *(31)*

In *salt*, Thompson effectively demonstrates how comparatively small scale inter-personal acts of aggression feed into and perpetuate racism, but are symptomatic of a drive to perpetuate a colonialist, capitalist status quo. The rock-smashing scene effectively demonstrates the institutional power of the shipping company, which in turn is part of the established system of capitalist commodity exchange, reliant on exploitation of resources and human labour for its success. Thompson's performance with the sledgehammer performatively enacts her awareness of intersectional oppression. As Patricia Hill Collins has explained, 'oppression cannot be reduced to one fundamental type' (Hill Collins 2000: 18). Each social group can be seen to be emblematic of a 'paradigm' of power which 'work together to produc[e] injustice'. For Collins, the 'matrix of domination', such as the model displayed by Thompson, 'refers to how these intersecting oppressions are actually organised. Regardless of the particular intersections involved, struc-tural, disciplinary, hegemonic, and interpersonal domains of power reappear across quite different forms of oppression' (18).

At the close of the performance Thompson does not claim to be transformed or denuded of her anger. She states: 'I am not healed. But I do decide to keep living.' She shares a sense of being 'pull[ed] back into being', of appreciating anew 'the need to continue to live' and of recognising 'how sacred it is to be a descendent of those that were never supposed to survive' (Thompson 2017: 51). These words illustrate the intensely arduous nature of Thompson's journey and articulate the resurfacing of a subject who entertained a fantasy of drowning. Despite her asser-tion that she is not 'healed', the performance can be seen to represent an act of self-care because she has measured and processed her experience in order to make sense of the injustice she has experienced. She intimates that she can never be 'healed' because the scars run too deep, but she can make the decision to stop being inca-pacitated by her wounds. Her decision to choose to continue living marks a ther-apeutic turn towards the future. By creating this performance she is passing on a language to identify and describe systematic oppression, sharing a resistant vocabu-lary and vision with her audiences and rendering her act of self-care a resistant weapon of warfare against myopic, liberal complacency.

In addition to maintaining an actively political stance, Thompson's perfor-mance resists being co-opted into a neoliberal version of self-care by drawing upon an aesthetics of the 'erotic', which Lorde has described as a political tool (Lorde 2007: 53). Throughout the performance Thompson's controlled demea-nour is shown to take its toll physically and mentally. She feels as if her skin has been 'torn off'; she feels as if she is 'carrying a weight I can't bear much longer' (23). She relates racist incidents in Brighton, Leeds, Birmingham and Bristol, in which people stare, aggressively ask her questions about race and perform acts of racist exclusion (Thompson 2017: 21). She has remained silent during these incidents, feeling the sense that 'Europe pushes against me' but living with the knowledge that, in the words of her nan, 'white people are like this' and attempting to reconcile the 'two halves of who I am, a body that works, educated in white institutions, and a body that feels, nurtured in black homes' (20). The language she uses to articulate her pain and frustration is one of sensuality and powerful eroticism. She states, for example, that her experience of conflict is akin to the two halves of her body 'smash[ing] together like tectonic plates', that she is, 'filling with this pain and rage and death, can't see, can't think, can't breathe' (21). At key points in the piece her thoughts trail off, she begins 'and something in me – ' but does not complete the sentence, leaving the audience to imagine how it might end. This caesura indicates that what she experiences cannot be rationally contained or articulated by language.

Thompson repeatedly returns to affective experience and how she feels physically and emotionally. Visiting Elmina castle in Accra, Ghana, she draws attention to how the women's dungeons 'reek' and how 'rotting wreaths' have been left 'too late' 'surrounded by flies'. She tells the audience, 'Elmina heaves, and then I am home, scraping grit and dust and sweat and tears off my body' (36). She speaks of the agony of waiting for an overdue period, stating '[m]y period sits thickly inside my body'. She confesses that she is 'waiting for a period that just won't come' (27). During the voyage she described how she stopped eating and stayed in her cabin. She said, 'I curl into the corner of my bed and make myself as small as I can, and sometimes, if it is too much, and the writing does not help, I claw at my chest' (27). On the final leg of her journey home she imagines becoming 'a dead living thing' and her body 'plung[ing] into the depths'. She envisions the body sinking:

> down to those that wait for me
> down to be preserved in salt
> down to be in all three parts of the triangle, and in the centre of it
> down to be where I have always been, down to the only place where I can be
> down to my own end of the world
> There is no peace to be had, no homes to be found.
>
> *(50)*

In addition to her affective account of suffocation and hopelessness Thompson uses sensual, celebratory language to describe a sense of relief at arriving in Jamaica. She describes eating 'buns, cheese, fish', noting how there are 'fruit pushing out buds everywhere – ackee and apples and breadfruit and mangoes and guava and pimento and oranges' (43). She celebrates Jamaica as a place of 'fecundity':

> Fecundity defines Jamaica, it is bursting everywhere, life, and I rest: fecundity, fertility, bursting and exploding tiny pale white green butterflies surrounding bright pink and orange flowers, my appetite coming back, a tugging of the womb out of sluggishness, pressure lifting, my legs are scarlet, shiny sticky … period. At last
>
> *(43)*

For Lorde, women have been taught to 'distrust th[e] power which rises from our deepest and nonrational knowledge'. For her the erotic is a 'resource within each of us that lies in a deeply female and spiritual plane, firmly rooted in the power of our unexpressed or unrecognized feeling' (Lorde 2007: 53). The erotic functions for Lorde as an 'underlining' of the 'capacity for joy' (56). Thompson's use of sensual language and her deployment of textured stone, plants and cloth on stage is indicative of a drive to foreground affective language and focus upon sensual and emotional experience. Far from 'distrusting' this resource, Thompson draws upon it as an alternative form of power. Not only is she resisting what Lorde has identified as 'male' suppression; she is resisting the suppression of a female language deemed 'essentialist' by white feminism.

salt. is a politicised and political piece of performance. Thompson grounds her experience in the personal, bringing stories alive by focusing on the way Eurocentric racism affects her personally and emotionally. At the outset she actively welcomes Black audience members and People of Colour. Her anecdotes focus on interpersonal exchange and subjective sensual experience whilst her performative actions physicalise and give substance to interlinking paradigms of power. As she smashes the sledgehammer against the blocks of salt she identifies different matrices of domination. She identifies colonialism and capitalism as ideologies responsible for normalising sexist and racist ideology and states, 'this is my grief. But it is *our* burden'. She asks the audience to 'sit with it. Sit with the pain' saying 'it won't go away. But I am sitting with you' (Thompson 2017: 52 my emphasis). Hoping it would help alleviate the burden British racism had conferred upon her, Thompson shares her experience of a transformative personal journey. The journey was intensely traumatic but part of a politically active model of self-care. She avoids perpetuating a populist neoliberal model by identifying and naming dominating matrices of power, asking her audience to 'sit with' her and drawing upon an affective, erotic language associated with Black womanhood.

Bryony Kimmings is a UK artist, currently based in Brighton, and has been creating work since 2009. Her practice is 'multi-platform' and incorporates elements of stand-up comedy, song, autobiographical story-telling, filmmaking and social activism. In 2013 Kimmings galvanised online debate about fair pay for arts work with a blog post entitled 'I'll Show You Mine'. This post instigated a wide-ranging debate between artists and venues about fair pay. In 2017 she set up the 'Working Class Artists' Group' on What'sApp and Twitter along with Scottee and Selina Thompson.

Kimmings' performance work is autobiographical, combining serious and light-hearted approaches to topics such as sexual health; alcoholism; pre-teen gender stereotypes; mental health; and cancer. Her best known works include: *Sex Idiot* (2009), a solo piece in which she shared her chlamydia diagnosis and stories emanating from the subsequent decision to contact previous sexual partners. *Credible, Likeable Superstar Role Model* (2013) featured other performers, including theatre company Figs in Wigs and her nine-year-old niece. It was the culmination of a period of research in which she set out to construct an alternative teen pop star and teen role model with integrity. She collaborated with Complicité on *The Pacifist's Guide to the War on Cancer* (2017), which took the form of a large-scale musical at

London's National Theatre. In addition to creating work for performance spaces Kimmings has featured in TV documentaries. In 2018 Channel 4 broadcast *The Sex Clinic: Artist in Residence*. The programme followed Kimmings as she built relationships with visitors to the Whittall Street sexual health clinic in Birmingham and put forward her argument for 'the healing power of art'.

I'm a Phoenix, Bitch (2018) (hereafter *Phoenix*) outlines Kimmings' experience of becoming a mother, moving into an idyllic country cottage with her partner and discovering that her three-month-old son Frank had West Syndrome, a form of epilepsy. The performance has been designed for middle- to large-scale theatre spaces and features a large gauze/projection screen towards the rear of the stage. It includes a series of small activity or workstations, which allow Kimmings to live-stream close-up images of her performing her songs along with images of a model version of her rural cottage. The performance focuses upon Kimmings' own experience, but is a show about 'what women do in the face of trauma' and a means of inviting audiences to think and talk about mental health (Bradbury 2018). She has noted:

> If you see postnatal depression played out in dramas, the woman ends up killing her kid or gets sectioned. Actually postnatal mental health is part and parcel of a huge change in your life. I wanted to talk about it without making it overly dramatic. To have the conversation about it and it be acceptable. But mostly also just to hear a woman talking about her experience and it not be reductive.
>
> *(Bradbury 2018)*

Kimmings sets out to formulate questions for each show, and for *Phoenix* she asked, 'When trauma is over how do you wear that on your skin, in your bones, in your tone of voice and deep within your thoughts and actions without losing it?' and, 'How do you even begin to marry your personal selfish self with your universal activist head without sending yourself mad or simply laying on the floor and crying?' She wants to 'delve into the universal of my personal' and to 'figure out what might be a progressive new thought and unifying'. The title of the performance came from her desire to 'scream from the rooftops: "I am a phoenix, bitch!"' after recovering from the mental breakdown and distress caused by the onset of her son's ill health (Gardner 2018).

Like Thompson, Kimmings speaks directly to the audience, drawing upon autobiographical experience, but demonstrating a self-conscious scepticism about what she is saying and how she is presenting her *self*. This piece shows multiple 'Bryonies' – some from the past and some lodged in an imaginary landscape. She plays audio recordings of her mother's voice and creates 'survival' voice recordings for her son Frank. She refers to the other figures in her life, such as Tim, Frank's father, her therapist and a number of doctors and other medical professionals who helped treat her son. *Phoenix* is based on stories about her life, so they are auto-biographical, but they are relayed in a self-reflexive manner that clouds the sense of them as definitive reports. Reflecting upon autobiographical performance Deirdre Heddon has warned against being seduced by the artist's 'unmediated presence' and putting too much faith in the illusion of self-possession and authority that is the product of language. For Heddon:

> Autobiographical performance brings to the fore the 'self' as a performed role, rather than an essentialised or naturalised identity [...] it is a property much capitalised on by many performers as a means to reveal not only the multiplicity of the performing subject, but also the multiplicity of discourses that work to forge subjects (and the contradictions within discourses that enable some degree of agency).
>
> *(Heddon 2008: 39)*

Kimmings plays with the notion of 'self' as a performed role. At the beginning of the performance she runs on to the stage in a red sequinned dress, which she tells the audience is from 'ASOS', a low-budget online clothing supplier. After describing her previous performances she takes off this particular costume and packs it away in a suitcase, saying 'away you go Old Bryony' (Kimmings 2018a: 10). A further version of her inner 'self' takes the form of a character listed in the script as 'MALE' and 'MAN'. When she takes on this role her voice is broadcast at a much lower pitch, the electronic alteration causes a slight echo and in addition to the lower pitch it appears to be relayed at a higher volume. Introducing 'MALE/MAN' Kimmings explains, 'sometimes in this show I will talk in a man's voice [...] I chose this voice because I feel like my internal monologue is a cis-gendered straight white middle-aged TV exec' (11). This internalised voice, another 'version' of Kimmings, is shown to be judgemental and cruel. He is without empathy or compassion and repeatedly lambasts Kimmings for being a 'failure'. In Act one Scene ten, for example, when she is at her lowest ebb with Frank in hospital, the inner voice criticises her for sharing her vulnerability. He tells her, 'Get up you stupid bitch, stop playing the victim' and asks, 'Why are you telling people this? Attention seeking' (28). Furthermore, in Act two Scene five the male voice tells her, 'You are a piece of shit [...] you don't deserve to be alive' (44–45). MALE/MAN is shown to be patronising and critical. He exacerbates Kimmings' increasing anxiety and self-doubt. This internalised voice is interesting as an example of a self-scrutinising Foucauldian subject. It also represents a split subject in conflict with itself. As Heddon suggests, Kimmings exploits the notion of multiple selves in order to draw attention to the ways in which popular mythologies about white femininity and motherhood construct an impossibly idealised mystification. *Phoenix* can be regarded as a performance stemming from and about self-care but, as in the case of Thompson, Kimmings provides political distance by calling out what Heddon has called the 'multiplicity of discourses that work to forge subjects'. Michaeli criticises the assimilation of self-care into a neoliberal discourse of individual responsibility and argues that the neoliberal version of self-care depoliticises the phenomenon of mental distress and trauma by taking attention away from the social and economic reasons for distress. I will argue that Kimmings avoids employing a populist model of self-care by using a number of different strategies. Firstly, although her work starts from a point of individual distress it works to raise awareness of post-natal depression for a wider community; secondly, she draws attention to the ways in which she has experienced pressure to take up a number of conservative, idealised subject positions; thirdly, she amplifies and shares a version of her own inner voice of criticism, one deliberately constructed to represent patriarchal power.

Kimmings creates a rich imaginary landscape to depict her idealised version of the world, and an ominous, threatening landscape as she begins to experience heightened anxiety and mental distress. When I saw the production in the renovated Great Hall at Battersea Arts Centre, the stage was furbished with four distinct covered piles, contents hidden by white sheets. The script reveals these to be 'stations'. Like Thompson, Kimmings addresses the audience directly, speaking in a conversational tone, explaining that she has put some 'safety measures' in place as part of the creative process: she has asked to wear her own, everyday clothes, to consult a therapist and for her mother to accompany her. Her mother is present in the show via pre-recorded audio, and these contributions add to a layered montage of anecdote, Kimmings' apocalyptic survival tips for Frank and cartoon-like vignettes projected via live-relay. Each of the stations helps create and broadcast an image of 'perfection' that Kimmings has internalised. The first station features a backdrop to suggest a 1960s domestic kitchen, the second a 1970s bedroom, the third a window of a 1950s style house and the fourth a scale model of her Oxfordshire country cottage. Kimmings animates each station in turn, performing a different version of idealised white femininity at each one. As mentioned in relation to *salt*, Foucault employed Bentham's Panopticon as a potent metaphor for the sense of 'conscious and permanent visibility' the subjects of hegemonic discourse experience (Bartky 1988: 131). Kimmings' sense of visibility relates to received ideas about what it means to be a 'good' girlfriend and mother. For Sandra Lee Bartky this,

> 'state of conscious and permanent visibility' is a sign that the tight, disciplinary control of the body has gotten a hold on the mind as well. In the perpetual self-surveillance of the inmate lies the genesis of the celebrated 'individualism' and heightened self-consciousness which are hallmarks of modern times.
>
> *(Bartky 1988: 131)*

Kimmings uses the word 'perfect', to describe the image created at the first station; she describes it as a 'picture of perfect sexy domesticity'. She describes the cottage as 'that perfect home'. The visual reference to earlier decades shows her sense of idealised white Western domesticity as seductive yet anachronistic. At the first station she dresses, 'her top half. *A beehive, sexily disheveled wig, a man's pyjama top, lashes, nude lip etc.*' (Kimmings 2018a: 14). She sits sideways inside the constructed set-within-a-set, facing a digital camera. She breaks into song and the performance is relayed live on to the large screen hung towards the rear of the stage. Stage directions state: '*The live version is from the side and you can see all of the tricks BRYONY is using to make the video, but on the screen above her head the picture is of perfect sexy domesticity, a total contrast*' (14). The song details the measures this fictionalised version of Kimmings goes to in order to persuade her latest sexual conquest to stay. She sings:

> I'm making you breakfast/ the kind that is heavy
> and sticks to the pan/ so that you feel lazy and
> kinda pathetic and you decide not to go
> I'm dressing up my body/ in the clothes that make
> you see a good combination
> Half like your mother and half like Babe Station so
> you can't leave me alone.
>
> (15)

The song is amusing and light-hearted and yet describes an internalised compulsion to capitulate to male desire and conform to a version of femininity that promises an eerie amalgamation of maternal solace and sexual satisfaction. The second station draws upon the Wiccan icon of the Earth Mother, part of an 'Earth-centred religion' which 'honor[s] the life-giving and life-sustaining powers of Nature' and sees Kimmings crowned with a flower-wreath and sporting a loose, flowing garment (Wicca Living 2019). This song apes the notion of the ideal mother who will eat her placenta and, effortlessly, 'breathe him out in one push'. She describes being 'so full of milk I'm soaked right through' and welcomes 'the blissed out paradise of motherhood' (21). The song refers to a practice popular with 1970s radical feminists and yet is brought up to date with the appearance of 'filters and emojis' floating across the surface of the screen. The use of emojis enables Kimmings to gesture towards the way that social media exacerbates the sense of 'perpetual self-surveillance' marked by Bartky. The third station features another small construction, this time featuring a window. Stage directions state that Kimmings puts on '*a plaited wig, a 50s house coat, wonky lipstick, beauty spot. All 50s movie victims rolled into one*' (26). This time she does not sing, but instead speaks into an old fashioned telephone pleading for help. Her performance at this station references iconic Hitchcock heroines such as Tippi Hedren and Priscilla Lane. Notably, Hitchcock's women are figured as the ideal recipients of the 'male gaze' in Laura Mulvey's seminal essay 'Visual Pleasure and Narrative Cinema'. They represent the 'leitmotif' of erotic spectacle and yet can only ever be passive recipients of male desire (Mulvey 1999: 62). Each of the characters created at the workstations bring to life idealised white Western archetypes of femininity, whilst showing the labour, props and artifice required to construct and maintain the illusion.

The fourth white sheet covers a model of a country cottage. The audience is told that it is a replica of the rural Oxfordshire cottage Grayling and Kimmings moved to after touring their joint show *Fake It Til You Make It* (2015). The model

FIGURE 3.1 Bryony Kimmings performs to camera in *I'm a Phoenix, Bitch* (2018)
Photograph: The Other Richard

is the size of a large doll's house and hinged in the middle so it can be cracked in half to allude to Kimmings' fractured dream. Throughout the performance Kimmings associates her anxiety with the stream that runs at the bottom of the road by the cottage. Introducing the house she relayed how the estate agent warned her about the stream, telling the couple it was likely to rise and cut the house off from the road in winter. Captivated by the 'perfect [thatched] cottage on a hill' with 'white paint, wisteria, the front porch, roses over the front', Kimmings deliberately dismisses the warning, saying, 'He was literally pointing at a trickle … I don't care estate agent man' (19). However in Scene five as Frank becomes increasingly ill, she repeats 'Heed the warning, the stream will rise' as if it is a mantra (44). The rising level of the stream exacerbates Kimmings' anxiety about the health of her child. She regrets not heeding the estate agent's warning and dismissing her sense that she was 'going overboard in [her] faith in maternal intuition' (20).

Kimmings describes the idyll of their early months in the house, '[w]e moved in late Spring 2015. The garden was awash with flowers, the trees lush and green and the little stream about an inch. We spend a lot of time in the bedroom' (19). She leans over the replica cottage as she reminisces. Each of the four workstations represents a similarly constructed idyll or idealised archetype, in the other three stations the projected image excludes the apparatus of representation, presenting the audience with a seemingly faultless image of beauty, and yet the nature of the workstations themselves, replete with costume, mirrors, built-in lighting, props and make-up, enables the audience to see the artifice behind the ideal. The workstations hold props and prosthetics, filters enhance the on-screen image and the giant doll's house cracks apart as if a glacier had sliced through its roof. Part of Kimmings' project of self-care builds upon her self-conscious deconstruction of archetypal notions of white feminine domesticity and part of it upon her confession that prior to becoming pregnant she actively invested in attempting to uphold those archetypes.

Kimmings further resists the assimilation of self-care into the neoliberal model by foregrounding the resilience she has learned from her mother and which she, in turn, teaches Frank via a series of recorded messages. At the moment she realised she was pregnant she stated that, 'getting pregnant suddenly made me completely vulnerable' and that 'something shifted … Under the surface of me, like tectonic plates, only I felt the rumble … I felt like I'd always known who I was, but the responsibility of a new life changed all that' (20). It is significant that Kimmings comes to associate pregnancy with vulnerability because, apart from her protective instincts for her child, she must factor in her shift in status in the eyes of a neo-liberal economy. Although women may be welcomed into the workforce in a wide range of Western professions, once they become pregnant, they cease to be the ideal, self-sufficient citizen, and instead are figured as a potential liability. Health and Safety practices in the UK advise employers to check the pregnant employee's workstations for compatibility with her newfound status and Human Resources departments are required to put in place measures to cover the

FIGURE 3.2 Bryony Kimmings shows her dream cottage split in half in *I'm a Phoenix, Bitch* (2018)
Photograph: The Other Richard

temporary 'loss' of a member of the workforce and ideally remunerate the employee with maternity pay. The woman who is pregnant is no longer an ideal, resilient neoliberal citizen who can take responsibility for her own health and wellbeing; instead she requires the paternalistic care of the State and medical profession. As Bracke has stated above, 'in a neoliberal political economy, resilience has become part of the "moral code": the "good subjects" of neoliberal times are the ones who are able to act, to exercise their agency, in resilient ways' (Bracke 2016: 62). Bracke describes how the 'resilient subject' is 'considered individually responsible for her survival' indeed, 'we might call her a subject of postfeminist resilience' (66). Kimmings' sense of foreboding then, can be seen to be exacerbated by a premonition that she is no longer the 'good citizen' of the neoliberal economy and by becoming vulnerable/pregnant can be seen to be 'failing'. *Phoenix* represents a way of coming to terms with vulnerability and the realisation that anxieties were caused by external social and economic forces. As such it remains politically motivated and represents a way of insisting, after Lorde, that self-care can act as a mode of resistance and 'warfare' against white patriarchal hegemony.

Kimmings performs her resilience in a more literal way during Scene five in which she works with dumbbells and lifts bar weights. Stage directions indicate that she '*fishes under the gauze and pulls out a selection of weight training gear and begins to set it up onstage. A bench, a belt, chalk powder, dumbbells, a large bar with weights*' (Kimmings 2018a: 43). The weights are those associated with professional weight training and she manipulates the equipment deftly. After training with the dumbbells she loads the bar with increasingly heavy weights and, despite showing signs of significant strain, executes the lifts. As she works out she describes the different medication prescribed for Frank and relays conversations held with his doctor. The voice of 'MALE/MAN' interrupts, telling Kimmings, 'You are weak', 'You are a piece of shit', 'You don't deserve to be alive', 'You are nothing'. Tension builds during the scene as she noisily drops the weights and begins to roar with the pain of exertion. Stage directions demonstrate that she is 'turning into an animal' and at the end of the scene '*she loses it, full animal now, screaming up into the sky*' (46). This scene uses an act of extreme physical exertion to articulate a heightened sense of anguish. As with Thompson's sledgehammer, Kimmings' weights crash down to dramatically refute the pessimism of the doctor and her internalised oppressor. Both artists are driven to a state of fury by white male authority figures. Their fury takes them to the brink of insanity and they use their anger to summon hidden reserves of energy. Thompson's violent crushing of the salt rocks and Kimmings' dropping of the weights represent climactic turning-points that mark a refusal to be subjugated any longer. Physical strength is equated with mental strength and the artists discover a newfound strength and resilience and ultimately a means of moving beyond trauma.

The title of Kimmings' work makes reference to the phoenix, a mythical bird born from the ashes of its predecessor. At the start of the piece Kimmings had referred to the 'old' Bryony, the sparkly, sequin-clad predecessor from whose ashes the new, wiser Kimmings emerges. Ironically the 'old' Bryony wears the colour of flames, whereas the 'new' Bryony sports a black exercise kit. Kimmings has shared different versions of her previous self who felt compelled to show herself to be the perfect examples of a fecund, nurturing mother, an epicurean expert and gymnastic lover. She has relayed the voices of those who love and sustain her, her mother and her own voice as it provides survival advice for Frank. She has also shared the voices of those who oppress: the medics and her internalised middle-class male TV executive. She has charted a journey through extreme anxiety and into restored mental health as she comes to believe in her own sense of resilience. Kimmings' piece represents an act of self-care and radical softness because she deliberately renders herself vulnerable and, like Thompson, provides detailed insight into the horror of the journey and the relief at coming through the experience. It avoids falling into the trap of solipsistic, neoliberal self-care because she demonstrates that she is sharing her experience for the benefit of others, she is setting out to 'demystify' post-natal depression (Bradbury 2018). In actively identifying as a feminist she shares her experience as an example of a female subject resisting subjugation by white male authority figures and draws attention to the need for support networks to sustain and support the working subject.

My third example, *How (Not) to Live in Suburbia*, was written by Annie Siddons in 2015 (published in 2017). Siddons is a writer, musician and theatre maker based in London. She describes herself as 'boho-in-suburbia, middle class, single mother in her 40s with a mixed background' and 'unrepentantly showbiz … from humble origins' (Stewart 2017). She has been outspoken about the predominant middle-class bias of the UK arts industry, observing that 'the industry is so snobby… loads of press people won't even come to the Oval or the Albany [theatres]'. She has worked as a writer and dramaturg with a number of different UK companies and venues, collaborating with Kneehigh Theatre on her production of *Rapunzel* in 2006 and writing for the Unicorn Theatre. Recent work includes *Raymondo* (2014), *How (Not) to Live in Suburbia* (2015) (hereafter *Suburbia*) and *Dennis of Penge* (2018). Siddons' writing draws material from the experience of working-class South London life. She combines the details of contemporary urban life with magical realism. In *Suburbia* she uses olive trees to represent her daughters and personifies loneliness as a walrus and shame as a seal. She states, 'I don't want to make realist work in the sense of the genre of realism, but I do want to present as much of human realism as I can' (Worthington 2017). Siddons is critical of the precarity of the UK arts labour market and part of *Suburbia* focuses upon the pressure to be creative in a hostile, commercial environment. Celebrating her Arts Council award, Siddons described how, for her, the lack of financial sustainability in playwriting had become 'pathological'. She wrote:

> I need to become a benevolent Tony Soprano, providing for my family, but despite regularly working 16 hour days, working through sickness, and making art I'm proud of, I seem to be encountering many ceilings. My work doesn't have the impact or growth potential I'd like it to, and I'm dangerously unsupported. Although the neoliberal way is to put that responsibility on the

self, I'm an old fashioned socialist and I'd like us, collectively, to come up with some solutions to offer to funders, venues and each other so we can be heard.

(Siddons 2019)

Suburbia is Siddons' first autobiographical piece. It is largely humorous, focusing upon a time when she experienced extreme mental distress as a result of feeling isolated, lonely and creatively stifled. The performance uses live performance, music and pre-recorded film and features one other live performer playing Siddons and other characters as required.[2] Siddons speaks into a microphone delivering rich, emotive imagery and imaginative, gritty, vignettes. In a similar manner to Thompson and Kimmings, Siddons speaks directly to the audience, although her demeanour is more reminiscent of a singer or spoken-word poet as she cradles the microphone and plays with its lead. She speaks with focus and control, smiling in an affectionate, almost bemused way, at the versions of herself she sees recreated on stage. As with Kimmings and Thompson we hear of the tension between the central performer's desire to rail against societal pressure and her actual performance of tolerance and pragmatism. At regular points Siddons states that she struggled to believe how isolated she had become and how nobody around her picked up on what was going on:

> After Jay left, I was a pure insomniac. It got so that I couldn't hear or see properly. I was underwater. My life was a dyspraxic subaqua ballet. I couldn't believe that the clipboard ladies still weren't coming, and that I was allowed to – no – expected to – take care of the Olive Trees all by myself.
>
> *(Siddons 2017: 32)*

Suburbia asks questions about why and how people become chronically lonely and raises awareness of the role of organisations such as the Samaritans who support and counsel those in need. Siddons trained as a Samaritan as part of her work around the project and has organised workshops and seminars to raise awareness of loneliness. In 2016 she collaborated with Krissi Musiol and Pamela Qualter from the University of Central Lancashire to set up a cross-disciplinary symposium on loneliness. Siddons' website reveals that, 'it look[ed] at loneliness from the dual perspectives of performance and psychology' (Siddons 2016).

At the close of the performance Siddons' alter-ego, played in the version I saw at the Soho Theatre, London, by Nicki Hobday, comes on stage to share her idea for a new show: 'Idea for a new autobiographical show. Idea for a new autobiographical show performed by me' (Siddons 2017: 50). This marks a significant breakthrough, as one of the main stumbling blocks cited previously had been her failure to produce a new play for Verity, her literary agent. Siddons has said that she felt that the autobiographical approach was 'the right thing to do' and that it allowed her to 'get up close and personal with [the] audience' (Costa 2018). She has not described the work in terms of 'self-care' but rather as an airing of 'my most befouled laundry' with the intention of making 'good, accessible, art'

FIGURE 3.3 Annie Siddons holds her olive tree daughters in *How (Not) to Live in Suburbia*
(2017)
Photograph: Claire Nolan

(Siddons 2017: Foreword). However, the piece is clearly driven by a desire to rail against the stigma associated with loneliness and has been life affirming and therapeutic to create. In a similar manner to Thompson and Kimmings, Siddons renders herself vulnerable by sharing stories of herself at her lowest ebb. She shares the voices of those subjugating her: the upper middle-class agent, nursery leaders, middle-class mothers and book group members. She details the ways in which she debased herself and began to cease caring about social propriety. Like Thompson and Kimmings she shares her journey through extreme anxiety, loneliness and depression and shows creating art to be part of a therapeutic process that enables her to achieve a sense of perspective and reach out to community members and collaborators.

In terms of the representation of self-care as political warfare, Siddons draws attention to societal pressures put upon white Western women to parent within small, nuclear family units; to suppress signs of intelligence; to have sex within a monogamous heterosexual relationship. In the Foreword to the script Siddons cites the work of John Cacioppo, who describes loneliness as a 'biosociological phenomenon' and emphasises the multiple internal and external reasons for the experience (Cacioppo and Patrick 2008). She foregrounds the imperatives passed down through the predominantly middle-class art industry, whereby the artist needs to be prolific in order to keep their work in the public eye. As Thompson pushed back against Europe and the Master, and Kimmings against her internalised

TV executive, so Siddons pushes back against Verity, her upper middle-class agent, and the fashionable arts enclave represented by New Cross. *Suburbia* represents performance making as self-care but, as with *salt.* and *Phoenix*, it remains critical of neoliberalism and resists the populist model of self-care. Siddons argues that communities need to look out and care for one another and that self-care should not be the sole responsibility of the individual. She details how her status as a single mother, and her need to find affordable childcare, sits in tension with her potential to earn a living. She criticises the precarity of employment within the UK arts industry, stating that the 'exhaustion' and 'lack of sustainability' can become 'entrenched and pathological' (Siddons 2019). Finally, she politicises the economic and social sources of her mental distress. Her status as a single parent and artist marks her as an outsider in what she perceives to be the predominantly middle-class, monocultural suburb of Twickenham. She lives in an affluent part of London, surrounded by beauty parlours and gyms whilst struggling to make ends meet. Siddons lends an insight into her individual predicament but points to the importance of community and social structures to support those in need.

Working along similar lines to Kimmings, Siddons presents multiple Annies, or 'split' selves. She performs a version of Annie as the storyteller and host of the evening; Nicki Hobday plays a version of Annie and we see another version, played by Siddons herself, on screen. Hobday appears as an exaggerated caricature of Siddons – her hair is larger and more violently red, her clothes tighter and the South London accent exaggerated. As Heddon has noted above, the representation of multiple selves on stage draws attention to the 'multiplicity of discourses' influencing those subjects (Heddon 2008: 39). The fracturing of selves here is extremely effective. In part it makes the piece more light-hearted and accessible to a wider audience. The live, or 'real' version of Siddons smiles indulgently at Hobday's comedic performance, seeming to approve, and so affirm this larger, more confident version of herself. Furthermore, the creation of multiple selves works as a distancing technique; Siddons narrates the story of something that has taken place in the past as if its threat has been recuperated or resolved. When Siddons-as-narrator turns to watch the film footage, she looks slightly bemused as if she is struggling, in the live moment, to believe that her past life took such a turn. When Hobday appears as Annie, she represents a version made momentarily real; her playful performance undermines the sense that the storyteller is necessarily being truthful or 'authentic' and celebrates artistic licence. Most notably, the 'real' version of Annie is no longer lonely; she is restored to her former glory and artistic productivity. She is also working to reach out to others in a similar situation. The fractured selves act as an effective critique of the idealised humanist subject, one who experiences a sense of self-definition and completion and is able to negotiate all terrains, unencumbered by baggage or misfortune. Siddons is shown to be subject to many conflicting external pressures, which rob her of a sense of agency and the capacity to work.

Kimmings and Thompson have represented internalised social forces by characterising them as particular figures or entities. For Thompson, Eurocentric racism is characterised as 'Europe' and specific instances of racism are condoned and encouraged by the 'Master' – the captain of Thompson's first cargo ship. The character listed in the script as 'MALE/MAN' represents Kimmings' internalised sense of white patriarchal supremacy – in this incarnation he is modelled as a TV executive. Siddons' oppressors are realised through the character of Verity, an upper-middle-class literary agent and a pair of sea animals: 'Loneliness' is personified as a walrus and 'Shame' as a seal. The Walrus of Loneliness appears on film as a hooded human figure wearing a rubber mask. Recalling her sense of anxiety about writing Annie narrates, 'this is the point at which the Walrus of Loneliness crashed unannounced into my life'. Stage directions state: '*WALRUS and ANNIE on the bus. He is harassing her. She tries to placate him with biscuits and drugs and booze. He is aggressive*' (Siddons 2017: 20). Siddons explains:

> From the moment he barged through my front door, the Walrus of Loneliness came everywhere with me. He was a total pain the arse – a constant, smelly, socially unskilled, anarchic and laceratingly critical companion. Some kind of yeti or bear, a Wild Thing but without the consolation of having James Gandolfini inside him.
>
> *(21)*

Siddons describes loneliness as an unwanted companion. As with Kimming's TV executive, Siddon's walrus is a 'laceratingly' critical male voice she has internalised as a form of self-surveillance. The walrus tells her that her loneliness has become pathological, consolidating a fear that stymies her ability to write. The walrus is joined later in the piece by the Seal of Shame. This time the character is female, and, according to Siddons:

> The Seal of Shame has no mercy; she will annihilate you with her sweet nothings. The Seal of Shame saw an opportunity that day, and she seized it; the shame of the fellatio, the shame of the random fucks of blindness, the shame of my fiscal failure and my professional paralysis, the shame of my daughter's illness, the shame of my failed marriage, the shame of ageing, the shame of being rejected, the shame of wanting, the shame of refusing to settle, the shame of fighting for a life that was not hemmed in by a picket fence of respectability and compromise …
>
> *(44)*

The walrus and seal serve a clear function – they allow Siddons to externalise sentiments experienced cognitively and express the feelings of abjection and shame that accompanied isolation and loneliness. She writes that, 'the seal of shame is the one that turns you from someone struggling to someone no longer struggling' (44). By externalising the critical voices, Siddons allows the audience to get an insight into the exhaustion accompanying the niggling self-doubt and fears of self-worth. A third voice in the piece acts in a similarly critical way.

Whilst the walrus and seal use a process of attrition to chip away at her sanity, the character of Verity makes clear threats and unceremoniously drops Siddons from her books when she has not been able to produce a new play. Verity appears as a disembodied voice, accompanied by projected images of her skiing. She is said to smoke 'long, thin cigarettes'. Her first appearance sees her leave the following message for Siddons:

> Theatre is a Darwinian profession. It's survival of the fittest. I know you have been having some little personal problems but you're going to have to pull your finger out and write something quickly that I can sell. I'm not interested in having one hit wonders on my books. The other day someone said 'Annie who?' and I can't have that so put your head down and write. I know you can do it. Lickety Split.
>
> (8)

The literary agent distils the predicament of an artist who has been taken on by an agent – it is not enough to have produced successful work in the past, the pressure remains to keep producing commercially successful pieces. Verity's messages report back on the success of other clients, one of whom has 'three plays running concurrently all the time' (20). Her reference to theatre as a 'Darwinian' profession refers to the theory of Social Darwinism, which, as Gregory Claeys has argued, normalises the idea that some members of society are 'fitter' and more likely to survive than others (Claeys 2000: 229). Siddons' lack of 'fitness' in this instance is due to her sense of social isolation and caring responsibilities, suggesting that those with a steadfast sense of self-containment and no duty of care have the clearest potential to succeed. Throughout the piece Siddons recalls her sense of bewilderment that she was being expected to raise her children by herself, a criticism of how normalised the image of a struggling yet resilient single mother has become.

Along with the tyrannical Verity, the personified Walrus of Loneliness and Seal of Shame work effectively to deprivatise a sense of responsibility for self-care. They are shown to be the product of social and economic forces imposed externally but internalised into a form of self-surveillance. By using personification in this way Siddons politicises the notion of self-care, the impossibility of unconditional resilience the need for wider social support. For Butler, Gambetti and Sabsay, neoliberal notions of resilience 'cover over the structural conditions of accelerated precarity, inequality, statelessness, and occupation' (Butler et al. 2016: 6). In *Suburbia* Siddons personifies these structural conditions and in doing so uncouples the responsibility for nurturing and support from the individual and on to the community at large.

Three very different female artists created the performances under discussion; each draws upon a distinct aesthetic, politics and style. Despite differences, they have many themes in common. Each piece is autobiographical and narrated by the central artist. Each artist describes the experience of mental distress as a result of a series of traumatic experiences exacerbated by social pressure to conform to idealised archetypes. It is significant that each performance includes a reverie around water and drowning. Thompson imagines herself leaping off a cargo ship at the central point of the Transatlantic Slave Triangle. Stymied in her attempt to find a 'home' she states:

> There is no peace to be had, no homes to be found
> [...]
> This body plunges into the depths, fathoms deep, and as
> it falls it changes
> Becomes a dead living thing
> Is reshaped and reformed by the ocean, into chunks of
> salt, falling like snow into the sea.
>
> *(Thompson 2017: 50)*

Stage directions state that, '*The Woman drowns, and her body becomes salt ... But something calls to her*' (50). Thompson is pulled back from the brink of death by the voice of her late grandmother calling to her, lending much needed solace. Kimmings' scenario sees her rescued from a burning cottage by the torrential influx of the stream that has been threatening to invade her life since her son fell ill. In Scene four stage directions show, '*For a moment she is relieved to be saved from the burning cottage but now she cannot breathe under the water, and she dies*' (Kimmings 2018a: 41). Kimmings describes how she, 'floated dead under the water for what felt like an eternity/Gently bobbing./I could hear the rational voices of doctors above my head/Muffled from the air above the water/But not clear enough to take heed' (41). Kimmings' renewed desire to live similarly emanates from a distant disembodied voice; it is that of her old-self. Stage directions state:

> Old BRYONY *arrives under the water in the video. In the sequins, with the wig and the shoes. And she dances. Real* BRYONY *watches herself. She stares longingly at her former self, it's sad. She reaches for her, joining in with the dance, lost in the fantasy of the past. Then she stops. She makes the decision to leave the nightmare world and comes down from the platform and watches herself from in front of the gauze.*
>
> *(41–42)*

Siddons' experience of drowning relates to her insomnia after the departure of JAY. She explains, 'I was underwater. My life was a dyspraxic subaqua ballet [...] I was entering a progressive degeneration phenomenon. A Downward Spiral' (Siddons 2017: 32). Solace comes in the form of the emergency services. After committing an act of self-harm she finally recognises that she needs urgent help and calls for an ambulance. She reports, 'the winning took time ... An intervention [was] necessary. An awareness. A naming of the parts' (50). As part of her healing process she undergoes training for a mental health charity and writes her 'Anniefesto' which plots the following aims:

1.   Be a good enough mother.
2.   Make good art. Collaborate.
3.   Love and connect, in as many different ways as you can.
4.   Keep your integrity.   (50)

Each of the artists are 'saved' by the voice of another (albeit another version of herself in Kimmings' case) and by 'connecting' and experiencing support from others. Even though the artists emerge from a state of anxiety and distress the performances show individualised resilience to be an impossible mystification and the support of a wider, empathetic community to be the only way forward. Thompson, Kimmings and Siddons share moments of extreme vulnerability in order to represent 'softness' or human vulnerability without shame. The activity of making the performances represents an act of self-care, a process of measured reflection and distanciation. Each artist lays bare the matrices of domination, the institutional and disciplinary authorities materially affecting their lives. They find themselves the subject of class, racial and sexist discrimination; they are advised to eschew instinctual knowledge and to champion rational thought above all else. They find themselves robbed of resources to support others and shunned from elitist cultural groups. Each has internalised the expectation that they should take individual responsibility for self-care but external pressure proves too heavy to bear. Thompson's work reveals the unsupportable pressure of living in the UK as a member of the African diaspora; she finds solace in the words of Black feminist writers and activists and feels their words/hands support her and bring her back from the fantasy of death. Kimmings experiences anxiety and post-natal depression. She internalises a sense of failure, feeling that she should be able to cope alone; feeling that she has is somehow responsible for her son's illness, and feeling that she has failed him when she becomes overwhelmed. Siddons' piece shares her experience of isolation and loneliness as she finds herself ostracised by a monocultural suburban community and pressurised to produce commercially successful plays whilst struggling to care for her ill daughter. A feeling of being apart or distanced from other people precipitates crisis in each case. The neoliberal drive to eschew vulnerability and softness and privatise resilience and self-care exacerbates this sense of isolation. Each story begins with an individual narrative and yet each performance is ultimately a celebration of community rather than individualised self-care. Thompson reaches out to the People of Colour in her audience, stating that she is 'sitting with' them; Kimmings, in sharing her story, works to reduce the stigma around the topic of post-natal depression; and Siddons, at the close of her performance, raises awareness of mental health charities such as the Samaritans who provide a crucial support network. Ultimately each artist surrenders to a sense of vulnerability and 'softness'. They embody Thompson's advice to: 'stay soft. Cry lots, demand and expect love and care and gentleness, and give all of those things to others, abundantly' (Thompson 2018). This celebration of softness and vulnerability ultimately champions Lorde's assertion that self-care, far from being an act of indulgence, is in reality a counter-cultural act, an act of 'political warfare'.

The invocation to 'stay soft' in the work of Thompson, Kimmings and Siddons is at odds with the 'coldness' of the irony which Lehman argues is a 'key feature of Post-dramatic theatre' (Lehmann 2006: 118). In performing a version of themselves and drawing attention to the apparatus of mimetic illusion the three artists can be seen to be working with cognisance of postdramatic or postmodern performance techniques. However they are anything but cool in their relationship to the material. Neither do they obfuscate their relationship to intention or meaning in the manner of Holstein, Lee and GETINTHEBACKOFTHEVAN. They show themselves interpellated by hegemonic discourse and robbed of agency at certain junctures, but show themselves capable of transcending the depths of despair by drawing upon the writings, advice and support of women close by and women who went before. By investing in a recognisable category of identity, such as Black or white working-class, the artists accrue the ability to recognise their own limitations as partly the responsibility of wider social forces. Fortified by this knowledge they choose to resist and live well.

As I mentioned in the Introduction Lavender has charted a 'return to a self that is somehow sincere'. For Lavender this self is a reaction against the laconic aloofness of postmodern performance, which he states 'appeared to sweep away the tainted procedures of dramatic characterization' (Lavender 2016: 118). Thompson et al. reconstruct centred images of 'the self' in order to address social and racial inequality. By dramatising their own experiences, and putting themselves at the centre of the work they create an illusion of sincerity and perhaps even authenticity. At times they experience an overwhelming sense of failure, they are depicted fractured and broken but ultimately return to a sense of stable self-hood, which in turn allows them to reach out to others. The images of being reborn after drowning, and what Thompson refers to as a sensation of being pulled 'back into being', tally with Muñoz's argument for the generative potential of failure. He writes,

> within failure we can locate a kernel of potentiality. I align queer failure with a certain mode of virtuosity that helps the spectator exit from the stale and static lifeworld dominated by the alienation, exploitation, and drudgery associated with capitalism or landlordism.
>
> (Muñoz 2009: 173).

In the next chapter I will examine the work of four artists seen to be employing elements of postmodern performance praxis whilst speaking via a centred self. Like Thompson, Kimmings and Siddons they describe the experience of feeling marginalised by hegemonic white patriarchal society, but in this case their work demonstrates an increased preoccupation with space and a questioned sense of belonging. I will consider the work of Rachael Young, Project O and Lucy McCormick all of whom have created work around the experience of feeling unwelcome. In particular I discuss Young's *Nightclubbing* (2018), McCormick's *Triple Threat* (2016) and Project O's *Voodoo* (2016). I argue that each production works to create a heterotopic world within a conventional theatre space in order to draw attention to how their bodies are perceived in different performative contexts. Each production creates an environment customarily associated with a cabaret or nightclub in order to challenge the limitations put upon certain body types and codes of behaviour. The heterotopic space-within-a-space encourages a reevaluation of ideologies which suggest some bodies 'belong' more than others.

Notes

1 Thompson took on the role of 'The Woman' in the productions I saw at Stage@Leeds, 2016 and the South Bank Centre, 2017. Rochelle Rose took on the role in the run at the Royal Court, London in 2019.
2 Films made by Richard Dedomenici.

Bibliography

Allen, Amy (2016) 'Feminist Perspectives on Power', *The Stanford Encyclopedia of Philosophy*, Fall 2016. Available at: https://plato.stanford.edu/archives/fall2016/entries/feminist-power/ (accessed 5 March 2019).

Ahmed, Sara (2014) *feministkilljoys.com*. Available at: https://feministkilljoys.com/2014/08/25/selfcare-as-warfare/ (accessed 12 March 2019).

Bartky, Sandra Lee (1988) 'Foucault, Femininity and the Modernization of Patriarchal Power', in *Feminism and Foucault: Reflections on Resistance*, Irene Diamond and Lee Quinby (eds.), Boston: Northwestern University Press, pp. 129–154.

Bracke, Sarah (2016) 'Bouncing Back: Vulnerability and Resistance in Times of Resilience', in *Vulnerability in Resistance*, Judith Butler, Zeynep Gambetti and Leticia Sabsay (eds.), Durham: Duke University, pp. 52–72.

Bradbury, Sarah (2018) 'Bryony Kimmings Interview: Imagine If We Were Living in a Matriarchy? That Would Be Amazing', *The Independent*, 3 October. Available at: https://www.independent.co.uk/arts-entertainment/theatre-dance/features/bryony-kimmings-im-a-phoenix-bitch-battersea-arts-centre-interview-tickets-a8564761.html (accessed 11 March 2019).

Body is Not an Apology, The (2019) website. Available at: https://thebodyisnotanapology.com/magazine/reflections-of-black-women-who-lived-radical-self-love/ (accessed 8 March 2019).

Butler, Judith, Zeynep Gambetti and Leticia Sabsay (eds.) (2016) *Vulnerability in Resistance*, Durham: Duke University Press.

Butler, Season (2017) 'Divesting From Whiteness', paper given to Roehampton Centre for Performance and Creative Exchange, 13 December, Roehampton University, London.

Cacioppo, John and William Patrick (2008) *Loneliness: Human Nature and the Need for Social Connection*, 2nd Edition, New York: W.W Norton and Company.

Cochrane, Kira (2013) *All the Rebel Women: The Rise of Fourth Wave Feminism*, London: Guardian Books.

Costa, Maddy (2018) 'Annie Siddons: "We Need To Be Raging"', *Exeunt Magazine*, 2 October. Available at: http://exeuntmagazine.com/features/annie-siddons-interview/ (11 March 2019).

Claeys, Gregory (2000) '"The Survival of the Fittest" and the Origins of Social Darwinism', *Journal of the History of Ideas*, 61(2), 223–240.

DiAngelo, Robin (2019) *White Fragility: Why It's So Hard for White People to Talk about Racism*, London: Penguin.

Eric-Udorie, June (ed.) (2018) *Can We All be Feminists? Seventeen Writers on Intersectionality, Identity and Finding the Right Way Forward for Feminism* [Kindle e-book] London: Virago.

Felman, Shoshana (2002) *The Scandal of the Speaking Body: Don Juan with J.L.Austin, or Seduction in Two Languages*, Palo Alto: Stanford University Press.

Flare (2017) *Flare.com* website. Available at: https://www.flare.com/living/self-care-is-a-radical-act/ (accessed 8 March 2019).

Foucault, Michel (1979) *Discipline and Punish: The Birth of the Prison*, translated by Alan Sheridan, London: Vintage.

Gardner, Lyn (2015) 'Dark and Lovely Review – Black Hair Story, Told Straight', *The Guardian*, 11 October. Available at: https://www.theguardian.com/stage/2015/oct/11/dark-and-lovely-selina-thompson-review-ovalhouse-london (accessed 21 August 2019).

Gardner, Lyn (2018) 'Interview: Lyn Gardner Talks to Bryony Kimmings about the Tough Stuff', *RunRiot.com*, 18 September. Available at: http://www.run-riot.com/articles/blogs/interview-lyn-gardner-talks-bryony-kimmings-about-tough-stuff (accessed 10 March 2019).

Goddard, Lynette Leni (2007) 'Middle-Class Aspirations and Black Women's Mental (Ill) Health in Zindika's Leonora's Dance, and Bonnie Greer's Munda Negra and Dancing on Blackwater', in *Cool Britannia? British Political Drama in the 1990s*, Rebecca d'Monte and Graham Saunders (eds.), Basingstoke: Palgrave Macmillan.

Goop (2019) Goop website. Available at: https://goop.com/beauty/makeup/self-care-cubicle-bound/ (accessed 29 August 2019).

Gorman, Sarah (2017) 'You Can Say Much More Interesting Things About a Scar, Than You Can About a Wound: Interview with Selina Thompson', 15 August. Available at: https://readingasawoman.wordpress.com/ (accessed 16 August 2019).

Hartman, Saidiyah (2008) *Lose Your Mother: A Journey Along the Atlantic Slave Route*, New York: Farrah, Strauss and Giroux.

Harvey, David (2005) *A Brief History of Neoliberalism*, Oxford: Oxford University Press.

Harvie, Jen (2017) 'Episode 6: Interview with Selina Thompson', *Stage Left with Jen Harvie*. Available at: https://soundcloud.com/stage_left (accessed 12 March 2019).

Heddon, Deirdre (2008) *Autobiography and Performance*, Basingstoke: Palgrave Macmillan.

Heddon, Deirdre (2012) 'Feminist Performance: Legacies and Futures', Opening Plenary presentation at Performance Studies International Conference, Leeds University, 25 to 28 June.

Hill Collins, Patricia (2000) *Black Feminist Thought: Knowledge, Consciousness, and the Politics of Empowerment*, New York: Routledge.

Jones, Amelia (2012) *Seeing Differently: A History and Theory of Identification and the Visual Arts*, Abingdon: Routledge.

Kimmings, Bryony (2013) 'I'll Show You Mine', Blog post, 21 November. Available at: http://thebryonykimmings.tumblr.com/post/67660917680/you-show-me-yours (accessed 18 March 2019).

Kimmings, Bryony (2017) 'Looking Through Glasses of Water', Blog post, 16 July. Available at: http://thebryonykimmings.tumblr.com/ (accessed 18 March 2019).

Kimmings, Bryony (2018a) *I'm a Phoenix, Bitch*, London: Oberon Books.

Kimmings, Bryony (2018b) *The Sex Clinic: Artist in Residence*, 60 min documentary, Producer/Director – Vic Silver, July, The Garden Productions.

Lavender, Andy (2016) *Performance in the Twenty-First Century: Theatres of Engagement*, Abingdon: Routledge.

Lehmann, Hans-Thies (2006) *Postdramatic Theatre*, translated by Karen Juers-Munby, Abingdon: Routledge.

Lorde, Audre (1988) *A Burst of Light and Other Essays*, Mineola: Ixia Press.

Lorde, Audre (2007) 'The Uses of the Erotic: The Erotic as Power', in *Sister Outsider: Essays and Speeches by Audre Lorde*, Berkley: Crossing Press, pp. 53–60.

Marlborough Theatre (2019) The Marlborough Theatre, Brighton website. Available at: http://www.marlboroughtheatre.org.uk/event/radicalsoftness/ (accessed 14 March 2019).

Mathis, Lora (2015) Lora Mathis website. Available at: http://www.loramathis.com/ (accessed 14 March 2019).

Michaeli, Inna (2017) 'Self-Care: An Act of Political Warfare or a Neoliberal Trap?' *Development*, 60, 50–56.

Mulvey, Laura (1999) 'Visual Pleasure and Narrative Cinema', in *Film Theory and Criticism: Introductory Readings*, Leo Braudy and Marshall Cohen (eds.) New York: Oxford University Press, pp. 833–844.

Muñoz, José Esteban (2009) *Cruising Utopia: the Then and There of Queer Futurity*, New York: New York University Press.

Nash, Jennifer C. (2013) 'Practicing Love: Black Feminism, Love-Politics, and Post-Intersectionality', *Meridians: Feminism, Race, Transnationalism*, 11(2), 1–24.

Siddons, Annie (2016) 'Loneliness Symposium at UCLAN', *Annie Siddons Blog*, 22 November. Available at: http://anniesiddons.co.uk/loneliness-symposium-at-uclan/ (accessed 29 August 2019).

Siddons, Annie (2017) *How (Not) To Live in Suburbia*, London: Oberon Books.

Siddons, Annie (2019) 'DYCP Grant Super Grateful Yes Yes Yes', 3 February. Available at: https://anniesiddons.co.uk/dycp-grant-super-grateful-yes-yes-yes-yes/ (accessed 20 March 2019).

South London Gallery (2019) South London Gallery website. Available at: https://www.southlondongallery.org/ (accessed 21 August 2019).

Spicer, André (2019) '"Self-care": how a radical feminist idea was stripped of politics for the mass market', *The Guardian*, 21 August. Available at: https://www.theguardian.com/commentisfree/2019/aug/21/self-care-radical-feminist-idea-mass-market (accessed 21 August 2019).

Thompson, Selina (2017) *salt*. London: Faber and Faber.

Thompson, Selina (2018) 'Selina', in *The Outsider's Handbook*, Scottee, Travis Alabanza, Selina Thompson and Emma Frankland (eds.), London: Live Art Development Agency. Available at: http://www.thisisliveart.co.uk/publishing/the-outsiders-handbook/ (accessed 1 March 2019).

Stewart, Greg (2017) 'Interview: Annie Siddons: How (Not) to Live in Suburbia', *theatreweekly.com*, 29 August. Available at: https://theatreweekly.com/interview-annie-siddons-how-not-to-live-in-suburbia/ (accessed 11 March 2019).

tucker green, debbie (2018) *ear for eye*, London: Nick Hern Books.

Waldman, Katy (2018) 'A Sociologist Examines the "White Fragility" that Prevents White Americans from Confronting Racism', *The New Yorker*, July 23. Available at: https://www.newyorker.com/books/page-turner/a-sociologist-examines-the-white-fragility-that-prevents-white-americans-from-confronting-racism (accessed 12 March 2019).

Wicca Living (2019). Available at: http://wiccaliving.com/what-is-wicca/ (accessed 19 March 2019).

Worthington, Amy (2017) 'Interview: Annie Siddons', 24 January. Available at: http://www.thenationalstudent.com/Arts_and_Theatre/2017-01-24/interview_annie_siddons.html (accessed 11 March 2019).

4

NIGHTCLUBBING: QUEER HETEROTOPIA AND CLUB CULTURE

In 1967 Michel Foucault presented 'Of Other Spaces', a lecture in which he shared his vision for alternative social spaces, or 'counter-sites' which come into being in order to contain, or give voice to, human states or behaviours considered somehow apart from or 'deviant' by hegemonic society. Examples include: ships, retirement homes, brothels, prisons, army barracks, cemeteries, fairgrounds, gardens and museums. He cites 'theatres' as heterotopic places in which several 'incompatible' sites can be 'juxtaposed' (Foucault 1984: 6). According to Foucault, heterotopias have the potential to contest or resist values associated with hegemonic culture; they create an alternative space of opposition in the midst of mainstream culture.[1] I will argue that my chosen artists Rachael Young, Lucy McCormick and Project O recreate or borrow from a club aesthetic in order to transform conventional theatre spaces and create an oppositional, heterotopic space-within-a-space. This alternative space has the potential to foreground normative expectations imposed upon their bodies and draw attention to the way social context exaggerates cultural meaning. This work occupies a space of 'failure' because each performance draws upon an experience of rejection, and can be seen to animate José Muñoz's sense of 'queer virtuosity'. By deploying tropes of amateur performance, impossible tasks and metatheatrical confession each practitioner draws upon what Sara Jane Bailes has described as the postmodern praxis of performing failure. They draw upon a negative experience in order to create an alternative world, setting out to deliberately occupy the margins of mainstream culture.

This chapter will explore the work of four contemporary London-based British artists who have forged an oppositional sense of agency through performance in response to an experience of rejection or marginalisation. Alexandrina Hemsley and Jamila Johnson-Small both make up Project O, a dance and performance company; Lucy McCormick's work straddles popular and experimental performance; and Rachael Young draws upon a rich visual, live art and theatre practice.

Several of the artists identify as queer but most have expressed frustration with the practice of identity labelling and present themselves in a number of different ways in order to challenge the imperative to fit into a definitive social category. Lucy McCormick's *Triple Threat* (2016) is an hour-long cabaret in which she attempts to re-enact the New Testament, playing each of the main roles. She describes the 'whole central premise of the show' as 'completely absurd and sort of impossible' (Winer 2017). Rachael Young describes her performance, *Night-clubbing* (2018), as an Afrofuturistic 'visual poem' (Masso 2018). It features musicians Mwen Rukandema and Leisha Thomas who provide a sonorous and immersive electronic sound track. Rukandema and Thomas layer live and pre-recorded music on to samples of vocal transcript as Young sways hypnotically and murmurs into a microphone. The visual impact of *Nightclubbing* is heighted by futuristic costume pieces designed by Naomi Kuyck-Cohen. Project O's *Voodoo* (2016) is an 'immersive experiential work' which fuses an Afrofuturistic layering of heritage and popular culture. Audience members are invited to leave all timepieces outside the performance space and participate in a collective, meditative experience. In terms of cultural and spatial context, I have visited these performances in a range of settings: end-on theatre spaces such as the Arnolfini, Bristol, London's Chelsea Theatre, Camden People's Theatre and The Place, London as well as spaces customarily reserved for stand-up comedy, such as London's Soho Theatre, and the Trinity Centre, a live music venue in Bristol. To a large extent these works maintain what Benjamin Wihstutz regards to be a key aspect of the 'topology' of theatre; that is the 'dual differentiation of space' between audience and performers. These performances begin with audience and performers in separate parts of the space, however each piece makes a number of sonic and spatial interventions that confront the conventional relationship between 'observers and those being observed' (Wihstutz 2013: 4). In *Triple Threat* McCormick leaves the stage to make physical and verbal contact with the audience; in *Nightclubbing* Young's use of looped sound encourages an otherworldly, somnambulistic experience; and in *Voodoo* Hemsley and Johnson-Small invite the audience to join them on the stage-as-dance-floor. Each piece incorporates an act of spatial subversion, which I argue amounts to a 'queering' of the conventional theatre space, and lends itself to an interrogation of the terms upon which these female bodies are welcomed into or ejected from mainstream social spaces. Each performance contains explicit and/or contextual reference to a moment in which the artist felt directly or indirectly excluded from a white and/or male dominated space. The pieces have been shaped, in part, by this experience, and the subversion of the conventional theatre space helps forge a sense of agency whereby the artists deliberately take control of how they present their bodies and represent themselves.[2] Each production is galvanised by Young's assertion that 'nightclubs should be places where we can let go and allow our unbridled selves to be free, they should be spaces of liberation and revolution, not spaces of oppression' (Prashar-Savoie 2018).

Muñoz's work on queer culture and aesthetics has been hugely influential in the emerging discourse of performing failure. Writing in opposition to 'antisocial queer theories' which set themselves against a reproductive futurity as hetero-normative and assimilationist, Muñoz has developed a theory of 'queer utopian-ism' that interrogates the 'ontological certitude that [he] understand[s] to be partnered with the politics of presentist and pragmatic contemporary gay identity' (Muñoz 2009: 11). Influenced by Ernst Bloch he argues for the importance of a sense of a productive future for 'minoritarian subjects' who, he believes, 'are cast as hopeless in a world without utopia' (97). He analyses Kevin McCartney's gay stages as part of a 'punk/queer utopian scene' and argues for performance's potential to 'generate a modality of knowing and recognition among audiences and groups that facilitates modes of belonging, especially minoritarian belonging' (98–99). For Muñoz a 'generative politics' can be 'distilled from the aesthetics of queer failure'. He 'align[s] queer failure with a certain mode of virtuosity that helps the spectator exit from the stale and static lifeworld dominated by the alienation, exploitation and drudgery associated with capitalism or landlordism' (137). Influenced by Paul Virno he recognises potential in its seeming opposite, a 'queer virtuosity'. He writes, '[i]t too, is going off script. Virtuosity debunks production-based systems of value that make work and even cultural production drudgery and alienated debasement' (178). Muñoz has celebrated queer failure and virtuosity in the work of Vaginal Davies, Dynasty Handbag and Jack Smith, celebrating its 'rejection of normative ideas of value' (173). I will argue that Young, McCormick and Project O deploy recognisable acts of amateurism and failure in order to demonstrate how they are perceived in a range of different social and cultural contexts. Their stories lend insight into how they are received as: white femme bodies; dark-skinned black bodies; mixed-race bodies; queer bodies in the context of mainstream contemporary dance; mainstream theatre; live art; commercial nightclubs and gay clubs. Their performances animate stories of intersectional exclusion due not only to sexism but also to colourism; gay misogyny; cultural elitism; and racism. Rather than construct their work as 'uto-pian' I want to borrow Foucault's notion of 'heterotopia' in order to capitalise on his assertion that heterotopia is an example of a 'real' rather than imagined place and explore how alternative club spaces created within mainstream theatre spaces interrogate and contest the way conventional, mainstream theatre itself might reject or alienate these bodies. Muñoz's theories of queer virtuosity and queer failure play an important role within each heterotopia.

As mentioned above, theatre, for Foucault, is one of a number of sites capable of 'juxtaposing in a single real place several spaces, several sites that are in themselves incompatible'. For him theatre 'brings onto the rectangle of the stage [...] a whole series of places that are foreign to one another' (Foucault 1984: 6). As a heterotopia theatre's role is to 'create a space of illusion that exposes every real space' or, 'create a space that is other, another real space, as perfect, as meticulous, as well arranged as ours is messy, ill constructed and jumbled' (8). Several theatre theorists have borrowed Foucault's determination of theatre as utopian or 'heterotopian'. Stephen

Farrier sees utopian potential in the way that the 'copresence' of the performer enables a performer's otherwise sublimated queerness to influence characterisation on the realist stage. He writes, '[t]his virtual/not-virtual copresence is a site of queer utopia because it offers utopic structures that momentarily propose a resolution to the problem of queer and its relation to identity politics and queer agency' (Farrier 2013: 49). Cathy Turner cites Mike Pearson and Jen Harvie who have described performance events as 'heterotopic' or 'micro-utopian' (Turner 2015: 14). Whilst drawing attention to the 'cryptic' and 'vague' nature of Foucault's description of heterotopia, Joanne Tompkins describes theatre as a kind of 'laboratory' and Benjamin Wihstutz celebrates theatre's utopian potential to represent events that 'cannot take place within everyday social life' (Tompkins 2014: 6; Wihstutz 2013: 188). While contemplating theatre as a 'form of utopian enclave' Turner warns that,

> we might … be on firmer ground with the term 'heterotopia' [because it] is often more compatible with the views of some of the artists themselves, for whom, like many others, utopianism appears dangerously connected to authoritarianism, or, alternatively, fatally detached from the real.
>
> *(Turner 2015: 17)*

For Tompkins theatre as heterotopia helps contemplate it as a 'world-making space'. She writes:

> when audiences perceive heterotopia in theatre, they are presented with a sample of what spatial, structural, and political options might be tried out for evaluation, whether or not they are accepted as actual possibilities. Even rejecting selections affords the opportunity for audiences to decide which options are a step too far. Heterotopic theatre that is engaged politically – and aesthetically – offers a model for (re)fashioning the present and the future.
>
> *(Tompkins 2014: 7)*

Turner's suggestion that utopias might be associated with a more recidivist version of humanist discourse is extremely useful here, considering that utopias have been associated with Humanist ideology and within Humanism women have traditionally been constructed as incapable of transcendence, anchored and determined primarily by their 'natural' and nurturing bodies.[3] Tompkins' distinction is also useful because she qualifies '*when* audiences perceive heterotopia in theatre' rather than constructing theatre as always automatically providing an interrogative stance (Tompkins 2014: 7 my emphasis). Indeed, Wihstusz warns that 'the heterotopia of the theatre runs the risk of merely simulating other relations or encounters and, ultimately confirming the old boundaries and divisions' (Wihstutz 2013: 191). I will argue that the artists in question actively engage with a club aesthetic in order to create a queer heterotopia within an otherwise conventional theatre space. Although Foucault cites theatre as a heterotopian space, I would argue that, for theatre, as I am sure for many of the other types of space he lists, this designation is too general and obscures the work that different types of theatre and performance spaces make possible. He states that he is interested in 'certain [sites] that have the curious property of being in relation with all the other sites, but in such a way as to suspect, neutralize, or invent the set of relations that they happen to designate, mirror or reflect' (Foucault 1984: 3). Although I do not see large-scale commercial theatre work as incapable of rendering society 'suspect', I do believe that it is rare to find the same sense of self-reflexivity in mainstream venues as in alternative spaces. Clearly not all theatres are 'counter-sites' or demonstrate a drive to 'represent, contest' or 'invert'. I do not want to repeat the notion that smaller scale fringe, performance or live art spaces automatically create work that is ideologically resistant or radical but I feel it is important to pay some attention to the neoliberal structures supporting large-scale commercial venues.[4] Foucault's designation of certain spaces as 'real' is, as Tompkins points out, frustratingly vague and surprisingly naïve. However, flawed as it may be, when Project O, Rachael Young and Lucy McCormick bring practices associated with nightclubbing and club culture on to the stage Foucault's vision of heterotopia provides an invaluable tool for theorising how a microcosmic space-within-a-space holds the potential to foreground the cultural production of meaning.

The artists create a sense of club culture by: inviting the audience to dance with them on stage; performing intimate acts close by in a part of the space customarily designated for the audience; playing music to drown out the spoken word. They reproduce behaviours and ways of looking associated with a range of different subcultural practices. These practices are designed to cater for and attract a more youthful, diverse, queer audience and may remain illegible to conventional theatregoers. By recreating subcultural practices the artists create an alternative enclave, a marginal space within a larger, more widely recognised institution. The artists under discussion are customarily programmed by small-scale subsidised theatre venues, some of which provide a mixed programme of work for a wide range of audiences, some of which cater for a specialist, queer audience. In smaller queer venues such as the Marlborough Theatre, Brighton, their subcultural practice will be legible and easily recognisable; however for theatres with a broader programming base, some of the club-based practices may appear alien and even taboo. The artists deliberately create a marginal practice or space, as if to say that in order for them to feel a sense of agency, they must control the context of reception and production. In 'Choosing the Margin as a Space of Radical Openness' bell hooks has argued for the importance of a 'politics of location'. She writes:

> As a radical standpoint, perspective, position, 'the politics of location' necessarily calls those of us who would participate in the formation of counter-hegemonic cultural practice to identify the spaces where we begin the process of re-vision [...] For many of us, that movement requires pushing against oppressive boundaries set by race, sex, and class domination.
>
> (hooks 2015: 223)

For hooks the creation of a marginal space is a way of escaping a 'colonizing mentality' and of creating access 'where there is unlimited access to the pleasure and power of knowing, where transformation is possible' (223). She cites this practice as a 'radical openness, a margin – a profound edge' (229). The artists in question all seek to subvert the white, patriarchal, colonising gaze whilst giving voice to the contradictory, joyful and sensual experience of their lives.

Based in London, Lucy McCormick is, as Harvie has pointed out, 'prodigiously talented' (Harvie 2016). She works across mainstream and experimental performance contexts. In 2018 and 2019 she appeared in plays such as *Collective Rage* by Jen Silverman and *Dear Elizabeth* by Sarah Ruhl at the Gate Theatre as well as touring internationally with GETINTHEBACKOFTHEVAN and her own, solo piece *Triple Threat*. She appeared in The Famous Lauren Barri Holstein's *Splat!* at the Barbican, London and regularly appears in alternative gay and live art venues such as Royal Vauxhall Tavern, Bethnal Green Working Men's Club, Steakhouse and Dalston Superstore. She identifies as queer, but is wary of reductive identity categories. In conversation with drag performer Jonny Woo, McCormick stated: 'I'm queer and my sexuality is fluid. […] It's funny, being queer is partly about fluidity and acceptance – but I think we also love titles and sometimes we're the first to box each other in' (QX Team 2017). Tongue firmly in cheek, she describes *Triple Threat* as a 'play' in three acts and cites the importance of context to her work,

> I think really specifically about the venue and context of what we're doing, so I can both go in knowing how to play the audience, but also mess around with expectations. I really like to make work that is in turns really slick, and a total mess.
>
> *(QX Team 2017)*

Of the gay venues she frequents, she has said, 'these spaces are my church, [*Triple Threat*] is about this being my religion' (Segalov 2017). She draws upon trash and pop culture and is attracted to female performers often described as 'divas'. Responding to a question about the feminist potential of her work she agrees that it is 'pro-actively feminist' but qualifies this by saying, 'I also like to think it's about the human condition – not always about gender. It's like how the fuck do you make sense of life anyway? It's about femininity as well' (Harvie 2016). She has stated that her work is about 'how I fit into these roles that this story is giving me; if that's even really possible in a socio-political way: being in a woman's body and being in a historically patriarchal society' (Winer 2017). A sense of agency and control is important to McCormick and this determines the venues she will agree to play. She states that it is crucial for her to 'have the agency over the action – always orchestrating the power but also always [to be] the butt of the joke' (Harvie 2016). Inspiration for *Triple Threat* came out of a request to create a ten-minute performance for a gay cabaret, which happened to be programmed at Christmas time. McCormick had been working closely with two male dancers (Sam Kennedy and Ted Rodgers) and chose to create a Nativity scene, featuring them dressed as the Three Kings delivering gifts to Baby Jesus. In terms of negotiating the context of each performance space, McCormick has stated that often she works in 'male-heavy' spaces, full of 'really hot gay guys'. Within this context she noticed that the situation sometimes felt 'a bit fanny-phobic' and that in this type of space whilst male nudity was acceptable, a 'vagina is more naughty or wrong than a penis' (Harvie 2016 and QX Team 2017). This sense of feeling 'othered' or marginalised by the cultural norms of a particular performance environment has directly contributed to some sections of *Triple Threat*, with McCormick deliberately setting out to 'ruffle a few feathers' (QX Team 2017). She is keen to subvert expectations that both queer and straight audiences might bring, stating that,

> I feel that we tie ourselves down to titles too much and sometimes there might be certain expectations on me as a conventional looking female. For me, the queer identity of the performance is about challenging expectations and thinking about my identity.
>
> *(Winer 2017)*

McCormick's celebration of gay venues as her 'church' maps conveniently on to the idea of her performance space being a type of 'heterotopia'. Although she works across a range of venues and contexts, she ensures the atmosphere and topology of the seating arrangements reference those of a queer nightclub or cabaret venue so she can encourage positive ways of looking and thinking about what she represents as a femme woman setting out to recreate the New Testament. I will argue that her use of space and the acts she performs invite audiences 'to suspect, neutralize, or invent the set of relations that they happen to designate, mirror or reflect' (Foucault 1984: 3).

Triple Threat is an interdisciplinary performance incorporating elements of electropop and dubstep, contemporary dance, ballet, stand-up comedy style direct address, performance art and intimate bodily acts of touching and sex play. McCormick explains to her audience that the promotional material describes the event as a 'play' but she would prefer to call it 'trash-step-dub-punk-nu-wave-post-popular-non-binary-socially-engaged-experiencial-experience'. She states her intention to perform the New Testament in three acts, taking on most of the key roles herself. The piece capitalises on a low-budget aesthetic, with McCormick referring to their limited means and her attempts to 'make do' by substituting shop-bought items for the gifts of the three kings. She explains that for myrrh she has substituted meringue, for frankincense, frankfurter sausages, for gold, Gold Blend instant coffee. McCormick takes control of the stage in the role of a highly energetic, self-deprecating host, who wryly asks the audience to remain respectful and remember that she is relaying religious stories, which remain sacrosanct for some. The 'triple threat' of the title refers to McCormick's talents as an actor, singer and dancer and the piece incorporates moments of rehearsed ineptitude and mess alongside performances of extreme virtuosity and skilful emotional simulation.

The piece features a number of expertly choreographed dance routines, performed by the male dancers and as a threesome. A different popular song accompanies each section with McCormick delivering a virtuosic vocal performance. McCormick directly addresses the audience throughout, delivering explanations and asides about what she has just done or what she intends to do and how it relates to the New Testament. She deliberately creates chaos and mess: throwing coffee granules about the stage and flinging frankfurters and meringue into the audience. She rifles through piles of props and costumes, her clothing becoming increasingly soiled as the show unfolds. In the final moment of the Ascension, a point when she asks the audience to physically hold her above their heads, she is partially naked and covered in chocolate spread, beer and sweat. McCormick juggles a fascinating balance of self-deprecation and ego-centrism, poking fun at the ludicrous nature of the project, whilst acknowledging that the story remains of significance to many.

As mentioned above, I have seen *Triple Threat* in a range of venues, most notably at the Soho Theatre, London and the Arnolfini, Bristol. The Arnolfini is known as an experimental arts venue; it contains a range of different exhibition and performance spaces as well as an arts bookshop and a café. The seating bank featured a solid block of seats, with aisles up either side of the space and a gantry of extra seats towards the top of the seating bank. The performance space is fairly deep and wide and enabled a good amount of space between the different changing stations and prop piles McCormick accesses throughout the show. The Soho Theatre is also a multi-space venue with an adjacent bar. It is known for promoting stand-up comedy, small-scale experimental theatre and queer performance. McCormick presented *Triple Threat* in the downstairs space on a stage customarily used by stand-up comedians. It contains a shallow raised stage and a number of round tables in a cabaret-style configuration. A wide aisle separates the two areas of seating. The reduced size of the stage resulted in fewer changing stations and gave more of a sense that the props and costumes were haphazardly organised. In the Arnolfini space the audience looked across or down at McCormick, in the Soho space they looked up. At the Arnolfini she entered from a side door next to the stage, at the Soho she entered via the back of the seating area and walked down the central aisle up on to the stage. At key moments McCormick goes into the seating bank to be close to or interact with the audience. For example, whilst Rodgers and Kennedy reset the stage in Act one McCormick leaves the stage to chat to audience members. She asks about jobs, tells someone she likes their sunglasses and asks them to 'bear with her' as she has not 'really been to [insert name of town] before'. She confesses:

> At first I didn't want to align myself with capitalist systems where the labour/ value exchange was quite problematic … but then I just got over it! The thing is, the world is all about money, isn't it? Clearly I don't do this for money, I just want to be famous – fuck the system!
>
> *(McCormick 2016)*

During one section in which she staged Judas' kiss and betrayal, Rodgers and McCormick began to kiss passionately on stage. In the Soho version they moved off stage so that they were positioned halfway up the central aisle. McCormick straddled Rodgers and they kissed and gyrated passionately on the floor for approximately five minutes, whilst Kennedy sat on a chair in the corner of the stage looking increasingly fed up. Part way through the embrace, McCormick broke off, looked over at Kennedy, and asked, 'what's he doing?' She then directed him to 'just look natural' and went back to kissing Rodgers. Another example of her making an incursion into the space of the audience took place, towards the end of the show, when she confessed that she had used 'artistic licence' in order to imagine that Jesus' mother Mary would have been present at his death. She began by cradling Rodgers, recreating the Pietà, then left the stage and walked to the back of the auditorium. She began to sing *Run* by Snow Patrol and selected one specific audience member, asking them to 'pretend [they're] Jesus'.[5] Singing with conviction she knelt and delivered the song to one audience member before breaking away to wail and howl in desperation. Breaking off from singing, but with the backing track continuing to play, she returned to the stage and writhed in agony, emitting loud groans and cries. This is one of several excursions between the two areas that make up what Wihstutz has described as the 'topology of theatre'. She moves from the playing-space, customarily the preserve of the performers, to the auditorium, customarily the preserve of the audience. At the end of the performance McCormick experimented further with the conventional topography of theatre. She summoned the audience to their feet and told them:

> OK guys, it's time to wrap up the play and think about what we have learned. At the core our story is one of democracy, it's one of community. A community that believes in something, that works together to make something happen. I thought it would be nice to end the show with the final ascension scene with a participatory crowd surf.
>
> (McCormick 2016)

McCormick directed the audience to stand up and fill the central aisle, or, in the case of the Arnolfini performance, the far left aisle. Still giving directions via the microphone, McCormick was hoisted aloft, initially by Rodgers and Kennedy, and then passed, hand by hand, over the heads of the audience towards the back of the auditorium. As she was carried along she shouted comments such as 'fill the gaps, madam!' or 'it's about no one being bigger than anyone else. No one is above anyone else!' At this point she was extremely dirty and in a state of semi-undress. Her leotard had come undone at the crotch and had ridden up around her waist, her pubic hair was exposed and one of her breasts was hanging out of her bra. She wore the remains of smoothie, lager and chocolate spread and looked extremely hot and sweaty. The audience experienced her dishevelled body in unusually close proximity and was asked to celebrate her symbolic ascension by carrying her through the performance space. McCormick's relationship with the audience is crucial to this performance, and it is her bodily proximity and inclusion of fluids and unguents that sets it apart from conventional theatre. *Triple Threat* came out of a short ten-minute version of the Nativity, created for Duckie and the Royal Vauxhall Tavern. McCormick retains some of the licence and intimacy of the Vauxhall Tavern's gay club nights by celebrating both her and her dancers' bodies, performing acts of physical intimacy and trying to get as close to the audience as possible.

Two further elements of *Triple Threat* specifically challenge the types of performance activity conventionally associated with theatre. At two different junctures McCormick inserts or facilitates the insertion of foreign objects into her body. Critic Michael Segalov referred to one of these sections as an actual 'sex act' whilst others have described them in less explicit terms as 'taboo challenging' (Harvie 2016). McCormick calls them 'irreverent bodily acts', stating that she is interested in the idea of 'what's sacred and what's not – I like the idea of the untouchable – like very bodily acts … I like the idea of the body being a prop' (Harvie 2016). The nature of these acts would be in keeping with playful and sex-positive performances associated with gay club venues such as the Royal Vauxhall Tavern in London, but would be extremely rare in mainstream theatre venues, in which onstage sex would be simulated rather than enacted for real. I want to argue that these 'irreverent' acts draw attention to the context of the performance space. In Foucault's terms the acts juxtapose the behavioural codes of several incompatible sites in one 'single real place' in order to foreground the cultural boundaries associated with both theatre and gay clubs (Foucault 1984: 6). McCormick has revealed that her interest in using penetrative acts on stage came partly from changes in government legislation, which determined what could or could not be shown as part of pornographic performance. For her the legislation was 'anti-queer' and when performing these elements on stage in a gay club setting she contexualises it as a response to porn legislation (Harvie 2016).[6]

The spatial organisation of the stage plays a key part in framing moments of irreverent body play. The performance opens with loud, operatic choral singing with Rodgers and Kennedy performing a rapid, balletic dance routine. McCormick enters wearing a long white cape, in the style worn by boxers as they enter the arena. McCormick stands enigmatically with her back to the audience, hand held triumphantly aloft before launching into a heartfelt rendition of *DNA*, an electro pop song by UK girl band Little Mix.[7] She invests passionately in the performance, thrusting hips forward and projecting strenuously into the microphone. However her 'microphone' turns out to be a large purple dildo. Seemingly unaware of the substitution McCormick continues to perform with focus and commitment, pushing her index finger into her ear as if to adjust her earpiece, and allowing a slight frown to cross her face. She signals subtly to the sound engineer that she wants the volume increased so she can hear herself sing. She repeats this gesture with increasing frustration a number of times. Continuing to sing, she points to the microphone/dildo and to the ceiling to indicate that the engineer should turn the volume 'up'. After several minutes Kennedy approaches her to inform her of the 'mistake'. At this point she breaks off, as if to confer, and then half smiles-half grimaces at the audience before deciding to, in colloquial terms, 'style it out' and pretend that she intended, all along, to bring her dildo on stage. To reinforce this decision she opens the flap in her off-white Y fronts and inserts the dildo into her vagina. She begins to gyrate with the dildo until Kennedy brings her a 'real' microphone, at which point she asks Kennedy to manipulate the dildo for her, raising her leg into his arm to facilitate access. Whilst forcefully delivering the remainder of the song she guides his hand, qualifying her enjoyment with an 'ouch' or 'that's better' as he attempts to pleasure her. As the song draws to a close she whisks the dildo out of her vagina and gestures to the operator to cut the music. Once the backing track has been silenced she launches into a deferential and enthusiastic welcome speech, thanking the audience for coming. She reveals that the opening section, whilst ostensibly resembling a moment of failure, has enabled her to perform the Immaculate Conception, with Kennedy, clad in fancy-dress wings, appearing to Mary as the Angel Gabriel. One of the most arresting aspects of this section of the show lies in the explicit performance of a 'real' sexual act, whereby a performer inserts a sex toy into her own vagina. This type of explicit activity would not normally be encountered in mainstream theatre venues, being reserved for sex and gay clubs. The actual nature of the insertion is clear to all, but those close to the stage are able to witness the intimate nature of the act. McCormick's experimentation with the dildo/microphone works effectively to foreground expectations about the type of behaviour associated with female artists. Heteronormative pornography customarily represents women as passive recipients of male desire and penetration; the sounds they emit would serve to amplify the perception of their pleasure. McCormick pushes back against such expectations by inserting the dildo herself, then assertively directing her partner in order to maximise her pleasure. Once in possession of the 'proper' microphone she refused to be 'shamed' by the sexually explicit act and switched instantaneously into the persona of charming host in order to brief the audience on what they should expect from the remainder of the show.

Throughout the performance McCormick, Kennedy and Rogers enjoy physical contact with one another in a variety of ways. They lift one another as part of expertly choreographed routines; the male dancers hold each other affectionately as they wait on the sidelines; they kiss passionately and stroke one another's bodies. The performers' physical intimacy is fluid, in so far as it is not restricted by sexuality or sexual orientation. During the 'Temptation of Christ', the biblical story of Jesus fasting for 40 days and nights in the Judaean Desert, Kennedy 'tempts' McCormick with cigarettes and beer, eventually breaking her willpower by forcing chocolate spread into her mouth and smearing it around her face. The second of the more intimate instances of 'irreverent touching' occurs during the 'Incredulity of Thomas', a scene in which Kennedy, as Doubting Thomas, demands proof that Jesus has come back to life. In the Gospel of John Thomas is cited as saying, 'except I shall see in his hands the print of the nails, and put my finger into the print of the nails, and thrust my hand into his side, I will not believe' (John 20:24–29). McCormick appears as Jesus, with Kennedy as Thomas. They exchange a series of meaningful looks, with McCormick exhorting Thomas to 'believe' by encouraging him to return her affirmative nod. Thomas refuses to return the nod and instead shakes his head insistently. He bears two fingers aloft in a ceremonial manner, and McCormick systematically introduces them into different orifices, starting with her ear, then nostril, umbilicus, vagina and anus. With the examination of each 'wound' McCormick, as Jesus, repeats a series of symbolic nods, only to be rejected by Kennedy's Thomas over and over again. It is not until he inserts his fingers into her anus and performs enthusiastic frottage that he is 'convinced' and his dour demeanour transformed to joy. As with the Immaculate Conception, the scene plays out on a dual level: as Thomas exploring Jesus' wounds and as a woman seducing a gay man. Responses from the audience at the shows I witnessed were testament to the subversive nature of these kind of sexual encounters within a theatre space. I heard loud gasps and cries of surprise as Kennedy progressed from umbilicus to vagina and then to anus. McCormick has stated that part of her intention with the acts of intimacy was to 'ruffle' feathers and confound expectation about the types of behaviour she would enact on stage as a femme. As mentioned above, her decision to display her vagina came out of experiences in 'male-heavy' gay clubs, which felt rather 'fanny phobic'. Coverage in LGBTQIAA newspapers such as *Vice* and *Gay Express* and more mainstream newspapers such as the *Guardian* and *Independent* has drawn attention to the phenomenon of 'gay misogyny', which McCormick appears to be referencing here. Journalist Jamie Tabberer has written of 'gay male privilege', articulating his sense that,

> Gay men of a certain age and disposition are becoming increasingly repulsed and scared by femininity – unless it's safe, a joke, a release valve in the form of a reality show … until gay men start recognising our misogyny problem, true equality will elude us forever.
>
> *(Tabberer 2017)*

McCormick has used her experience of being 'othered' in a male gay context as a point of resistance in her work, and choreographed a scene in which she is in control of how her body is perceived. Ultimately she has forged a sense of agency out of her desire to push back against gay misogyny and has created an alternative, queer, playful environment in which to foreground women's presence in patriarchal biblical narratives and patriarchal 'fanny-phobic' narratives. By introducing sex acts into more conventional performance venues McCormick not only draws attention to the marginalisation of gay, sex-positive experience on the British stage, but points to the way in which women continue to be marginalised within ostensibly gay friendly and queer spaces. She creates a heterotopia within the theatre space by juxtaposing a set of performance acts strongly associated with other venues: concert venues, gay clubs and live art venues. This is a heterotopic space, which, in Tompkins' terms is 'distinguished from th[e] actual world, but resonates with it'. Furthermore, McCormick can be seen to provide an 'examination of locations in which cultural and political meanings [are] produced spatially' (Tompkins 2014: 1).

Rachael Young is a British performer currently based in London, having developed the early part of her practice in Nottingham. Like McCormick she works across a range of platforms and describes herself as making 'theatre, live art, interactive installations and socially engaged projects'. She remarks that she 'likes to work in the space between disciplines and discover new languages for performance through collaboration' (Young 2019). Of her approach she states, 'I guess my work is activist – I get really funny about labels. I waited so long to be given that place to speak. Work allows me and other femmes to claim space to say what they want to say' (Young 2018b). In interview she has stated, 'I'm a black woman and in some ways, a black woman on stage is a political act itself' (Manning 2016). Her work is a mix of collaborative and solo performance, often drawing upon her own life experience. In *How I Wear my Hair* (2014) she drew upon her experience as a hairdresser, exploring racial archetypes and the potential for experimentation and reinvention Afro-Caribbean hairdressing allows. As described in Chapter one, *I, Myself and Me* (2016) drew upon Young's experience of internalising the social and cultural expectations of her family, local working-class community and society at large. She shared stories of repressed grief over her mother's death and railed against behavioural codes and rules she felt pressured to observe. *OUT* (2017) was created with dancer and choreographer Dwayne Antony and took the form of a queer, ambient, meditative dance performance. The pair danced, semi-clad, in a dimly lit space, referencing choreographic movements from Vogue and queer club culture. The piece spoke out against homophobia within Afro-Caribbean culture and communities. As part of the piece Antony and Young peeled a large basket of oranges, a reference, Young says to the fruits' association with queerness. She has shared insights into her choice of oranges, explaining that:

> In the Caribbean oranges are not orange, they are more of a green colour. There's an idea in black culture about assimilation – when you try to speak to your parents about queerness there's an idea that queerness is a Western thing. This is what oranges mean in the show. Also the idea that queerness can spread, so when you eat the oranges you are complicit.
>
> *(Young 2018b)*

Nightclubbing (2018) continues to develop the theme of internalised societal pressure, drawing upon the story of two black women deemed to breach the admission policy of London's DSTRKT nightclub. The women were told they could not come in and would have to 'go home' for ostensibly being 'too dark' and 'too fat'. *Nightclubbing* borrows from a number of different performance forms. To a certain extent it resembles gig theatre because it features musicians playing live on stage and sound is exaggerated and amplified through a large PA system; however it also borrows from contemporary live art and dance and the language is lyrical and poetic. The piece has toured to small-scale theatre venues and audiences customarily watch the performance from a raked, end-on seating bank. *Nightclubbing* interweaves the story of DSTRKT nightclub with stories of artist Grace Jones and Young herself. Young describes it as a 'visual poem' and revealed that she 'spent a lot of time researching Jones, feminism and Afrofuturism before working with a dramaturg to see how it would work with musicians' (Masso 2018). The Afrofuturistic influence can be seen in the richly textured costumes, shoes and headgear Young dons as she relates her stories; the influence of Jones is channelled through Young's borrowing of her statuesque, proud authority and rendition of *Nightclubbing* towards the end of the show. For Young,

> [when I was] growing up, Jones was always this person breaking away from the norm and doing her own thing, she has always managed to be authentic. She's dark-skinned, androgynous, and she's always ahead of her time, she can be – is – Afrofuturist.
>
> *(Minamore 2018)*

Bridget Minamore has attributed the term 'Afrofuturism' to cultural critic Mark Dery, who in 1993 identified it as, 'a movement in literature, music art etc. featuring futuristic or science fiction, themes which incorporate elements of black history and culture' (Minamore 2018). For Bolanie Austen Peters, 'given the sometimes bleak present-day circumstances of Afro-descended people, Afrofuturism is a chance to envision a radical and progressive vision of blackness… one in which black creativity is mystical and fascinating' (Austen Peters 2018). *Nightclubbing* borrows aspects of autobiographical performance, gig theatre and live art as it interweaves biographical material with real-time performance tasks and feats of virtuosity. Mojisola Adebayo cites Jones as a fascinating exponent of queer/black culture who clouds the distinction between 'where queer begins and black ends' (Adebayo 2016: 134). Critical of the whiteness of British queer theatre, Adebayo coined the term 'Afri-Quia', a term poignant and relevant in relation to Young.

The stage is furnished with the paraphernalia one would associate with a live concert: amplifiers, microphones, microphone stands, mixing desks and instruments are placed at intervals around the space. A television monitor is positioned in front of the sound desk; it remains dark, with sporadic white tracking lines crackling across its surface. A silver glitter curtain hangs down the back wall and giant pieces of costume fill the rest of the stage. Young slowly emerges from what looks like a large black tarpaulin pile. Her hand emerges first, crooked at right angles into a voguish gesture, then her upper body follows until she is wearing the tarpaulin like an enormous crinoline. The material of the skirt is rough, black and faintly glossy. Visible from the chest up, Young performs a series of choreographed movements: she holds her arm perpendicular to her body and uses her hands to create star shapes either side of her face. Having wriggled from beneath the tarpaulin Young stands before the audience in an off-the-shoulder leotard. It is half-silver, half-black with a triangle cut out of the side. Her hair is curled into tightly wound buns or clipped closely to her scalp with hundreds of golden Kirby grips. Once free of the giant skirt Young climbs into a pair of high, platform flip-flops. The exaggerated scale of these items, along with the amplification of her voice and music, works to create a sense of proximity, as if we are witnessing Young in close-up.

Young's homage to Jones takes a number of forms. She copies her virtuosic hula-hooping as she recites a list of heartfelt apologies into a microphone;[8] she dons a headdress and tabard constructed from multiple black, rubber coils; she sings Jones' eponymous song, *Nightclubbing*, before reciting a closing verse about Black-love.[9] At the beginning of the show Jones' voice is sampled so that it effectively begins with a recording of Jones announcing, 'do what you feel, if you feel like it, when you feel like it' and ends with her saying, 'No! I have the last word, and you don't get it unless you go through me' (Young 2018a). Young's hula-hooping represents an excellent example of Muñoz's 'queer virtuosity'. It presents a high-risk scenario, which she knowingly employs to exaggerate her vulnerability. The attempts to hula-hoop take place alongside a simultaneous attempt to rationalise her place in the world. She approaches a microphone suspended from the lighting rig and moves towards the front of the stage. Skilfully rotating the hoop, she begins to recite a list of apologies:

I'm sorry for breathing
For taking myself too seriously
For laughing too loudly
Sorry for being able to ride the beat
Sorry for my love of colour
For my queer outlook
Sorry for *Black Panther* and *Get Out*
Sorry for poverty
Sorry for looking good in neon pink
Sorry for being too outspoken
Sorry for heteronormativity
Sorry for having a chip on my shoulder
I'm sorry you feel uncomfortable
Sorry for my features, for my muscles
I'm sorry for moving in next door
Sorry for questioning your authority
Sorry for my vulnerability – for fighting back; for this armour
Sorry for your fragility
Sorry for not turning the other cheek
I'm sorry for taking up space
I'm sorry for this skin
I'm sorry for being sorry.

(Young 2018a)

Young's demeanour during this section is markedly different from sections in which she occupies or channels the persona of Jones. As she delivers her inventory she looks pained and uncomfortable. When the hoop falls, as it does at on a number of occasions, the lapse amplifies and heightens her discomfort. Through repetition the list of apologies acquires accumulated gravity. As Muñoz suggests, her failure is 'generative', her activity enacts the politics of attempting to assimilate, attempting to complete a set task and yet foiled by an inability to remain sincere and keep the hoop aloft. The hula-hooping represents an example of what Muñoz would call 'a queer utopian aesthetic practice: failure and virtuosity' (Muñoz 2009: 169).

As in the case of *Triple Threat*, Young takes the experience of 'othering' as generative material for her performance. As McCormick pushed back against gay misogyny in *Triple Threat*, so Young pushes back against racism, colourism and misogyny in commercial London nightclubs. She has taken the story of Zalika Miller who, along with her friend, was refused entry to DSTRKT nightclub. Security personnel told the women that they had been refused entry because, in relation to the club's entry policy, their skin tone was found to be 'too dark' and they were deemed 'overweight' (Oredein 2015). The story was widely reported in the press, and the club issued a denial, insisting that they did not observe racist or colourist door policies. Young includes recorded testimony from Miller in the performance. She is heard to say,

> People had to die. People had to battle, go through pain and suffering even to this day because of their skin colour … and then you … just because of the image of a club, you're not going to let people in based on their skin colour. It's disgusting.
>
> *(Young 2018a)*

As a way of pushing back against racism and colourism Young creates an alternative, inclusive, club-world within the theatre space. This world features virtuosic black women performing, celebrating heritage and singing the praises of dark brown 'light-catching' skin and the beauty of 'blackness'. Choreography, lighting, music, props, costume and poetry work to beautify Young in her split persona as herself/Jones. In hooks' terms, Young can be seen to be harvesting a deliberately exaggerated sense of self-esteem as a way of proactively practising self-love. By fusing multiple perspectives she rejects narratives of the past about 'holding on to grief about the past or holding on to a narrative that places blame on others' (hooks 2001: 54–55). By collaborating exclusively with black performers, rejecting narratives of shame and championing the experiences and words of black women, Young is creating a heterotopic space of exception that draws attention to the conventional demographic associated with Western theatre-going and colourist veneration of lighter skin tones. Like McCormick she challenges the expectations of how a queer femme body will behave on stage and invites consideration of how, as Tompkins would say, cultural and political meanings are enacted, or are 'produced spatially' (Tompkins 2014: 1).

As McCormick drew attention to conventional theatre practices through a process of deviation, so Young breaks with convention by employing sound and acoustics to amplify and enhance interweaving narratives and poetry. Rukandema and Thomas stand towards the back of the stage, working at a raised table containing mixing equipment and musical instruments. Thomas plays live guitar, recording looped notes, which contribute to a repetitive, all-encompassing sound scape. Rukandema incorporates pre-recorded excerpts of Jones and Miller speaking and weaves them into an original composition. As Young delivers poetry into a microphone Rukandema enhances its affect, adding reverb, echo and loops. The amplified volume, heighted visual spectacle and declaration of self/black-love in this piece create a narrative of camp celebration and rejection of shame. Adebayo has cited the work of queer theorist Kathryn Bond Stockton who calls camp an 'aesthetic delight' that has been 'fostered from sharing black/queer feeling of shame' (Stockton 2006: 24). Adebayo explains that she is,

> weary and wary of the recent western tendency in queer theory towards placing black and queer people in the depressing paradigm of shame; I am much more interested and invested in the more positive approach of black cultural studies scholars, such as bell hooks, who explore self-love.
>
> *(Adebayo 2016: 147)*

Young can be seen to be working in tandem with this sensibility, her work a potent example of Adebayo's vision of Afri-Quia. Towards the end of the performance Young recites an associative list celebrating all things Black. She lists:

> Moving Black; seeing Black; feeling Black.
> Blacksplaining; speaking Black; loving Black; Black love; moving through space and time Black; ride the beat Black; sowing Black; holding Black; evolving Black.
> Seen through Black eyes.
> Ceramic Black; titanium Black.
> Drifting on the black sea under cover of moonlight Black;
> Black history; the sovereignty of Black future.
> Majestic Black; liquid Black; reclaiming Black.
> Seductive Black; erotic Black. Sexy as fuck; reclaiming space Black;
> Deep Black; hard Black; obsidian glass.
> Black holes that drink deep from the light of the universe. Sleek, slick black.
> Black that stops the clocks and leaves time suspended. Nourishing midnight.
> Secret places; sacred objects.
> Dreaming, dreaming, dreaming, dreaming Black.
>
> *(Young 2018a)*

Young's verse imbues Blackness with a sense of overwhelming positivity; the notion of 'blackness' is not, at any point qualified or diminished by its binary pairing, instead it stands alone. In this speech Blackness glories in a reflective, erotic majesty. Earlier in the piece, Young is heard, via audio recording, to recite a list of quasi-scientific questions about skin colour and tone. She asks:

> What are you? What planet are you from? Did your people grow up closer, or further away from the sun? Do your melanocytes cling together to form one, continuous brown hue? Are you Eumenalin or Pheomelanin? Are you a light-catcher? Like early human you developed the ability to catch the sunlight. Are you sub-Saharan? Your melanin functions as a shield against ultra violet radiation.
>
> *(Young 2018a)*

The quasi-anthropological tone serves to cool the emotive topic of difference, distancing it from emotive narratives of racism, colourism and white fragility. The scientific tone enables Young to articulate the factual complexity of pigmentation in an objective manner. She subverts and contradicts Social Darwinist theories of 'evolution' by emphasising that a higher level of eumelanin protects the body from the harmful effects of the sun's ultra violet rays and therefore promotes survival and longevity.

Young's celebration of queer Black femininity takes place in a performance space that, according to Torreggiani, would ordinarily be occupied by a white, middle-aged demographic (Torreggiani 2016). *Nightclubbing's* heightened rhetoric removes it from a normative everyday context and creates an alternative world, albeit one that can only exist for the duration of the performance. Young includes Miller's ostensibly everyday narrative of 'othering' but gives her time to express the story using articulate and persuasive anger. Young's alternative world is akin to Muñoz's queer utopia – it shows a blueprint for a world that celebrates rather than denigrates Blackness; it presents a 'horizon of possibility' (Muñoz 2009: 97). However, the fact of it being created as a 'real space', albeit a temporary one, enables us to imagine it to represent a queer heterotopia. As Tompkins would have it, the performance 'depicts other possible spaces and places live in front of an audience' and 'offers spectators specific examples of how space and place might be structured otherwise' (Tompkins 2014: 3). This heterotopia, being a 'real' space, an alternative enclave within a more conventional, hegemonic space, invites audiences to consider how the heterotopic space stands in tension with the more conventional theatre space. It invites audiences to revisit narratives of Blackness experienced in those spaces and contemplate how they might be refigured in light of this celebratory event. Young's heterotopia acts as a potent challenge to conventional narratives around diversity and representation, creating queer utopias and heterotopias to celebrate Black self-love and draw attention to the tensions created when those narratives are articulated as part of the contemporary British theatre scene.

Project O is a London-based company comprised of Alexandrina Hemsley and Jamila Johnson-Small, who met at the London School of Contemporary Dance. The artists have been working together since 2011 and in addition to producing work as

Project O they produce solo work and collaborate with other artists. Together they have produced *O* (2013), *SWAGGA* (2014) and *Benz Punany* (2014) along with several other pieces. The company produces work for the stage, for gallery and performance spaces, drawing upon a shared dance training and attraction to popular culture. Whilst frustrated with the risk of over-simplification, they describe their work as being about the experience of inhabiting and representing Black female bodies, making those experiences visible and creating a space in which those stories can be heard. Their style of dance has been described as: 'improvised non codified'; 'bedroom'; 'nightclub'; and 'minimalist' (AQNB 2018, Cochrane 2016, Burt 2016). Johnson-Small has stated, 'I'm not interested in the conventional aesthetics of virtuosity – but I am interested in the concept of expansion or of pushing to the edges of things' and Hemsley feels that, 'the traditional aesthetics of virtuosity […] exclude so many. Any sort of virtuosity is an impossible ideal and I don't know if I want to spend my life trying to reach impossibility in that way' (Osunwunmi 2017). Whilst making *Voodoo* Project O deliberately adopted a different approach to that used in *O* because they felt many had misinterpreted the gender and racial politics of the piece. Their use of nudity had led to a sense that they reaffirmed rather than problematised the sexualisation of Black women's bodies, and they were accused of claiming, according to Johnson-Small, 'some bullshit egotistical narrative of privilege' (Johnson-Small 2015). Kirsten Cochrane clarifies:

> While it may be obvious that Hemsley and Johnson-Small are speaking and dancing back to these fantasies of the Black female body, critics did not notice these nuances. In *London Dance*, Hemsley and Johnson-Small claimed that they were 'a bit let down by the well-intentioned early readings of our first work *O* – a dance duet inspired by our experiences of racism and over-sexualisation as mixed race women. Apparently when we dance, we look like we are having loads of fun as opposed to suffering under the weight of racial and sexist stereotypes'.
>
> *(Cochrane 2016: 143)*

The company is keen to challenge the freighted stigma of identity politics. Johnson-Small has shared her sense that,

> a lot of what I do reads as personal because of the 'identity' situation – my blackness, perceived queerness and I guess my working with improvised non-codified dancing. [However] a lot of the practices I am working with are not *about* me. I don't make things for myself personally; I make them for 'myself' politically.
>
> *(AQNB 2018: my emphasis)*

Hemsley confessed, 'the desire to make a "black piece" emerge[d…but] it is a real trauma to make a piece which is *about* something. Who on earth in 2011, 2012 and 2013 would be so stupid?' (Project O 2013: 30, my emphasis).

Voodoo employs Afrofuturistic imagery and creates a layered, multiperspectival performance about ancestry, time and embodiment. It is a durational and immersive piece, giving audience members the opportunity to participate for approximately two hours at a time, whilst the performers repeat their performance up to four times in a row. I saw this piece at Chelsea Theatre, London in 2016 and at the Trinity Centre, Bristol in 2017. I have also reviewed footage of the Chelsea Theatre version using the British Library's Sound Archive. There were marked differences between the performances; I will chiefly refer to the Bristol version.

The performance began before the audience entered the theatre space with participants asked to put all time-keeping and monitoring devices such as watches and smart phones into black bags. These were retained by front of house staff until the end of the performance. The audience was ushered into a medium sized black-box studio and asked to sit on a series of benches organised in front of a projection monitor. The screen featured a scrolling list of historical events, some referring to personal experiences of company members, such as the reading of a book ('Jamila and Alexandrina both read Caitlin Moran's *How to Be a Woman*: It is bad'); attendance at professional development workshops ('Alexandrina attends a workshop with Shobana Jeyasingh. Epic fail'); or the death of Johnson-Small's father. They refer to news events ('unelected Prime Minister Theresa May is pictured holding Donald Trump's hand') and historical events such as the abolition of slavery in the US and the cessation of death sentencing in the UK. The audience watched the list scroll repeatedly for approximately 20 minutes before being asked to move into a larger space, towards the back of the studio, and remove their shoes. The rear space contained benches on either side of an illuminated performance area. A complex tapestry of small bones, woven and tied into rows and knots of string and flax was suspended above the performance area. Hemsley and Johnson-Small appeared dressed in white quilted trousers, cream polo necked shirts and fake leather jackets. They wore head mounted microphones, which amplified whispered messages. They murmured, 'tonight we have no masters. We are not slaves to time. We move slowly'. At different junctures they dragged different items into the performance area. First they dragged two large chrysalis bags, into which they climbed; then two large black sacks replete with animal bones. White balloons were scattered about the floor. The performers ceremonially punctured each one with long hatpins drawn from their hair. They approached individual audience members, placing hands on knees, shoulders, backs and transmitting a sonorous 'hum' which reverberated from body to body. Towards the middle of the performance they asked the audience to lie down in a meditative state for ten minutes, and then to stand in the performance area with eyes closed and to 'feel the pulse' of the music, allowing the body to sway and eventually dance. Front of house staff, clad in black versions of the performers' costumes, approached with trays of vodka. In both of the performances I experienced, audience members approached the stage area/dance floor and danced with varying degrees of enthusiasm and skill. Sanjoy Roy described the music as 'an extended sequence of club tracks – techno, drum 'n' bass, dancehall'. He felt 'the performers [were] dancing among us like shamanic presences' (Roy 2017). The final section of the piece comprised the audience joining Helmsley and Johnson-Small and dancing on stage for an extended period of time. The company described it as 'an ode to the present, [a] durational unfolding [that] becomes a science fiction that addresses the desire, confusion and responsibility of being a single subject who is also a symbol of many long-persecuted people' (Unity Theatre 2017). For Anna Winter it was, 'the ultimate plunge into an unexpected vortex of visibility and vulnerability' (Winter 2017).

Both of the performances of *Voodoo* I witnessed were presented in the context of UK performance festivals – 'Sacred' at the Chelsea Theatre and 'Inbetween Time' at the Arnolfini. Project O's use of an immersive club experience stood in contrast to other festival spaces and the audience's customary experience of performance going. For immersive theatre expert Gareth White the 2010s represent a 'golden age of participatory culture', which pushes against recognised rules of behaviour associated with the 'conventional theatre event'. White states, 'the social structure of the conventional theatre event is coded and exhibited through a domestication of noise-making, chiefly through the silence of the audience, and through their use of approved vocalisations and other bodily noises' (White 2011: 199). In *Voodoo* the audience remain silent but not immobile. Instead, they move between different states of sitting, lying, standing and dancing. For Adam Alston immersive theatre audiences are important co-producers of meaning, they 'augment the productivity of watching as a prospectively participating spectator' (Alston 2016: 5). Project O are keen to involve the audience in the co-production of meaning, they have presented the audience with a series of references to time and ancestry and they wish to leave it to the audience to navigate the composite signs as they see fit.

Project O exaggerate the sense of *Voodoo* being in a time and place apart from the 'real world' encouraging a sense of temporal dislocation. As outlined above, they ask audience members to give up watches and smart phones before they enter the space so they are unable to keep a check on horological time. The audience is invited to remove shoes, effectively delaying any attempt at early departure, and asked to temporarily jettison the external social world of 'work'. Costumes worn by the performers are futuristic, reminiscent of costumes worn on films such as *Star Trek* or *Star Wars,* they map a route into the future and yet bones of dead animals hang above audience members' heads indicating death and past lives.[10] For Winter *Voodoo*, as the title of the show, points to 'a historic miasma of white misunderstanding and fear surrounding black culture' and the large bags of bones the performers lug on stage suggest 'ancestral burdens' that are 'cast off, leaving performers to dance blithely' (Winter 2017). By referring to the US abolition of slavery and key moments of Black history at the beginning of the piece the performers actively engage with an ancestral past. This is amplified by the inclusion of dead animal bones associated with voodoo, or 'black magic', and whispered assertions that, 'we are not slaves to time. We move slowly'. Their dual engagement with, and rejection of, ancestry is reminiscent of Saidiya Hartman's exhortation to 'lose your mother' in her eponymous book. In the story of her four month tour of West Africa Hartman tells how she was always recognised as an American 'daughter of slaves' and that people were 'kinder and less severe' about slavery than they would have been otherwise (Hartman 2008). She noted, to her surprise:

> the slave was the only one expected to discount her past […] everyone told me a different story about how slaves began to forget their past. […] In these stories, which circulated throughout West Africa, the particulars varied, but all of them ended the same – the slave loses her mother.
>
> *(Hartman 2008)*

Voodoo encourages a similar forgetting; despite the invocation of magical practice through animal bones hung above the audience's heads, the performers advise 'cast off your demons' and remind 'tonight we have no masters'. J. Jack Halberstam has appropriated Hartman's directive in their theory of queer failure. For Halberstam,

> Hartman's title indicates a loss that has always already happened for African Americans, but it also argues against a simple genealogical account of history that stretches back in time through the family line. Losing one's mother […] actually enables a relation to other models of time, space, place and connection.
>
> *(Halberstam 2011: 123–124)*

As a result, 'broken mother-daughter bonds' give way to 'an anti-Oedipal feminism' that offers 'modes of unknowing, failing and forgetting as part of an alternative feminist project' (124). Halberstam's queer failure is aligned with Muñoz's sense of queer failure and virtuosity. They each represent a paradigm shift away from neoliberal, heteronormative, white supremacist logic. Within their designated black-box studio the company build an alternative world, away from the neoliberal imperative to align oneself with a fixed, individualised identity and a recognisable, codified system of dance. Project O borrow key elements of queer virtuosity and failure in order to create this alternative world. As the company state, they produce work in order to 'dance themselves out of the desire for and expectation of an aesthetic assimilation that upholds a system of white supremacy' (Unity Theatre 2017).

As in the case of Young and McCormick, Project O creates an alternative space within a conventional performance studio. They recreate a club atmosphere by replicating movement patterns and music associated with that environment. In contrast to *Nightclubbing* and *Triple Threat* they employ an immersive element, inviting the audience to take off their shoes, lie down and eventually join them on the dance floor. During the Chelsea Theatre performance, they announced,

Dearly Beloved, we are gathered here today to get through this thing called life. We are telling you about the afterworld. We don't know how to DJ but in the time we have left we'll mix you some tunes. Cast out your demons; leave your seats and dance with us!

(Project O 2016)

The nightclub-within-a-theatre functions as a heighted sensory space apart from the world Foucault designates as 'real', away from everyday life. The futuristic costumes and exhortation to 'move slowly' enhance its sense of being like a laboratory. As Selina Thompson asks her audiences to 'sit with' or digest what she has to say in *salt.* so Project O ask their audience to move with them and be moved by them (Thompson 2017: 52). For Tompkins the context of experimentation and enquiry with this alternative space-within-a-space is a key feature of Foucault's heterotopia:

> A heterotopia, then, does more than simply mark politics or ethics or conscience: it is a technique for exploring theatrical space that enacts a 'laboratory' in which other spaces – and therefore other possibilities for socio-political alternatives to the existing order – can be performed in greater detail than Foucault's conventional definition of theatre as heterotopic. This enactment of space in performance has the capacity to demonstrate the rethinking and reordering of space, power, and knowledge by locating world-making spaces and places tangibly, albeit transiently.
>
> *(Tompkins 2014: 6)*

By mounting a dance performance entitled *Voodoo* Project O invite freighted expectations only to overturn them by refusing to represent themselves in any easily recognisable manner and by subverting the conventional relationship between observer and observed. This subversion amounts to the enactment of sociopolitical alternatives that return the colonising gaze and invite the audience to participate in the creation of meaning.

Project O's desire to explore theatrical space comes in part from a rejection of a virtuoso model of dance but also from a desire to query the programming policies of performance festivals as a whole. Whilst many of the quasi-historical 'facts' shown towards the beginning of the piece refer to key moments in Black history, they also stage the duo's ambivalence about being programmed and promoted primarily as 'Black' artists. Two of the scrolling 'facts' lent insight into the cause of their displeasure. The first read, 'Project O were thanked for bringing race to the table at X Festival' and the second, 'the number of Black artists on stage outnumbers those in the audience at Inbetween Time 2015' (Project O 2016). During an interview with *Rife Magazine* Hemsley and Johnson-Small express bewilderment at the marked visibility of their race, but unmarked nature of whiteness. They recalled, 'we were in a talk and someone spoke to us about having or bringing *the race question* to *the whole festival*. Like – we *all* bring *the race question* – we *all* have a race!' (Rife Magazine 2015: my emphasis). Johnson-Small has articulated her sense that on occasions invitations to share work amount to 'tokenistic gestures'. She pushes back by adopting the title 'Last Yearz Interesting Negro'. She asserts, 'I have to trust that the work is more than that [...] for myself I am the norm so I can't approach myself as "other"' (AQNB 2018). As Young cited London nightclubs which 'othered' women with darker skins and McCormick felt 'othered' by a male-heavy gay environment so Project O find themselves 'othered' within the context of festival programming and what Selina Thompson has referred to as the 'white supremacy' of the UK 'liberal arts scene' (Thompson 2015). The alternative club environment of each performance is representative of Muñoz's utopian world-making. Artists have a sense of control and agency and they invite the audience to experience the world through their eyes. Perspective is exaggerated by a sense that these artists are excluded, to a certain extent, from mainstream white, patriarchal culture and as a result need to create alternative spaces. These spaces encourage different rules of behaviour than the ones cited by White. According to his observations about conventional theatre, the interactive nature of these shows would represent a break from the 'domestic' practice of stillness and silence (White 2011: 199). The invitation to behave differently in the theatre draws attention to the ways that 'cultural and political meanings are produced spatially' both within the space of the nightclub and the mainstream auditorium (Tompkins 2014: 1). Furthermore the invitation galvanises the audience to reconfigure assumptions about the customary segregation of performers and spectators in the topology of theatre and conventional power relations between the 'observers and the observed' (Wihstutz 2013: 3–4).

Each of the artists speak from what Muñoz would describe as a 'minoritarian' position, however they express frustration with the practice of identity labelling, even within the productive space of queer culture. They deliberately complicate attempts to fix their identity and subject position in any simplistic manner. Each has taken the experience of being 'othered' by mainstream culture and used it as generative material to inform their practice. For McCormick this took the form of feeling marginalised by a male-heavy gay club environment; for Young it took the form of analysing racist and colourist entrance policies in London nightclubs; and for Project O, it was their experience of being promoted and programmed as 'racialised' subjects that led to a sense of otherness. Each artist has started from the experience of feeling 'othered' and worked to reconfigure conventional performer/audience relations in order to query normative expectations and practice, as such the sense of 'failure' or rejection has been generative. The artists all foreground assumptions audiences might make about their Black, femme, queer/straight bodies and subvert those expectations by behaving in an ambiguous and contradictory way. Although their work is largely programmed into conventional theatre venues each has organised onstage activity so that it draws upon club music and culture. It references clubbing rather than realist theatre practice and creates an alternative world, within and yet apart from, what Foucault calls the 'real' world. Each of the artists draws upon tropes of performance associated with a postmodern praxis and a poetics of failure. In Project O's case this amounts to a rejection of codified dancing, in Young's case the staging of real-time tasks as part of the performance and for McCormick setting herself the impossible task of staging the New Testament in three acts, whilst performing the majority of roles herself. This performance of failure and the drive to create a space-within-a-space is reminiscent of Muñoz's queer failure and virtuosity. I have deliberately chosen to describe their worlds as heterotopias rather than utopias because Foucault's heterotopias allow us to think of the artists' alternative worlds as taking up space in the 'real' world, rather than remaining in the realm of the imaginary. Furthermore, as Turner has pointed out, heterotopia has the potential to be anti-humanist and invites individuals granted entry to 'submit to rites and purifications' (Turner 2015: 17; Foucault 1984: 7). For Foucault the role of the heterotopia is to 'create a space of illusion that exposes every real space' and 'create a space that is other, another real space, as perfect, as meticulous, as well arranged as ours is messy, ill constructed, and jumbled' (8). The alternative worlds created within *Voodoo, Nightclubbing* and *Triple Threat* are all organised according to the world-view and agency of the artist, and as such 'expose' other real spaces that stymie or repress their sense of agency. They mimic the 'ill constructed' and 'jumbled' spaces of normative society, and yet are 'meticulous' and 'perfect' in so far as they allow for an alternative distribution of power and agency. An association between club culture and a sense of freedom drives the artists to create club-like environments on stage. They work to replicate the freedom of those alternative spaces within the context of a more conventional theatre environment, gestures which in turn invite a reappraisal of how they are perceived within a broader cultural scene.

Each of the artists recognises and celebrates the 'generative' potential of failure and enacts the type of 'queer virtuosity' elucidated by Muñoz. They perform a knowing form of postmodern self-reflexivity and yet eschew a postmodern scepticism of agency by aligning themselves with recognised identity categories. Project O, Young and McCormick draw upon a sense of marginalisation or othering in order to fuel the drive to create a politically resistant performance. Like Kimmings, Siddons and Thompson they draw upon autobiographical material and actively name and query identity categories imposed upon them by a white supremacist patriarchal society. Forging deliberate interventions into conventional spaces they create a subculture or heterotopic world-within-a-world that foregrounds how social expectations are formulated conservatively within certain spaces. In my next chapter I will move away from the focus upon space in order to explore the work of three artists who continue to draw upon autobiographical material, but who frame their work through their ambivalence about fixing gender identity. Lois Weaver has created the 'resistant femme' in order to query the phallic privilege of the butch lesbian, Kate Bornstein celebrates her joyful, erotic experience of being trans★ and Lucy Hutson details her drive to bind and suppress her breasts whilst resisting societal pressure to occupy a recognised identity category. All of the artists discussed in Chapters three and four have engaged with what Lavender has termed a 'return to sincerity;' they eschew the laconic or ironic attitude associated with postmodern performance (Lavender 2016: 118). However they continue to employ the metatheatrical techniques associated with postmodern praxis. Their work is often staged as an 'attempt' to communicate or share a story; their relationship to identity reveals a post-Brechtian facility to step in and out of character and a frustration with the societal compulsion to categorise. All of the artists described so far chronicle their relationship to a sense of failure. They may cite the impossibility of the task they have set themselves, deliberately obscure their intention, detail how they have been constructed as failures or lambast the paucity of positive paradigms available. The artists can similarly be seen to actively resist the negative associations of failure by using the experience to fuel the drive to form a creative response to the experience. The generative potential of failure runs through the work of all of the artists as they refuse to be shamed, labelled, ostracised or contained.

Notes

1 Jill Dolan has shaped a similar argument for the resistant yet utopic nature of theatre and performance. In *Utopia in Performance* she identifies transformative moments as 'utopian performatives'. For Dolan, '[u]topian performatives describe small but profound moments in which performance calls the attention of the audience in a way that lifts everyone slightly above the present, into a hopeful feeling of what the world might be like if every moment of our lives were as emotionally voluminous, generous, aesthetically striking, and intersubjectively intense' (Dolan 2005: 5).

2 In *Theatre & Audiences* Helen Freshwater rightly warns against the dangers of generalising about audiences and their perceptions of performances (Freshwater 2009: 5), however for the purposes of this piece I want to draw upon Anne Torreggiani of The Audience Agency's research in order to describe an approximate demographic of audience members visiting conventional theatre venues in the UK. Her research indicates that, 40% of all English households attend theatre, and of those 85% is white British and the average age is 52. Furthermore, her research suggests that the majority of theatre-goers wish to experience the event as 'educational' (Torreggiani 2016).

3 See, for example, Yoran (2010).

4 In *Acts and Apparitions: Discourses on the Real in Performance Practice and Theory* (2013) Liz Tomlin discusses her sense of a renewed 'anti-theatrical prejudice' which posits dramatic, text-based theatre as ideologically conservative and devised, non-text based theatre and performance as inherently 'radical'. She states that 'this binary opposition is played out in various calibrations, the most familiar of which include performance against theatre (when theatre is understood as dramatic theatre), performance theatre against dramatic theatre, devised theatre against text-based theatre, and Postdramatic theatre against dramatic theatre. In each opposition the first term is commonly aligned with a radical, oppositional narrative of deconstruction, the second term with a reactionary, traditional narrative of logocentrism, whilst the binary itself is underpinned by a poststructuralist scepticism of representations of the real' (Tomlin, 2013: 8).

5 *Run* by Snow Patrol, written by Gary Lightbody and Jonathan Quinn, 2003.

6 See, for example, Burnett (2014).

7 *DNA* by Little Mix, 2012, written by Thomas Barnes, Peter Kelleher, Ben Kohn, Iain James, Perrie Edwards, Jesy Nelson, Leigh-Anne Pinnock and Jade Thirlwall.

8 Grace Jones used a hula- hoop as she performed her 1985 hit, *Slave to the Rhythm* at both The Queen's Diamond Jubilee Concert, London, in 2012 and Brooklyn's Afropunk Festival in 2015. For information see: https://www.bbc.co.uk/programm es/p00tgwyj/p00th195 (visited 27 April 2019) and https://www.dazeddigital.com/m usic/article/26042/1/grace-jones-hula-hoops-topless-at-afropunk-festival (visited 26 April 2019)

9 *Nightclubbing* written by David Bowie and Iggy Pop, 1981. Jones' version produced by Chris Blackwell and Alex Sadkin, 1981

10 *Star Trek*, initially US television series created by Gene Roddenberry, 1966; *Star Wars*, George Lucas, 1977.

Bibliography

Adebayo, Mojisola (2016) 'Everything You Know About Queerness You Learnt from Blackness: The Afri-Quia Theatre of Black Dykes, Crips and Kids', in *Queer Dramaturgies: International Perspectives on Where Performance Leads Queer*, Alyson Campbell and Stephen Farrier (eds.), Basingstoke: Hampshire, pp. 131–149.

Alston, Adam (2016) *Beyond Immersive Theatre: Aesthetics, Politics and Productive Participation*, Basingstoke: Palgrave.

AQNB (2018) 'Different Angles: Jamila Johnson-Small on Last Yearz Interesting Negro, the Limits of Language and How those Limitations Might Speak', 12 November. Available at: https://www.aqnb.com/2018/11/12/different-angles-jamila-johnson-small-on-last-yearz-in teresting-negro-the-limits-of-language-how-those-limitations-might-speak/(accessed 5 April 2019).

Austen Peters, Bolanle (2018) 'This is Afrofuturism', 6 March. Available at: https://africana rguments.org/2018/03/06/this-is-afrofuturism/ (accessed 6 April 2019).

Burnett, Dean (2014) 'The UK Pornography Law: A Scientific Perspective', *The Guardian*, 5 December. Available at: https://www.theguardian.com/science/brain-flapping/2014/dec/ 05/uk-pornography-law-scientific-perspective-children-safety (accessed 29 April 2019).

Burt, Ramsay (2016) 'Jamila Johnson-Small "i ride in colour and soft focus no longer any-where"', 9 October. Available at: https://ramsayburt.wordpress.com/2016/10/09/jamila -johnson-small-i-ride-in-colour-and-soft-focus-no-longer-anywhere-8-10-16-rich-m ix-dance-umbrella-2016/ (accessed 27 August 2019).

Campbell, Alyson and Stephen Farrier (eds.) (2016) *Queer Dramaturgies: International Perspectives on Where Performance Leads Queer*, Basingstoke: Hampshire.

Cochrane, Kristen (2016) 'Schooling the Spectator in O. Project O: Alexandrina Hemsley and Jamila Johnson-Small. Forest Fringe Microfestival. Progress Festival, Theatre Centre, Toronto, Canada', *Performance Research*, 21(4), 142–144.

Dolan, Jill (2005) *Utopia in Performance: Finding Hope at the Theater*, Ann Arbor: University of Michigan Press.

Farrier, Stephen (2013) 'It's about Time: Queer Utopias and Theater Performance', in *A Critical Enquiry into Queer Heterotopias*, Angela Jones (ed.), Basingstoke: Palgrave Macmillan, pp. 47–70.

Foucault, Michel (1986) 'Of Other Spaces', *Diacritics*, 16(1), 22–27, translated by Jay Miskowiec. Available at: http://seas3.elte.hu/coursematerial/RuttkayVeronika/Foucault_of_ other_spaces.pdf (accessed 27 August 2019).

Freshwater, Helen (2009) *Theatre & Audience*, Basingstoke: Palgrave Macmillan.

Gorman, Sarah (2018) 'It Is From Failure that We Learn to Be Truly Amazing, Instinctual Artists: Interview with Rachael Young', *readingasawoman*. Available at: https://readingasa woman.wordpress.com/2018/05/11/it-is-from-failure-that-we-learn-to-be-truly-amazin g-instinctual-artists-interview-with-rachael-young/ (accessed 27 August 2019).

Halberstam, J. Jack (2011) *The Queer Art of Failure*, Durham and London: Duke University Press.

Hartman, Saidiyah (2008) *Lose Your Mother: A Journey Along the Atlantic Slave Route*, New York: Farrah, Strauss and Giroux.

Harvie, Jen (2016) 'Stage_Left with Jen Harvie: Episode 2: Lucy McCormick: Triple Threat', *Sound Cloud*. Available at: https://soundcloud.com/stage_left (accessed 10 April 2019).

hooks, bell (2001) *All About Love*, New York: HarperCollins.

hooks, bell (2015) 'Choosing the Margin as a Space of Radical Openness', in *Yearning Race, Gender and Cultural Politics*, New York: Routledge, pp. 222–235.

Johnson-Small, Jamila (2015) 'on silence and invisibility', Blog post, 4 June. Available at: https://jamilajohnsonsmall.wordpress.com/2015/06/04/on-silence-and-invisibility/ (accessed 29 January 2018).

Johnson-Small, Jamila (2016) 'Last Yearz Interesting Negro'. Available at: https://jamila johnsonsmall.wordpress.com/2016/01/02/dear-2015/ (accessed 5 April 2019).

Lang, Nico (2017) 'Casual Misogyny in Gay Men', *GayExpress.com*. Available at: https://ga yexpress.co.nz/2017/03/casual-misogyny-in-gay-men/ (accessed 27 August 2019).

Lavender, Andy (2016) *Performance in the Twenty-First Century: Theatres of Engagement*, Abingdon: Routledge.

Manning, Lucy (2016) 'Rachael Young on her One-Woman Show', *LeftLion.co.uk*. Available at: https://www.leftlion.co.uk/read/2016/june/rachael-young-on-her-one-woman-show-8294/ (accessed 9 April 2019).

Masso, Giverny (2018) 'Performance Artist Rachael Young: "Black Women are Still Having to Fight Oppression"', *The Stage*, 5 June. Available at: https://www.thestage.co.uk/fea tures/interviews/2018/performance-artist-rachael-young-black-women-still-fight-opp ression-inspiritation-grace-jones/ (accessed 9 April 2019).

McCormick, Lucy (2016) *Triple Threat*. Touring Production.

Minamore, Bridget (2018) 'Interview: Black to the Future: Afrofuturism Hits the Stage', *Guardian*, 4 May. Available at: https://www.theguardian.com/stage/2018/may/04/racha el-young-interview-nighclubbing-grace-jones-afrofuturism (accessed 27 August 2019).

Muñoz, José (2009) *Cruising Utopia: the Then and There of Queer Futurity*, New York: New York University Press.

O'Connell, Ryan (2013) 'Gay Men and Their Not-So-Cute Misogyny Problem', *VICE*, 21 May. Available at: https://www.vice.com/en_uk/article/nn4xpz/gay-men-and-their-not-so-cute-misogyny-problem (accessed 27 August 2019).

O'Flynn, Brian (2018) 'They Just Wanted to Silence Her: The Dark Side of Gay Stan Culture' *Guardian*, 4 September. Available at: https://www.theguardian.com/music/2018/sep/04/they-just-wanted-to-silence-her-the-dark-side-of-gay-stan-culture (accessed 27 August 2019).

Oredein, Tobi (2015) 'How One Club's Refusal To Let Black Woman In Says So Much More About Race In 2015…' *graziadaily.com*. Available at: https://graziadaily.co.uk/life/real-life/one-clubs-refusal-let-black-woman-says-much-race-2015/ (accessed 29 August 2019).

Osunwunmi (2017) 'Project O & Impossible Places', *realtime.org*, 10 May. Available at: https://www.realtime.org.au/project-o-impossible-places/ (accessed 27 August 2019).

Prashar-Savoie, Anjali (2018) 'Nightclubbing into the Future: Artist Rachael Young in Con-versation with Anjali Prashar-Savoie', *CUNTemporary.org*, 30 April. Available at: https://cuntemporary.org/nightclubbing/ (accessed 9 April 2019).

Project O (2013) *A Contemporary Struggle*, London: Live Art Development Agency.

Project O (2016) *Voodoo*. Touring Production.

QX Team (2017) 'Jonny Woo in Conversation with Lucy McCormick', *QXMagazine.com*, 9 October. Available at: https://www.qxmagazine.com/2017/10/lucy-mccormick/ (acces-sed 10 April 2019).

Rife Magazine (2015) '"Step, Ball – Change?" Project O's Dance Activism', *rifemagazine.com*, 18 March. Available at: https://www.rifemagazine.co.uk/2015/03/move-over-miley-p roject-os-dance-activism/(accessed 9 April 2019).

Roy, Sanjoy (2017) 'Voodoo Review – Project O's Shamanic Dance Bops with the Public', *Guardian*, 14 May. Available at: https://www.theguardian.com/stage/2017/may/14/voo doo-review-project-o-sadlers-wells-london-review (accessed 9 April 2019).

Segalov, Michael (2017) 'Lucy McCormick's "Triple Threat": The Nativity Reimagined, With LGBT Club Culture, Vibrators and Lady Gaga', *inews.co.uk*, 27 March. Available at: https://

inews.co.uk/culture/arts/interview-triple-threats-lucy-mccormick-on-her-subversive-new-play/ (accessed 10 April 2019).

Stockton, Kathryn Bond (2006) *Beautiful Bottom, Beautiful Shame: Where 'Black' Meets 'Queer'*, Durham and London: Duke University Press.

Tabberer, Jamie (2017) 'Gay Men Like Me Need To Start Acknowledging Our Misogyny Problem', *Independent*, 27 July. Available at: https://www.independent.co.uk/voices/gay-men-lgbt-50th-anniversary-misogyny-rupaul-drag-race-fishy-queen-lesbians-a7862516.html (accessed 27 August 2019).

Taylor, Amie (2017) 'Interview: Lucy McCormick', *LGBTQarts.com*, 5 December. Available at: https://lgbtqarts.com/2017/12/05/interview-lucy-mccormick/(accessed 10 April 2019).

Thompson, Selina (2015) *Race Cards*. Touring Installation.

Thompson, Selina (2017) *salt*. London: Faber and Faber.

Tomlin, Liz (2013) *Acts and Apparitions: Discourses on the Real in Performance Practice and Theory 1990–2010*, Manchester: Manchester University Press.

Tompkins, Joanne (2014) *Theatre's Heterotopias: Performance and the Cultural Politics of Space*, Basingstoke: Palgrave Macmillan.

Torreggiani, Anne (2016) 'Who Will our Audiences Be?', *theaudienceagency.org*. Available at: https://www.theaudienceagency.org/asset/1104 (accessed 1 September 2019).

Turner, Cathy (2015) *Dramaturgy and Architecture: Theatre, Utopia and the Built Environment*, Basingstoke: Palgrave Macmillan.

Unity Theatre (2017) 'Step, Ball – Change? Project O's Dance Activism'. Available at: www.rifemagazine.comhttps://www.unitytheatreliverpool.co.uk/whats-on/project-o-voodoo.html (accessed 27 April 2019).

White, Gareth (2011) 'Noise, Conceptual Noise and the Potential of Audience Participation', in *Theatre Noise*, Lynne Kendrick and David Roesner (eds.), Newcastle: Cambridge Scholars, pp. 198–207.

Wihstutz, Benjamin (2013) '"Other Space or Space of Others?" Reflections on Contemporary Political Theatre' *in Performance and the Politics of Space: Theatre and Topography*, Benjamin Wihstutz and Erika Fischer-Lichte (eds.), translation by Michael Breslin and Saskya Iris Jain, New York: Routledge, pp. 182–192.

Winer, Joseph (2017) 'Interview with Lucy McCormick – Lucy McCormick: Triple Threat', *londontheatre.com*, 8 December. Available at: https://www.londontheatre1.com/interviews/interview-with-lucy-mccormick-lucy-mccormick-triple-threat/ (accessed 10 April 2019).

Winter, Anna (2017) 'Review: Voodoo at Sadler's Wells', *Exeuntmagazine.com*, 12 May. Available at: http://exeuntmagazine.com/reviews/review-voodoo-sadlers-wells/ (accessed 27 August 2019).

Yoran, Hanan (2010) *Between Utopia and Dystopia: Erasmus, Thomas More, and the Humanist Republic of Letters*, Plymouth: Lexington Books.

Young, Rachael (2018a) *Nightclubbing*. Touring Production.

Young, Rachael (2018b) Presentation at Love, Pain and Intimacy in Live Art, CUNTemporary Events, 8 February, Queen Mary University of London. Available at: https://www.youtube.com/watch?v=Km6IDXaOjDY&index=5&list=PLYl8Hv8h0OeQH_S6Cuut8_L2rH372XhIg (accessed 27 August 2019).

Young, Rachael (2019) Website. Available at: http://www.rachaelyoung.net/ (accessed 27 August 2019).

5

TAKING PLEASURE: BINARY AMBIVALENCE AND TRANSGRESSION

Postmodern and poststructuralist theories have long espoused the need to challenge the way binary oppositions organise and reproduce oppressive systems of knowledge and power (Derrida 2002 and 1976; Foucault 1995). The strict distinction of 'either/ or' reduces complex phenomena into narrow, limiting categories and disguises the ideological superiority of one value over the other. Rather than tolerate binaries, postmodern theorists have argued for hybridity, indeterminacy, fluidity and play as a way of resisting closure and celebrating a process of 'becoming' (Hassan 1987; Bhabha 1994; Edwards 1998; Deleuze and Guattari 1987). In terms of postmodern gender theory, Judith Butler's theory of gender performativity revolutionised the field by arguing against fixity and promoting gender as part of a shifting continuum of masculine and feminine codes of behaviour (Butler 1990 and 1993).

Feminists, queer and trans★[1] theorists have found themselves at odds around questions of fixed gender identity, essentialism and the social construction of sex and gender (Stryker 2004; Koyama 2003 and 2006; Halberstam 2005 and 2011; Doyle 2009; Case 2009; Bornstein 2016b). Even within trans★ theory, tensions emerge between those who identify as either male or female rather than non-binary and those who, by necessity, identify with a stable gender identity in order to resolve a sense of gender dysphoria or access medical support. For trans★ theorists both gender and biological sex are social constructs (Koyama 2006). Tensions between feminist and queer theory have tended to revolve around feminism as a female-identified movement, evincing a continued investment in the binary distinction between male and female as meaningful, fixed identities (Case 2009; Koyama 2003; Merck, Segal and Wright 1998). Recent tensions between queer theory and trans★ theory have led to criticisms of Butler's theory of gender performativity for its tendency to prioritise a materialist analysis of gender and sublimate the embodied day-to-day experience of living with gender dysphoria, that is, living in a body whose sex does not tally with that designated at birth (Elliot 2010; Stryker 2004; Reilly-Cooper 2016).

Similar tensions have become evident between subsequent generations of feminists, with older, notionally anti-pornography feminists chastising younger generations for not paying due respect to the work of their forbearers and frivolously engaging with tropes of femininity paying little heed to how this might performatively reinforce normative culture (Halberstam 2011). A survey of theoretical developments across feminism, queer studies and trans★ studies over the past 30 years reveals that in spite of postmodernism's call for plurality and flux, a number of distinctions have caused rifts between activists and theorists who might otherwise unite to resist the oppression of a hegemonic binary system (Stryker 2017; Koyama 2006). For feminists, there are tensions between older and younger generations, tensions that have been characterised by the binary of mother/daughter and between those who are supposedly 'pro' or 'anti-sex'. For queer and trans★ theorists and activists there are rifts between those who believe gender should be celebrated as fluid rather than fixed and identifying as either: cis-gendered, transgendered, non-binary, queer or trans★ (Bornstein 2016b; Farrier 2013; Koyama 2003, Edgecomb 2016).

In terms of gender identity and its 'queer' relationship to failure, theorists such as J. Jack Halberstam and José Muñoz have re-appropriated the sense of failure many gender nonconforming people articulate. Halberstam calls for a 'shadow feminism' that is part of a 'counter-knowledge … grounded in negation, refusal, passivity, absence and silence, offer[ing] spaces and modes of unknowing, failing and forgetting as part of an alternative feminist project' (Halberstam 2011: 124). Muñoz has argued that 'a generative politics can be potentially distilled from the aesthetics of queer failure' (Muñoz 2009: 173). After Saidiya Hartman Halberstam proposes that shadow feminists 'lose [the] mother' as a way of freeing themselves from the disapproval of second-wave feminists and the heteronormative imperative.

The artists I have chosen can all be seen to interrogate and explore gender boundaries through performance, in Susan Stryker's terms they 'cross over (trans-) the boundaries constructed by their culture to define and contain that gender' (Stryker 2017: 1). They each articulate a different experience of gender identity and can be seen to draw upon the experience of shame, failure, marginalisation and misrecognition as generative material. However, I want to argue that their work does not readily correspond to arguments circulating in feminist, trans★ or queer discourse because they each resist hetero and homonormative categorisation. Their work celebrates the ingenious, creative and manifold ways they have found to exist as queer subjects in a binary heteronormative world. Each artist eschews the medical tendency to pathologise gender ambiguity and refuses to reiterate what Caterina Nirta has condemned as the depiction of trans individuals as 'miserable souls' that forge a 'lonely and unhappy' path through life (Nirta 2018: 2). The work is sensuous, erotic, celebratory, joyful, mischievous, intergenerational and articulates a thoughtful and complex relationship with family members, particularly mothers. Each artist wrangles with sexual identity and/or gendered subjectivities. Some hold back from giving their identity a name, some describe it as a 'home' or state of stability that has been attained only after a long, disorientating journey. Each attains a clear sense of agency from arriving at a stable position, however they thoughtfully map out and share their journey with the audience so as to ameliorate understanding about what it means to have arrived at sense of stasis. Each artist performs a sense of ambivalence about their sexual/gender identity and acknowledges decisions are the result of a period of profound introspection and contemplation. I will analyse and discuss the work of Kate Bornstein, Lois Weaver and Lucy Hutson. Bornstein is a US non-binary trans★ activist, playwright and performer who has been working in the field of performance and gender since the early 1980s; Weaver, a performer and artist who has worked in experimental theatre since the 1970s. She has worked as a solo artist, developing the persona of Tammy WhyNot and as part of a company with Spiderwoman, and lesbian feminist company Split Britches. Weaver is American but has worked between the UK and US for the past 30 years. She identifies as a femme lesbian. Lucy Hutson is a London based UK artist and writer, creating solo performance and installation work since 2007. In her work Hutson has identified as a male-presenting lesbian.

In order to contextualise the work of my chosen artists I will examine key theories informing feminist, queer and trans★ debates. Lois Weaver has spoken of being taken to task by radical lesbian feminists during the 1980s who did not approve of her co-option of signs associated with a frivolous and conventional femininity; Kate Bornstein has shared her experience of being criticised for exercising 'male privilege' after her transition from male to female (Gorman 2017; Bornstein 2016b: 97). The artists go out of their way to demonstrate that their lived experience of gender does not necessarily fit into recognised or sanctioned ways of being, even those developed within more radical disciplines. They find themselves at the interstices of feminist, queer and trans★ discourse and attempt to negotiate an idiosyncratic pathway despite, rather than thanks to, emerging discourse. Detailing the fractious relationship between 1970s feminists and trans★ people, Emi Koyama has written about the way radical feminists have historically constructed their oppression under patriarchy as '*the* most pervasive, extreme and fundamental of all social inequalities regardless of race, class, nationality and other factors' resulting in a 'cloistering blindness to oppressions outside their own immediate experience and a tendency to create a "hierarchy" of oppression' (Koyama 2006: 700 my emphasis). Koyama is keen for silenced women to come forward, explaining:

> Every time a group of women previously silenced begins to speak out, other feminists are challenged to rethink their idea of who they represent and what they stand for. Although this process sometimes leads to a painful realization of our own biases and internalized oppressions as feminists, it eventually benefits the movement by widening our perspectives and constituencies. It is with this understanding that we declare that the time has come for trans women to openly take part in feminist revolution, further expanding the scope of the movement.

(Koyama 2003: 244)

Working along similar lines Stryker explains some of the tensions between queer and trans★ theory and spaces. She recalls her early apprehension that 'queer ... seemed an anti-oedipal, ecstatic leap into a postmodern space of possibility in which the foundational containers of desire could be ruptured to release a raw erotic power that could be harnessed to a radical social agenda'. Stryker later revised her thinking, coming to sense that queer transmuted into a 'code word' for being gay or lesbian and led to a sense of exclusion for those who did not identify in those terms. She articulates her concern that 'transgender increasingly functions as the site to contain all *gender trouble*, thereby helping to secure both homosexuality and heterosexuality as stable and normative categories of personhood' (Stryker 2004: 213–214 my italics).

As mentioned above, Halberstam has imagined an alternative model of feminism, a 'shadow feminism' that celebrates 'knowledge from below' or a version of Foucault's 'subjugated knowledge' which uses forms of knowledge 'disqualified, rendered nonsensical or "insufficiently elaborated"' (Halberstam 2011: 11). They see the celebration of failure as key to a feminist poetics. Halberstam anticipates some of the piquancy of queerness in the work of my chosen artists when they write:

> [f]rom the perspective of feminism, failure has often been a better bet than success. Where feminine success is always measured by male standards, and gender failure often means being relieved of the pressure to measure up to patriarchal ideals, not succeeding at womanhood can offer unexpected pleasures.
>
> *(Halberstam 2011: 4)*

In the *Queer Art of Failure* and *Gaga Feminism* Halberstam articulates a resistant relationship to the radical feminism of the second wave. *Gaga Feminism* sees them record a public disagreement with Susan Faludi about the 'mother-daughter' dynamic. *Queer Art* states its intention to break away from the 'essential bond of mother and daughter that ensures that the daughter inhabits the legacy of the mother and in so doing reproduces her relationship to patriarchal forms of power' (Halberstam 2011: 124; Halberstam 2012: 1). Although I recognise the oppressive nature of the mother-daughter imagery within radical feminist discourse and am deeply sympathetic to, and excited by Halberstam's celebration of failure, their construction of the mother-daughter relationship strikes me as rather too deterministic because it assumes that patriarchal subjugation is always successfully transmitted in this way. If this were the case then there would be no counter-cultural or queer activity to celebrate. It constructs those who have come out as gay or queer as having exceptional powers of resistance. It assumes that *all* mothers are successfully subjugated by patriarchy and risks ignoring the myriad of alternative families and reproductive relationships in existence today. Hartman's exhortation to 'lose your mother' was written under very different circumstances, coming out of the devastating experience of travelling to Ghana to conduct research into the history of slavery.[2] Although I understand the assimilative role that the mother supposedly occupies, the designation of *the* mother risks constructing her anew as a misogynistic archetype, valued only for her reproductive capacity and denied other forms of identity or agency. Halberstam's construction of mother here strikes me as strangely conservative. Jennifer Doyle has been critical of the construction of motherhood in Lee Edelman's *No Future: Queer Theory and the Death Drive*. Developing a theory of the 'anti-social' Edelman writes in opposition to Muñoz's work on queer utopias, arguing he finds them assimilationist. Edelman critiques the heteronormative celebration of 'pro-life' discourse. Doyle describes how, for Edelman, 'radical queerness is achieved by the identification of homosexuality with all that is outside or against reproductive futurisms' (Doyle 2009: 28). The figure of the mother is charged with carrying the burden of all things reproductive, repeating, once again, the primary association of womanhood with sexual functionality or potential carrier of the heir to the patriarchal throne. Doyle has described Edelman's article as 'perhaps the most hotly debated text in queer theory published in the past decade', which,

> may come as a surprise to some readers not only because the text is almost totally uninterested in female figures or questions of femininity – but because, as far as I can tell, this fact has not been taken seriously in any of the critical responses to Edelman's book.
>
> *(Doyle 2009: 27)*

The reduction of mother to conservative demagogue in anti-social queer theory is problematic, and as a result I want to read the work of my chosen artists partly in relation to their construction of mothers and motherhood. It is my contention that these pieces represent a more generous and imaginative construction of parenting whilst refusing a homonormative or assimilationist drive.

As introduced above, Nirta's research into 'marginal bodies' has revealed that 'early studies of transgenderism describe trans individuals as "miserable souls"'. She observes:

> [i]n both theoretical and medical literature, trans identity has been framed within a paradigm made of minority stress, sense of awkwardness or discomfort, self-dislike due to genitalia being 'organ of hate and disgust' or dysfunctional mental health. This picture has created an impression of negative emotions such as rage, loneliness, denial, self-refusal, pain.
>
> *(Nirta 2018: 2)*

Whilst not wanting to undermine the trauma and increased risk of physical threat associated with an embodied trans★ experience I agree with Nirta that a relentlessly negative portrayal downplays the potential for the type of pleasure, which Halberstam claims can be garnered from the experience of not 'succeeding' as a man or woman. Many queer and trans★ artists take pleasure in subverting heteronormative gender codes. Trans-feminine performance poet and artist Travis Alabanza has written in a frank and open way of the experience of feeling perpetually 'othered':

the world others us, and we just learn to cope with that othering. We are not innately other, that is something done to us. The feeling of being other'd can be beautiful, but it can also be tough. And in those tough moments, I remind myself, this is something done to me, not something innate about me. I am as Other as I wish to be. I embrace the other. But I recognise it was not a choice. The world others us, and we just learn to cope with that othering.

(Alabanza 2018: 17)

Dhruva Balram consolidates Alabanza's aura of positivity by writing, 'their work may be rooted in trauma but Travis radiates joy, a feeling which is shared in abundance from the minute I meet them for a drink at a nondescript bar in South London' (Balram 2019). Whilst foregrounding a pervasive feeling of being under siege, Alabanza gestures towards the potential pleasure and sense of beauty that can be won by being defined in opposition to the norm and by actively 'embracing' the other. Alabanza's statement is provocative and uplifting and I would like to read for signs of a similar sense of beauty and joy in the work of my chosen artists.

Working along similar lines to Alabanza, Carol Queen and Lawrence Schimel argue for the transgressive potential of hybrid, multiple sexualities. Although perhaps a little dated, their 1997 publication championed 'pomosexuality' as the 'space in which all other non-binary forms of sexual and gender identity reside – a boundary free zone in which fences are crossed for the fun of it, or simply because some of us can't be fenced in'. For them the theory of pomosexuality 'acknowledges the pleasure of that transgression, as well as the need to transgress limits that do not make room for us all' (Queen and Schimel 1997: 23). Jen Harvie, in her discussion of Weaver's resistant femme, reifies this notion of pleasure when she describes how Weaver very deliberately 'enjoys and deploys femme attractiveness and its inherent power while refusing any intimations of subordination that are conventionally attributed to femme' (Harvie 2015: 84). Potential pleasure goes against the logic of the medical discourse, which has traditionally pathologised transgenderism as a type of 'identity disorder' and developed a theory of 'gender dysphoria', which, Stryker reminds us, is the *opposite* of 'euphoria' or joy. However, it is clear that queer and transgender artists have described a sense of pleasure and beauty that can come from the act of transgression. My chosen artists all wrangle with the contradictions of gender binaries and boundaries whilst giving voice to a playful, joyful, sensuous, counter-cultural experience.

Bornstein is a writer, trans★ activist and performer working between New York City and Rhode Island. Bornstein identifies as 'a non-binary femme-identified person' and when asked about their preferred gender pronoun has stated,

I've been blessed with living my weird identity for so long that I don't mind anymore. … I think it would be fun to alternate 'they' or 'them' and 'she' or 'her'. Those are the two sets of pronouns that give me the most tickle.

(Raymond 2018)[3]

Bornstein has created and toured performances such as *Hidden: A Gender* (1989), *The Opposite Sex is Neither* (1993), *The Seven Year Itch* (1993) and *Gender Outlaw: On Men, Women and the Rest of Us* (2016). Philip Auslander has written that, for all their celebration of pomosexualities, Bornstein is 'notable for the open sincerity of her performance persona and the absence of irony in her work' (Auslander 1997: 153). Queer activist Theda Hammel describes Bornstein's books as full of a 'wisdom' delivered with 'a candid lucidity and sweetness you won't find anywhere else. They leave no room for shame …' (Nichols 2017). As discussed in Chapter two, Bornstein appeared in the role of Person in Charge #1 on Broadway in Young Jean Lee's 2018 version of *Straight White Men*, one of two transgender people framing the performance.

I witnessed Bornstein's performance of *Gender Outlaw: On Men, Women and the Rest of Us* at the Soho Theatre, London in 2017. The performance took the form of a solo performance organised around the release of the revised version of Bornstein's book of the same title. Bornstein entered to the theme music from *Dr Who*, an indulgence they confessed did not work with US audiences.[4] They were dressed casually in black dungarees, a stripy long sleeved t-shirt and an Ankh pendant hung around their neck. They shared insights with the audience and spoke in warm, confessional tones about a range of different topics. Despite discussing suicidal episodes, anorexia and cancer treatment, Bornstein's mode of presentation was primarily light-hearted. Attempting to describe her gender identity, she said 'I call myself trans or a tranny and the latter angers a small but vocal group of transsexual women who see tranny as the equivalent of kike to a Jew' (Bornstein 2016a). They revealed:

> I was born male and now I've got medical and government documents that say I'm female – but I don't call myself a woman, and I know I'm not a man. That's the part that upsets the pope – he's worried that talk like that – not male, not female – will shatter the natural order of men and women. I look forward to the day it does.
>
> *(Bornstein 2016a)*

Bornstein has spoken and written about the politics of 'passing' as a transgender woman, articulating a sense that up until very recently there has been enormous pressure to pass successfully as either male or female. She has written: 'passing by choice can be fantastic fun. Enforced passing is a joyless activity' (Bornstein 2016b: 163). She asserts that 'real gender freedom begins with fun …' (111). She unpacks both the joy of passing and the shame associated with failing to pass:

> I identify as nonbinary trans. My most joyful gender expression is as female. I'm not genderqueer – I don't aim to mix up my gender expression. As out of the closet as I am on a very broad public level, I still make every effort to be pretty according to my own standards – and sometimes that means I pass as a woman. Honestly? I love that … I chose to pass in part because I didn't want

to get beaten up. I chose to pass because all my life it's been something I've wanted – to live as a woman – and by walking through the world looking like one, I have that last handhold on the illusion, the fantasy, the dream of it all. Passing is seductive – people don't look at you like you're some kind of freak.

(Bornstein 2016b: 161)

Bornstein acknowledges the elements of pleasure she derives from performing her gender identity, however it must be acknowledged that her joy does not necessarily map on to Alabanza's 'beauty' in being 'other'd' but is instead related to a sense of joy due to a *success* in passing. Relating the memory of being mis-gendered by an old associate, she described how she felt engulfed by an abject sense of shame:

[t]he word echoed in my ears over and over. Attached to that simple pronoun was the word *failure*, quickly followed by the word *freak*. All the joy sucked out of my life in that instant, and every moment I'd ever fucked up crashed down on my head.

(162, my italics)

Bornstein's testimony demonstrates the precarious nature of transgender joy; despite having successfully transitioned they still felt restricted and oppressed by the heteronormative gender imperative.

Bornstein repeatedly refers to her childhood and maternal relationship. She describes the key role her mother played in her life. Acknowledging her influence in *Gender Outlaw* she writes:

With special love and gratitude to Mildred Bornstein, who has put up with an awful lot from me. From my mother, I learned how to be gracious under fire, how to look for the laughter in any situation, and, most importantly, how to say no when no must be said. You kept the love there through all the hard times. Thank you, Mom.

(Bornstein 2016b: 293)

In terms of the relationship with their marital family, Bornstein has described how she was ostracised after having been expelled from the Church of Scientology. During *Gender Outlaw* they shared a story about a frustrated attempt to make contact with their daughter via their ex-wife, in order to pass on information about the daughter's increased risk of inheriting leukaemia. Bornstein relates her experience of getting through to her ex-wife on the telephone and saying, 'Hello. It's Kate Bornstein here' only to be rejected as her ex-wife replaced the handset without speaking.

Bornstein writes of being grateful to family and friends who got back in touch after gender reassignment because they provided a way to 'measure the continuity of my life' (Bornstein 2016b: 127). She has always been supported by her mother and has actively championed their relationship. *Gender Outlaw* the book features a photograph of her mother proudly holding Albert, her infant son. Bornstein has provided a caption to accompany the photograph: 'My mother was so proud to have given birth to a son. Our love and friendship grew into much more than either mother-son or mother-daughter' (4). Towards the beginning of the Soho Theatre performance Bornstein shared stories about a range of people who had posed the question 'who are you?' as if her trans★ identity presented something of a conundrum. She shared a piece of writing written for the *New York Times* about the experience of attending her mother's funeral in 1997:

> My mother never heard the blue-haired ladies ask 'Hoowahyoo?' of the tall-tall woman with mascara running down her cheeks. She never heard the producer from the Ricki Lake show ask me, 'Who are you?' when I told her I wasn't a man or a woman. My mother never heard the Philadelphia society matron ask me the same question when I tried to attend her private women-only Alcoholics Anonymous group. My mother only once asked me, 'Who are you?' It was about a week before she died. 'Hoowahyoo, Albert?' she asked anxiously, mixing up names and pronouns in the huge dose of morphine. 'Who are you?'
>
>   I told her the truth: I was her baby, I would always be. I told her I was her little boy, and the daughter she never had. I told her I loved her.
>
>   'Ha!' she exclaimed, satisfied with my proffered selection of whos. 'That's good. I didn't want to lose any of you, ever.'
>
> *(Bornstein 1997)*

As well as paying homage to an older generation Bornstein champions the young. In terms of her relationship with younger trans★ people and the new wave of feminists, Bornstein very deliberately resists the antagonistic mother-daughter relationship described by Halberstam. In conversation with Theda Hammel she acknowledged:

> Too much of our LGBTQetc generational interaction is based in pride. Too many old farts are proud of what they did years ago, and resent the changes that young things are bringing to the table […] As soon as we own pride in an accomplishment, that pride drags us away from the here and now and hampers out ability to navigate life as it unfolds.
>
> *(Nichols 2017)*

Bornstein's enduring affection for their mother and warning about the pride of 'old farts' or 'fuddy duds' marks them as an activist interested in intergenerational relationships, and open to the ideas of the next generation. Her life stories reach both forward and back in time, reaching back to experiences of talking to her mother, reaching forward to identify with a new generation of trans★ people. She shares stories of her mother in order to mark that which remains consistent in spite of a polymorphous, postmodern celebration of indeterminacy. In spite of her peers' tendency to view gender transformation in terms of a seismic ontological shift, the reports of her relationship with her mother and enduring affection for her family demonstrates that she is fundamentally unchanged in her desire and continued need for affection, affirmation, support and friendship.

Bornstein's performance and writing has been enormously important for the trans* and LGBTQIAA communities. Their frank and open style gives voice to the sense of apprehension, confusion, complexity and contradiction experienced by many trans* people. Her confession that 'after the change it all felt like a lie again' throws into relief the tense relationship trans* people have with medicine and psychology and draws attention to the problematic of the binary gender model. She acknowledges that in '1987 there was no word for non-binary' and that it took her seven years to find a language to be able to articulate her experience of gender. Her performance and writing is optimistic, humorous and joyful and pushes back against the tendency, observed by Nirta, to construct trans* people as 'miserable' (Nirta 2018: 2). She does not go so far as to describe the experience of being othered as 'beautiful' but does articulate the pleasure and joy to be found in 'passing'. She shares her pleasure in the erotic, discussing sexual practices and the cognitive and somatic pleasure to be found in gender play. Bornstein takes both pleasure and pain in failing to become a woman and failing to be content as a man. She shapes narratives with transformative potential for those interested in pushing against the boundaries of conservative hetero-normative and homonormative sexuality.

The next artist to challenge gender boundaries and binaries is Lois Weaver, cited by Harvie as 'one of the most important feminist artists of the twentieth and twenty-first centuries' (Harvie and Weaver 2015: 8). Weaver has been engaged in performance, activism and theatre making since the late 1960s and has worked as both solo and collaborative performer. Weaver co-founded Spiderwoman Theater in 1975, a company for native, indigenous, African-American and working-class white women. She went on to found Split Britches with Peggy Shaw and Deb Margolin in 1980. Weaver created her alter ego Tammy WhyNot in 1977 as part of Spiderwoman's *The Lysistrata Numbah!* and has called upon her services as compere, chair and hostess for numerous subsequent events. Weaver recently held an Engagement Fellowship with the Wellcome Institute and performed as WhyNot as part of this work. Weaver co-founded the WOW Café Theatre in New York in 1983 and was Joint Artistic Director of Gay Sweatshop in London, between 1993 and 1997. Split Britches has toured internationally with performances such as *Dress Suits to Hire* (written with Holly Hughes in 1987); *Belle Reprieve* (1991); *Lesbians Who Kill* (1992); *Faith and Dancing: Mapping Femininity and Other Natural Disasters* (Weaver's solo show in 1996); *Miss Risqué* (with Clod Ensemble 2001); and *Unexploded Ordnances* (UXO) (2017). I will focus upon Weaver as a solo female and femme-identifying artist who pushes back against conservative gender boundaries and binaries and challenges some of the more recent binary constructions of gender, such as the emerging binaries between cis-gender and transgender or cisgender and non-binary.

As Peggy Phelan charts in 'A Femme on her Own', Weaver became frustrated by the diminished sense of agency she felt in being recognised *in her own right* as a 'femme' lesbian. Weaver was alert to the different degree of attention garnered by Peggy Shaw when they toured two solo shows together as a double-bill in 1994. She articulated her sense of invisibility, that 'no one sees the femme unless she's on the arm of a butch' (Harvie and Weaver 2015: 165). Weaver observed that Shaw's show *You're Just Like My Father* (1994) 'got a completely different kind of attention' from *Faith and Dancing*. She recalls,

> someone said to me, 'well, Peggy *demands* attention. You *command* attention.' I go, 'Oh.' In a certain way if I look back at the pieces, maybe the pieces were that way. Then that became, 'No, no, no. We got to work this out. I've got to figure this out.'
>
> *(Gorman 2017, my italics)*

Weaver experienced further frustration during their co-production of *Belle Reprieve* in which Split Britches teamed up with drag artists, Bloolips. Of male drag-artist Bette Bourne Weaver has said:

> I realised I just couldn't *take stage* from Bette. I just couldn't do it. It wasn't going to happen. Whether it was down to my ability as an actor, but I don't think so. I just thought it was that distance between him as a man and his representation of female. I didn't have that much distance. The tension was not as great and so attention was not as great.
>
> *(Gorman 2017, my italics)*

As a solution, or means of 'figuring it out', Weaver created the 'resistant femme'. For Weaver, identifying and dressing as femme is erotic, playful and pleasurable and creates opportunities for some of what Halberstam has called the 'unexpected pleasures' of 'not succeeding at womanhood' (Halberstam 2011: 4). Halberstam has registered this tension, writing, 'if femme reads as lesbian only in the presence of a butch partner, then femme becomes a wholly dependent category, borrowing an aura of authenticity from the masculine woman' (Halberstam 1998: 176). For Weaver 'femme in and of itself is a *failure of femininity*, it's the acquisition of all the elements of femininity; a wearing and a putting on and performing that, but not quite getting it' (Gorman 2017: my italics). According to Harvie, Weaver 'is a femme who occupies, enjoys and deploys femme attractiveness and its inherent power while refusing any intimations of subordination that are conventionally attributed to femme' (Harvie 2015: 84). Weaver's femme is:

> fundamental to Lois Weaver's life and work. This may sound simple, but Lois's femme certainly is not. Femme is her dynamic identity, her persona, her politics, her erotics, and her playground. Femme is her career-long challenge to others, a secondhand satin glove thrown down gauntlet-style to second

wave feminism's widely held suspicion that femininity inevitably capitulates to heteronormative patriarchy.

(83)

Elin Diamond enthusiastically welcomed the subversive potential of Weaver's alter ego. She wrote:

> That's where Tammy comes back into the story. As a 'country music star turned solo performance artist' Tammy practices her big femme personality in her big blonde country music star wig. *Everyone sees this femme.* Because 'she needs to know', Tammy is never alone: her audiences have to participate, not just watch.
>
> *(Diamond 2015: 166, author's emphasis)*

Weaver's resistant femme provides a fascinating opportunity to consider female agency, performance, power and queer failure. Weaver's femme was influenced by Spiderwoman's celebration of the Hopi goddess Spider Woman, the goddess of pottery and weaving. According to Weaver 'she taught people to leave a hole in the design, to leave a flaw so that the spirit could come and go' (Gorman 2017). This approach to narrative encouraged Weaver to think about her resistant femme as a way to show the 'cracks' in constructed images of femininity. She recalls:

> I was always a femme. I felt that was part of me whether it's to do with class or whether it's to do with aesthetics … but I never could keep my fingernails clean. I never could keep my legs shaved. I never wore the exact right combination of things. I remember I was the treasurer for Spiderwoman Theatre and we put our money in The First Women's Bank in New York, which no longer exists. This was in the 70s […] Whenever I went up to make that deposit, it was at that moment I realised I hadn't met the criteria of the people. I didn't look like the people in line. I wasn't dressed like them. I had some element of 'failure' about me even at that point. We used to make jokes about it.
>
> *(Gorman 2017)*

Weaver created high-femme characters in *Miss Risqué* and *Faith and Dancing* in order to explore the potential of 'a femme on her own' (Harvie and Weaver 2015: 93). Weaver's experiments in what Lisa Duggan has called 'fem(me)nism' work to both champion and problematise the butch-femme aesthetic. Furthermore, her work as a resistant femme works to challenge the newly established binary between cisgender and transgender or non-binary and cisgender.

Patricia Elliot rightly acknowledges that the landscape of feminist, queer and trans★ theory is complicated and sees 'the trans body … as one possible site for exploring the chaos of our collective experiences of gender' (Elliot 2010: 4). She emphasises, 'those who experience some form of incongruity, whether it is welcome or unwelcome, are unfairly disadvantaged as a result of normative claims to the natural' and 'the lives of those who embody non-normative sex or gender depend, often quite literally, on what meaning gets made, the stakes for them are much higher than for others' (4). One of the key debates in trans* discourse revolves around the fixity or fluidity of the term 'trans'. For some 'trans' can be used in a similar way to 'queer', to signal an open, disjunctive, inclusive form of gender identification that resists binary oppression or closure. For others 'trans' should be particular to the transgender community and act as a point of identification and gathering-point for a coalitional politics. For example, Sean F. Edgecomb has summarised some of the tensions, explaining that:

> Stryker notes that 'transgender studies can be considered queer theory's evil twin' and Jack J. Halberstam argues that attempting to legitimize trans in the same way queer has been legitimised as a political stance may be potentially destructive, suggesting that trans should remain resistant and thus unintelligible.
>
> *(Edgecomb 2016: 345)*

Edgecomb's own work articulates the hope that 'a union of [trans and queer politics] might be formed through the development of performative and fluid post-identitarian notions of self' (Edgecomb 2016: 337). Arguing for gender inclusivity and fluidity Rebecca Reilly-Cooper takes issue with the way that some of the terminology around gender identity has become fixed. She asserts,

> you do not need to be genderqueer to queer gender. The solution to an oppressive system that puts people into pink and blue boxes is not to create more and more boxes that are any colour but blue or pink. The solution is to tear down the boxes altogether.
>
> *(Reilly-Cooper 2016)*

Reilly-Cooper takes issue with the binary opposition between 'cisgender' and 'non-binary', writing:

> There seems to be an immediate tension between the claim that gender is not a binary but a spectrum, and the claim that only a small proportion of individuals can be described as having a non-binary gender identity. If gender is a spectrum, doesn't this mean that every individual alive is non-binary, by definition?
>
> *(Reilly-Cooper 2016)*

Reilly-Cooper questions the idea that cisgender people experience a 'match' or congruity between the gender they identify as and the identity assigned at birth. For her this is problematic because it assumes that the binary gender categories of male and female are coherent and meaningful within themselves, and that nontransgender people are happy or 'at home' in the bodies and the gender roles to which they have been assigned. For her it is the binary male/female gender system itself that is problematic. For Reilly-Cooper:

> This desire not to be cis is rational and makes perfect sense, especially if you are female. I too believe my thoughts, feelings, aptitudes and dispositions are far too interesting, well-rounded and complex to simply be a 'cis woman'. I, too, would like to transcend socially constructed stereotypes about my female body and the assumptions others make about me as a result of it. I, too, would like to be seen as more than just a mother/domestic servant/object of sexual gratification.
>
> (Reilly-Cooper 2016)

I recognise that for some Reilly-Cooper may be employing a reductive and simplistic meaning of the word 'cis'. For Stryker the term 'cis' functions differently – it works to draw attention to the fact that people who identify with the gender/sex assigned at birth (trans★ approaches see both gender and sex as socially constructed) enjoy social and cultural privilege in a way that transgender people do not. She writes, 'being perceived or "passed" as a gender-normative cisgender person grants you a kind of access to the world that is often blocked by being perceived as trans or labeled as such' (Stryker 2017: xii). For Bornstein it means something different again, it introduces a third term to intercede between the binaries of cis and trans in a way that is 'deliciously problematic':

> In LGBTQ, nonbinary gender identities currently can occupy either the T or the Q. On the other hand, nonbinary genders can also be seen as the third that shatters the binary of cisgender and transgender.
>
> (Bornstein 2016b: xvii)

Weaver stands as an excellent example of a femme-identifying woman who shows the designation of cisgender to be dangerously reductive in ascribing the way that she, as a cisgendered woman, should experience and perform gender. Because Weaver identifies as a woman, the sexual designation given to her at birth, under the cis/trans binary she becomes associated with normative gender practice. For someone who has spent her life campaigning for queer and gay rights, raising awareness of lesbian sexuality and arguing for the right of the femme to occupy centre stage, the designation of 'cis' is violently reductive. Her identity would be better served by Reilly-Cooper's designation of 'nonbinary' as an inclusive term. The relationship of 'cis' to 'queer' is contentious. Disagreements around the fixity of sex and gender go some way to explaining Stryker's motivation in calling 'transgender studies' the 'evil twin' of queer theory (Stryker 2004: 212).[5] As part of her engagement work at the Wellcome Trust, Weaver, in character as Tammy WhyNot, delivered a session entitled 'What Tammy Needs to Know about LGBTTQQIAAP'. As part of this open, conversational event Weaver explored the multiplicity of sexual preference and identity. She reminded her audience of the dangers associated with policing boundaries and called for the queer community to be open and 'more gentle' with one another (Weaver 2017). If non-binary can be open to all who experience gender outside of heteronormative binary structures, rather than being limited to a coalitional group then the term and concept presents an unprecedented challenge to the status quo.

Performances such as *Miss Risqué* and *Faith and Dancing* show Weaver claiming agency, by putting the femme centre stage and foregrounding feelings of ambivalence associated with her journey towards claiming an identity as a lesbian femme. Like Bornstein, Weaver celebrates the sense of dislocation and 'queer-ness' she experiences when she starts to identify as a sexual being. She draws attention to a sensuality she discovers in dressing and undressing, the enjoyment of being watched and watching and the value of intergenerational connections between herself and older women. As Bornstein articulates her ambivalence about gender identity and her journey towards transition, so Weaver constructs substantial female characters full of contradiction and ambivalence. She draws upon metaphors of natural disaster, cartography and costume to articulate a bur-geoning sense of self.

In addition to her work as Tammy WhyNot Weaver's resistant femme is brought to life in performances such as *Miss Risqué* (2001) and *Faith and Dancing* (1996). *Miss Risqué* is set in fin de siècle Paris, its central character developed from the memoirs of historical figures such as Mistinguett, Maurice Chevalier and Collette (Harris 2002: 218). Lawrence Van Gelder describes the character as 'part Mata Hari, part diva', changing costumes from 'a Niagara of white gown to one of deep blue' (Van Gelder 2002). Weaver's actor-manager figure controls the acts on her venue's roster, hiring and firing as she sees fit. Peggy Shaw plays a socially awkward male detective known as Serpentine Cashmere. Cashmere is charged with establishing Risqué's identity as a spy. Shaw's character falls under Weaver's spell, periodically absenting himself to telegraph missives to his superiors. Weaver's character takes centre stage in a number of different ways. Firstly, the set has been designed to amplify her lavish sense of costume and ownership. Risqué poses atop a steep platform, alongside a luxuriant white gown suspended from the lighting rig. Her heightened and exaggerated manner of speaking indicates she inhabits a per-petual state of self-consciousness, stage-managing even her own death. At the close of the first number she announces:

> God, I thought that would never end … It's not like I don't like standing here. I do, I love being the centrepiece. The exquisite decoration on top of an extravagant cake. And I have loved every moment of my exposed thigh … from the first moment I lifted my skirt and the audience shouted 'higher' and I lifted it even more and I understood the relationship between what you wanted and how I felt. But everything, even good sex must come to an end.
>
> *(Split Britches 2001)*

Weaver's character shows herself to be fully in control of her appearance and demeanour; she gives voice to an active, desiring sexuality. She enjoys being watched and eliciting longing looks of desire. This piece demonstrates the company's deliberate attempt to contemplate how the femme might 'take stage' from a masculine presence. Shaw's character remains physically, culturally and socially subordinate to the high society dame. Cashmere is seduced by Risqué and robbed of agency, shown to be subject to the demands of his superiors. The piece pushes against conservative constructions of sexuality by foregrounding an active female sexual desire and employing the spectacle of a female Shaw in character as male, making love to a female character. It refuses to reinforce conservative constructions of the dominant male by showing Cashmere as a mere pawn in the operations of greater men.

Weaver's femme remains consistently centred and resistant. The visual effect of the scenography reinforces her air of superiority; indeed she has been placed on a pedestal, which holds her aloft throughout the show. The dramaturgical logic revolves around the character of Risqué and the stagecraft around the figure of Weaver's femme. The top of the 'Niagara-like' robe is in scale with Weaver's body and yet the skirt has been multiplied and extended to cover the rostra units making up the high platform. The platform is sufficiently high to allow Shaw to sit in one of the lower sections. Backlighting illuminates Shaw's figure so the audience can see a silhouette sitting, as if in front of a telephone exchange, sending reports to her commander. Weaver appears throughout as an 'exquisite decoration' in various states of undress and yet she is not reduced to the figure of mere spectacle. Towards the end of the performance, as Cashmere states he has no choice but to take the 'courtesan spy' into custody, Weaver steps into the suspended gown and Shaw gathers a sea of fabric in his arms as he clambers towards her. Risqué's final speech illustrates the consummate show woman expertly stage-managing every aspect of her appearance. She submits to Cashmere's order to accompany him to the police station, but before departing insists he helps her. She commands:

> help me get ready for my final number. I stand, suggestively, inadvertently, revealing my legs. I refuse a blindfold. The audience shouts, 'this lady knows how to die!' I thank them as the soldiers raise their guns. [*Sound of gunfire*] … the reviews are mixed. Some say I startle my executioners by throwing open my fur coat to reveal my body. Others say that my Spanish lover rides up on horseback and we disappear into the woods. Others say that a single bullet pierced my heart. Others say that I raise my hand to blow a kiss and as the bullets sound I disappear into a heap of petticoats. Oh, I did not threaten a nation, as some are kind enough to say, or conquer the world. But I did take up a little of your time.
>
> (*Split Britches* 2001)

Weaver's transcendence gives her license to break away from her figuration as Shaw's 'other' and to be seen as more than simply one element of what Sue-Ellen

Case called their Butch-Femme aesthetic (Case 2009: 31). Weaver's character is constructed so as to be culturally, socially and economically independent. Halberstam cautions: 'if femme reads as lesbian only in the presence of a butch partner, then femme becomes a wholly dependent [on the] masculine woman' (Halberstam 1998: 176). In role as Miss Risqué Weaver is able to counter and resist Halberstam's warning about the invisibility of the femme.

In her solo piece *Faith and Dancing: Femininity and Other Natural Disasters* (1996) Weaver draws upon autobiographical material. Weaver grew up as part of a religious Southern Baptist family in the state of Virginia, US. This performance shows Weaver sharing her experience of sexual awakening, a polymorphous, ambiguous desire and realisation that her desire meant relishing looking and being looked at. It dwells upon her relationship with her mother and a growing realisation that she needed to leave Virginia, meaning both her mother *and* the US state of Virginia. The language of the piece is sensuous and richly metaphorical, drawing upon the symbolism of natural geological and weather phenomena such as volcanoes and tornados. She describes the colour of the Blue-Ridge Mountains, the pink geraniums in Aunt Ame/Lucy's garden, the taste of sugar wrapped in a twisted handkerchief. She puzzles over the suppressed mystery of her mother's body and nurtures a deep pre-Oedipal desire. She articulates a sense of confusion about her burgeoning sexuality, explaining how she sought to educate herself by consulting *The Yellow Pages* and a dictionary. The performance begins with Weaver quoting Dorothy from *The Wizard of Oz*, clicking her heels and announcing 'I want to go home'. She introduces herself as 'Faith' – 'Faith, who had always lived in the stage of Virginia until the Tornado' (Harvie and Weaver 2015: 22).[6] The small stage is furnished with a combination of bench and swing and littered with dictionaries and copies of *The Yellow Pages*. Weaver wears a white girl-like frock made of paper.

Faith and Dancing focuses upon Weaver's adolescence and sexual awakening. Adolescence is regarded as a crucial stage of human development as the subject begins to experience the world with a sense of heightened sensuality. In this production Weaver describes the means by which she was socialised and brought up to be a 'good girl', and details how she subverts the rules whilst still managing to be perceived as 'good':

> I discovered religion or rather the Church the same way I discovered sex and infinity, and modern dance – by accident. [...] That is where I learned about power and what it means to maintain power and still behave like a good girl. I was going to try this out. I would be good.
>
> *(Split Britches 1996)*

Weaver's adolescent harbours fantasies of participating in the *Miss America* beauty pageant, she explains that her chosen 'turn' would be striptease. She dreams of wearing cut-off Levi jeans and brings her knees up to her chest to get a sense of what it would feel like to have breasts pressed against her. She stymies her mother's attempts to turn her against their messy neighbour Ame by mentally transforming her 'sorry' nature into a sense of worthiness. Faith's rich imagination and interest in sex fails to tally with her sense of herself as a 'good girl' – but she states that she deployed a dyslexic logic: 'that is how I learned to be a good girl. Dyslexia. I turned it inside out. I kept the frame of good and girl but reversed the picture. Pretty is as pretty does. I built a character ...' (Split Britches 1996). For Deanna Shoemaker the character Weaver created was one of self-conscious hyper femininity, she terms it 'female-to-femme drag', explaining that 'a female-to-femme drag of femininity potentially troubles essentialist, heterosexist discourses hailing "natural womanliness" because it assumes as its premise an inherent artificiality' (Shoemaker 2007: 321). Indeed, by making the confusion and skewed logic of her adolescence clear Weaver shows that there is no 'natural' logic to religion or desire and no ready or comfortable recognition of sexual preference or gender identity.

As in *Miss Risqué*, Weaver shares details of her desire and sexual experience. Her descriptions of childhood memories are infused with erotic suggestion. She celebrates: the blues and pinks of far off mountains and nearby geraniums; her enjoyment of having her hair and body brushed; the smell and squeak of her mother's rubber girdle; the pleasure she experiences wrestling with a group of boys. Her desires can be seen to be polymorphous: music, dancing, tasting sugar, revelling in physical contact, fantasies about Jesus and forbidden articles of clothing all awake a sense of quasi-sexual desire and longing. She recalls how the 'logic' of sexual enjoyment 'exploded' in her brain when she balanced on an associate's bike:

> the short-stop who was younger than me ... let me sit on his hand as it caressed the cool stiff frame of his bicycle. I'm not sure if it was his hand or the steel pipe inside it that felt so good between my legs.
>
> *(Split Britches 1996)*

She describes watching her mother's body as she hung out the washing, hoping to catch a glimpse of her pubic hair. Although her mother denied either of them had bodily needs, Weaver became supremely aware of both her own and her mother's sensual presence. When her older brother left home she wanted to tell her mother, '[d]on't worry Mama, I'll be your boy. I'll even be your husband. I would be your lover if the idea had ever occurred to us simultaneously' (Split Britches 1996). She found the proximity of her mother's body intoxicating, describing how:

> The closest we ever got was in the kitchen after returning home from Bible school or after going to town. We'd come home and sit down for a minute. V. would light a cigarette and I'd be near her or on her lap, but only if there were others there. It was too frightening to be alone and that close. I would remember the smell and force of the rubber in her girdle. It smelled like something sweet and tight. I would hear the sound her stockings made when she rubbed her tired legs together.
>
> *(Split Britches 1996)*

She recalls seeing her mother lying in bed next to the postman and imagining sexual desire as volcanic magma gathering in her mother's pelvis and threatening to explode in an all-encompassing climax. Weaver describes herself as having been the 'apple of her mother's eye, the object of her affection' but goes on to meditate on the complex interrelationship between subject and object. Tearing away her paper dress she positions herself in a crucifix position towards the rear of the stage. She asks:

> But what about the dancer? Is she the subject or the object? If she is the subject of this story what is the object? Does that mean what is the point? And if so doesn't that elevate the position of the object to the entire reason we are here? And in that case why wouldn't you want to be objectified if it meant you were the very reason for living? So what is the subject? The dancer or the one who is danced round?
>
> *(Split Britches 1996)*

Faith and Dancing offers a fascinating insight into the process of female socialisation. It foregrounds the role of the family, the Church and phallocentric language in reinforcing the 'natural' logic of hegemonic sexuality. Weaver suggests that her Aunt Lucy/Ame, who could 'tell a dirty joke' and had 'big hands that smelled of geraniums', showed her how to come to terms with a rounded sense of self and the role that lesbian sexuality could play in her life. She explains that it was Ame's 'recipe for cornbread that gave me the map I needed to navigate my way home' (Split Britches 1996). Weaver identifies with Ame's less conventional performance of womanhood. Her story reveals the material circumstances shaping her world-view but also dwells upon bodily experience and the exquisite and counterintuitive tension created by a culture of bodily suppression. Weaver demonstrates how she comes to identify as femme but holds back from automatically associating the femme with conservative womanhood. Weaver's version of femininity is far from the stable, fixed position that 'cisgender' implies neither is it non-binary. It is better understood via a spectrum of queer fluidity or Halberstam's model of trans★ as having the potential to defy stabilisation and intelligibility (Elliot 2010: 1).

Lucy Hutson is a solo artist working in London, UK. Key examples of performance include *Bi-Curious George and other Side Kicks* (2017); *Bound* (2015); *Britney Spears Custody Battle vs. Zeus in Swan Shocker* (2014) and *If You Want Bigger Yorkshire Puddings You Need a Bigger Tin* (2013). In 2018 she wrote *Everything in my Head at One Time in my Life* (2018) about her experience of the UK mental health system. Her work is autobiographical and explores the experience of feeling pressured to take on a fixed sexual and gender identity. She has described herself as a Marxist feminist and social agitator. She describes the performance *Bound* as being about 'the slippery nature of identities – the ones you give yourself, the ones forced onto you and the ones that were once strong and now you are just clinging on to' (Hutson 2015). Her performances employ everyday found or domestic objects such as cake ingredients, bandages, sketchpads, tampons, children's puppets and toys. In

Bi-Curious George she worked with her father, borrowing techniques from his children's Punch and Judy shows in order to explore their relationship. Hutson employs an open, interrogative style, using direct-address to talk to the audience. As Diana Damian Martin observes, Hutson '[s]peaks with candour and openness about her own discomforts to do with gender and the control we take to gauge its representation. [She talks about] the shifting categories she finds herself in and about learning not to cling on' (Martin 2015).

In *Bound* and *If You Want Bigger Yorkshire Puddings* Hutson draws upon her experience of growing up as a masculine presenting girl and woman. She is a lesbian, but confesses, 'I have never really identified as queer. Reclaimed words are something that confuse me' (Hutson 2015). In relation to her preferred pronoun she reveals, 'if I'm asked, I'm happy to tell the truth that I am a woman' but she states that she also enjoys 'jumping ship' and identifying as a trans man when required to 'do something feminine' (Hutson 2015). Like Bornstein and Weaver, Hutson shares a sense of ambivalence about the range of gender positions and identity categories on offer. She presents as masculine in the way she dresses and the tenor of her voice. She wears boys or men's clothing and occasionally binds her breasts. She asserts, 'I look more attractive as man than as a woman' (Hutson 2015).

In *Bound* Hutson sits alongside three large television screens which play footage of Hutson in a number of guises. On one of the monitors she can be seen wearing a long red negligée. She is in what appears to be a forest gathering sticks and attempting to build a shelter. On the central screen she is shown talking directly to camera and on the other she is caught in the act of burying objects such as tampons and a strap-on dildo in a plot of soil. Throughout the live performance she quietly sketches members of the audience, letting the drawings slide to the floor once completed. At the end she finds relevant audience members and hands over their portrait. In *Bound* Hutson explores her perception of her breasts. She confesses that she used to see her breasts as her 'best asset' but found that 'this feeling faded away when I got used to the idea of wanting to be a man'. She traces her interest in breast binding to her frustrated sense that:

> I want my breasts to be mine and I feel like they are. I think breasts are seen as something to be wanked over or tittered at, put on Page Three or just showing a little bit at the top of long dresses. I feel like my breasts have been taken away from me and made into symbols of femininity that I can't live up to. I want to let my breasts hang, let them bounce when I walk with my arms swinging and I want society to think nothing of that. I want to sit naked on the beach or in the park in summer – or just walking down the street when it's hot. And I want this just to be the same as if I had a flat chest.
> *(Hutson 2015)*[7]

Hutson shares her sense of frustration with gender categories and behaviours available to her. Articulating her sense of ambivalence she states: 'I'd like to talk

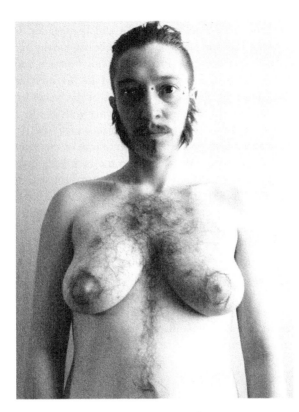

FIGURE 5.1 Lucy Hutson procures her chest hair in *If You Want Bigger Yorkshire Puddings You Need a Bigger Tin* (2013)
Photograph: Cheryl Wills

this evening about identities. There's loads of identities I have, but I don't really know how to be any of them, even the ones I feel it's really important I proclaim I am.' She speaks of wanting to be part of a sub-group such as a feminist or Marxist sub-group, but doesn't feel happy with the idea that Marxist feminism is 'named after a man' (Hutson 2015). Her suspicion of categories could, on the one hand, be seen as a rejection of the many different identity 'boxes' or identity labels Reilly-Cooper sees proliferating today, or it could be read as an assertion of an individual identity that has yet to find the right 'box'. Hutson's tone and demeanour on stage is quietly affecting. In *Bound* she is present both as a live and mediated performer. Her confessions are delivered directly to camera and the 'live' Hutson is silent, paying careful attention to the audience members she draws. By scrutinising her audience Hutson, like Weaver, can be seen to be resisting the customary relationship of subject and object; watcher and watched. Her meditations are measured, and although she articulates frustration she does not express anger. Instead, she behaves as if meditating before an audience on the nature of her own identity. Like Weaver she stands as an interesting example of a notionally cisgendered woman who problematises the distinction between cis and transgender, non-binary and cisgender. Hutson embraces and takes pleasure in her masculinity and confesses that she enjoys occasionally presenting as a trans man, however she returns to the fact that she is 'happy' to tell people she is a woman. Like Bornstein and Weaver her stories eschew the 'miserable' archetypal narratives of the trans* experience Nirta describes and celebrate instead the pleasure of playing with gender as a panoply of different possibilities. At the outset of her performance of *If You Want Bigger York-shire Puddings* she outlines her experience of taking one of the many 'gender tests' available. A series of images are projected on to the back wall as she describes the tests. They depict 'talking heads' style photographs of people taken in an urban street. Each photograph features the subject's name and 'breakdown' of masculine and feminine traits, for example: 'Josh: 60% masculine 40% feminine; Imogen: 70% feminine 30% masculine; Glinda: 90% feminine; 10% masculine; Lucy 60% masculine; 40% feminine' (Hutson 2013). Hutson describes taking a 'femme role test', which asked her to rate her 'feminine qualities' such as 'compassion and under-standing' and masculine qualities such as 'dominance and aggression'. Hutson tells the audience that her score suggested she was 'androgynous'. She goes on to describe the 'Transgender, Combined gender and Transsexuality inventory', a test designed to 'help doctors assess potential pre-transitioning transsexuals as "male" to "female"'. She draws attention to the fact that no such test exists to assess potential pre-transitioning female to males. Having outlined the details, she states: 'I have two reactions to the tests I took. Reaction Number One: these tests are fucked up stereotype reinforcing shit. Reaction Number Two: "Androgynous" – Wicked!' (Hutson 2013) Hutson's enthusiastic response to being identified as 'androgynous' can be seen to resemble Alabanza's joy and sense of 'beauty' in being 'other'd' (Alabanza 2018: 17). She describes her gender ambivalence in terms of the pleasure and joy it gives her but does confess:

> It has only been in the last four or five years that I haven't been embarrassed when people think I'm a man and it used to really make me cringe when people weren't sure and they wanted me to tell them. Now I feel quite happy, I feel there's less pressure. You don't really have to learn how to use a drill properly; you don't have to let your mates do your make up before you go out.
>
> *(Hutson 2013)*

Hutson describes coming to terms with the fact that for many people her ambig-uous identity presents something of a conundrum that needs to be resolved. She uses a prop, Lucy the Doll, to stand in for some of her more well-intentioned friends who try to reassure her that she *is* 'feminine':

> Lucy is always telling me how feminine I am and I don't know why because I don't see it. I think she's just trying to make me feel better, but it just makes things more complicated. When I am being honest and proud about claiming

my boyishness people think you are putting yourself down. No one has ever told me to leave the women's toilets. Lots of people have told me to leave the men's, but I don't care. There are few pleasures I enjoy more than casually strutting into the gents, exposing my penis-lacking womanhood before backing up against a urinal to relieve myself.

(Hutson 2013)

Hutson revels in the potential mischief mobilised by her androgyny and, rather than feeling embarrassed or ashamed, actively enjoys causing confusion. Like Bornstein and Weaver, she actively identifies as a feminist and capitalises on the subversive nature of her gender ambiguity. She celebrates the way her attempts to pass as a teenage boy confound expectations around gendered behaviour.

At the outset of *Yorkshire Puddings* Hutson describes her experience of joining the Stoke Newington branch of the Women's Institute (WI) – an organisation that is open to 'anyone who considers themselves a woman' and willing to pay £36 a year (Hutson 2013). The organisation is associated with domestic labour such as cake and preserve making. The WI website explains that it was founded in the middle of the First World War and:

> Under the auspices of the Agricultural Organisations Society (AOS) [the WI] played their part in increasing food production by making jams and preserves and bottling and pickling other fruit and vegetables. These tasks were second nature to most countrywomen – and very necessary if the excess produce from gardens and smallholdings were to be preserved. This was the war work for which WI members became renowned.[8]

The first section of the performance features Lucy, dressed in trousers and a collared t-shirt, making a cake. She mixes ingredients live onstage as well as appearing on film as part of a pre-recorded cooking demonstration. Her on screen actions are mirrored and intercut with footage of American food presenter Stephanie Jaworski who hosts the *Joy of Baking* website.[9] Hutson describes her enjoyment of the WI sessions, explaining, 'my favourite thing that we do, on the night before International Women's Day is creep out and decorate our favourite tree in green, white and purple' (Hutson 2013). She admits 'the kind of things I talk about are not the kinds of things I can talk about to the WI ladies' and confesses that she has been developing a practical demonstration session, in the style of the cooking demonstration, that might allow her to 'explain it to them'.

During one section of the show Hutson talks to camera, using a live feed, to project a close-up on to the screen. She draws attention to her facial and chest hair (which she has exaggerated with mascara), her breasts and her vagina. In a manner similar to the performance in *Bound* she describes her ambivalence about breasts, explaining she feels they constrain her movement and require containment and concealment in a way she finds oppressive. However she also reveals she would not consider surgery to reduce or remove her breasts 'for two main reasons. Number one: it is a really expensive and long process and Number two: I think having breasts helps when trying to get casual sex from lesbians' (Hutson 2013). In relation to her vagina Hutson speaks more positively. Naked, she draws up her legs before the camera to reveal a close-up of her vulva. She draws apart her labia to draw attention to different parts:

> I like the way these come out there, I like that bit there … I like the way it goes inside, like that … I don't feel any disconnection to this part of my body at all. I feel like I've got to know it over the years, all what it likes and that, because we are one and the same. I'm really relieved I don't feel any disconnection. Yes. It makes it a lot easier.
>
> *(Hutson 2013)*

Hutson again resists a narrative of unhappiness, confiding that she does experience a sense of unease about certain parts of her body but would not want surgical intervention to do away with them. Hutson's demonstration for the WI women takes the form of a live demonstration with practical assistance from audience members. She stands naked before the audience and starts to construct a prosthetic penis out of a ball of wool. She explains: 'you need your own strap, but once you have got that you can use any old ball of wool. It can be any colour, it can match your skin tone…' (Hutson 2013) She demonstrates how to use the spare wool to wrap around the strap so that it hangs securely but is free. Her final attempt successfully resembles a flaccid, woolly penis. Next she moves on to a demonstration of breast binding. She produces a familiar roll of plastic cling-film, recognisable from supermarkets and local grocers, and wraps it repeatedly around her chest. She explains:

> I find that cling-film works really well. If I'm honest, I do find it a bit of a turn-on, I'm not sure what that is about. The t-shirt you put over the top needs to be quite loose, not too tight. And smooth it out […] I think the W.I. would be proud of me!
>
> *(Hutson 2013)*

Hutson's exploration of gender is both embodied and performative. She describes her experience of living in an androgynous body throughout her formative years and her early sense of shame when asked to explain whether she was male or female. She confesses her most recent experiences of passing as a boy or man reveal it to represent a gateway to privilege rather than oppression. Her androgynous gender identity would customarily mark her as 'other' and yet she is able to enjoy the privilege of 'passing' as male and so experience a reduced degree of harassment. Her pleasure in identifying as a woman would customarily mark her as 'cisgender' and yet her sense that she looks more attractive as a man and feels more comfortable in men's clothing troubles this designation. For example, she explains that one of the advantages of passing is that she feels able to walk around at night without feeling afraid and does not receive unwanted sexual attention when alone in public spaces. Furthermore she champions a sense that things are 'less pressured now' and that even institutions such as the WI, traditionally considered to represent a conservative image of womanhood, have a more open and liberal understanding of gender.

Most positively and again, in a way that goes against received reports of intergenerational feminist tensions, Hutson demonstrates a close relationship with her family, going so far as to make her show *BiCurious George and Other Side-Kicks* (2017) with her father, Professor the Amazing Addrian. She uses family members as part of her 'focus group' who respond to questions about the advantages and disadvantages of being a woman. Her family is very supportive. Towards the end of *Yorkshire Puddings* Hutson shares an anecdote to illustrate her mother's solidarity. She relates a story about shopping for underwear:

> I used to cut down PJ bottoms to wear as shorts before I was confident enough to go into a shop and buy boxers. Not that long ago I was shopping for boxers with my Mum. And it was one of those days when it was really cold outside but the shop is really warm and you don't want to take your clothes off. And it was one of those shops that has loads of different departments, so my Mum asked the shop assistant directions. And she just pretended I was her son. We didn't talk about it before and we didn't talk about it afterwards. It didn't feel weird; we just took on the roles that made the most sense to her on that day and in that moment.
>
> *(Hutson 2013)*

Hutson's experience and articulation of gender would appear to fall in line with Butler's theory of gender performativity to a certain extent, but also speaks to an embodied experience. She enjoys dressing and 'passing' as a boy or man and enjoys her embodied experience as a woman. Stryker explains why Butler's work has come under criticism by some transgender writers. According to Stryker she is 'criticized, somewhat misguidedly, for supposedly believing that gender can be changed or rescripted at will, put on or taken off like a costume, according to one's pleasures or whim' (Stryker 2017: 10). Stryker explains that for many trans people their sense of self is 'ontologically inescapable and inalienable' a reality they consider marginalised by Butler's notion of the performative. Butler has articulated her sense that there are multiple ways of 'doing gender' and it is perhaps the sense that gender is something one performs rather than an ontological reality that is at stake in the transgender theorists' questions. Butler writes:

> the act that gender is … is clearly not one's act alone. Surely, there are nuanced and individual ways of doing one's gender, but that one does it, and that one does it in accord with certain sanctions and proscriptions, is clearly not a fully individual matter. […] The act that one does, the act that one performs, is, in a sense, an act that has been going on before one arrived on

the scene. Hence, gender is an act that has been rehearsed, much as a script survives the particular actors who make use of it, but which requires individual actors in order to be actualized and reproduced as reality once again.

(Butler 1988: 525–526)

Hutson's articulation of gender identity is resistant and oppositional because it fails to reproduce a normative reality of either male or female. As a result she does not, in Butler's terms, 'actualize' or 'reproduce' normative gender ideology. However, she does refuse some of the subject positions described by queer and trans★ discourses. She identifies as neither cis nor trans★ and rejects the alternative gender play offered by lesbian butch-femme identities, stating, 'I have never identified as butch in a butch/femme way and I don't know anyone who has. I've just read about them in fiction' (Hutson 2013). She could be seen to be putting forward a case of what Halberstam has called 'transgressive exceptionalism', a case whereby transgender subjects assert their unique position and compete 'over who is most oppressed or the most radical' and yet this is unlikely because Hutson points out the advantages that passing as a 'teenage boy' affords her and celebrates the way her female body gives her a sense of completion because 'we are one and the same' (Halberstam 2005: 20; Hutson 2013). Like Bornstein and Weaver, Hutson elides categories employed by feminist, queer and trans★ theorists. Her story is not one of exceptionalism, but rather one of affirmation and joy. She celebrates the potential of lesbian sex and desire, revels in the privilege she enjoys when passing as a young man or boy and thrives with the support of loved ones. She resists the boundaries of gender categories that would have her identify as male or female, cis or trans★. As Bornstein would have it, she remains 'deliciously problematic' (Bornstein 2016b: xvii).

The artists discussed above all use performance to articulate a different sense of their own sexual and gender identity. They share stories pointing to the importance of social groups and institutions in contributing to their socialisation; they describe an embodied experience of desire or feeling that their body did not fit with established gender patterns. They resist reductive male/female gender binaries but also confess to struggling to identify with the categories offered by queer and trans★ discourse. Each artist describes a type of journey towards acceptance or realisation of their 'otherness' and fortunately all detail an experience of finally arriving at a sense of completion or happiness. In addition to celebrating the dynamics of lesbian desire by using a butch-femme aesthetic, Weaver has invented a 'resistant femme' who is capable of taking centre stage and being recognised as subversive and playfully resistant without reference to a butch partner. Weaver's sense of the femme, as a woman who doesn't quite 'get it', capitalises on the creative potential of failure. She has said, 'femme in and of itself is a failure of femininity' (Gorman 2017). Her femme embraces what Halberstam has called the 'unexpected pleasures' found in failing to live up to the patriarchal ideals of womanhood (Halberstam 2011: 4). Bornstein has shared her long experience of negotiating a transgendered life, noting that even after gender reassignment surgery 'it all felt like a lie again. I ended up being a not man/not woman', a startling experience in the late 1980s when the term non-binary had yet to be coined (Bornstein 2016a). They embrace the potential of non-binary but assert they are not 'genderqueer' because they identify as female. For Bornstein the concept of non-binary is 'deliciously problematic', representing as it does a refusal to observe the authority of the binary gender system. Hutson has confessed she does not recognise herself as 'queer' or 'butch' but enjoys 'jumping ship' between identifying as a transgender man and a woman. She describes her work as being about 'the slippery nature of identities – the ones you give yourself, the ones forced onto you and the ones that were once strong and now you are just clinging on to' (Hutson 2015). Each of the artists experiences a mismatch between the identity categories available to them and their sense of embodied gender. As such their work is best understood via Stryker's inclusive use of the word 'trans*' which signals a desire to be 'inclusive of many different experiences and identities rooted in acts of crossing' without 'get[ting] hung up on fighting over labels or conflicts rooted in different ways of being different from gender norms' (Stryker 2017: 11). Alternatively they can be thought of as 'queer' as a 'fluid post-identitarian notion of self' (Edgecomb 2016: 337). Weaver's work presents itself as a potent challenge to the category of cisgender women. Her work chimes with that of Reilly-Cooper who questions the potential of women to signal an active refusal of heteronormative and homonormative gender norms when cisgender women always signify as normative.

Each of the artists has rejected a sense of overwhelming oppression, choosing instead to celebrate what Alabanza has called the 'beauty' of being othered and the pleasure in refusing to be fixed by conservative gender boundaries (Alabanza 2018: 17). Bornstein revels in the joy of passing as a woman; Weaver celebrates the depth of her sexual desire; and Hutson takes pleasure in confusing those who want to know definitively whether she is a man or a woman. They all identify as feminist and defy narratives about intergenerational tensions between different generations. They ultimately refuse to 'lose' or turn their backs on their mothers, choosing instead to dwell upon and celebrate the roles they play in their lives. The artists all refuse oppressive gender boundaries; they resist heteronormative patriarchal gender roles and push back against restrictive binaries. By not 'succeeding' at womanhood or manhood these artists embrace the potential of failure to open pathways for imagining multiple, shifting gender identities.

These artists, akin to those in previous chapters, can be seen to be questioning the experience and phenomenon of queer failure according to Muñoz's 'generative' project (Muñoz 2009: 173). By creating a performative space to celebrate the 'joy' of passing and the 'beauty' of being 'othered' they locate what Muñoz has called a 'kernel of potentiality'. These moments of pleasure 'help[s] the spectator exit from the stale and static lifeworld dominated by alienation, exploitation, and drudgery associated with capitalism or landlordism' (173). They can be seen to revel in Halberstam's 'queer art of failure', celebrating the fact that 'failing is something queers do and have always done exceptionally well …' (Halberstam 2011: 2–3). They illustrate the potential relief from oppression that comes from refusing to meet 'male standards' and demonstrate 'gender failure often means being relieved of the pressure to measure up to patriarchal ideals, not succeeding at womanhood can offer unexpected pleasures' (4). Like Young, McCormick and Project O the artists in this chapter push back against societal expectations by interrogating the way their bodies signify in certain socio-cultural contexts. Furthermore they create work out of the drive to interrogate the tyranny of binary gender categories and frustrate attempts to 'fix' and categorise. My next chapter will continue with and develop the theme of laughter and joy by investigating the work of four stand-up comedians. I will argue that my chosen artists repurpose the negative associations of anger and harness its energy to productive resistant laughter. I will scrutinise performances by Bridget Christie, Shazia Mirza, Lolly Adefope and Hannah Gadsby in order to argue that despite an initial reluctance to be perceived as difficult or 'angry' each artist has come to embrace its subversive potential. In Soraya Chemaly's terms the comedians refuse the pressure to 'put anger and other "negative" emotions aside' and realise their 'right to rage' (Chemaly 2019). They draw upon anger as a form of politically resistant vehemence. They reinforce Audre Lorde's sense that 'every woman has a well-stocked arsenal of anger potentially useful against those oppressions, personal and institutional, which brought that anger into being' (Lorde 2017: 26). Like the other artists featured in the book they articulate the frustration of being othered by hegemonic society and use the experience of failing to meet the standards of white, heteronormative, patriarchal society to procure subversive laughter. Rather than discuss the work of female comics in terms of the well-used tropes of self-deprecation and beauty this chapter will attend to changing attitudes within the work and exploit the negative emotion of anger as a forceful tool for change. These artists are repurposing failure by forging comic material out of oppression.

Notes

1   For the purposes of this chapter I will follow Susan Stryker's example and use the designation 'trans*' to refer to transgender theory and politics. Stryker notes 'Using trans* rather than transgender became a shorthand way of signalling that you were trying to be inclusive of many different experiences and identities rooted in acts of crossing, and not get hung up on fighting over labels or conflicts rooted in different ways of being different from gender norms' (Stryker 2017: 11). Stryker's revised edition of *Transgender History* provides an invaluable guide to the changing use of terminology around transgender and transsexual politics. Trans* is a shortened version of Transgender, which Stryker explains 'is a word that has come into widespread use only in the past couple of decades, and its meanings are still under construction. I use it … to refer to people who move away from the gender they were assigned at birth, people who cross over (*trans-*) the boundaries constructed by their culture to define and contain that gender' (Stryker 2017: 1). Kate Bornstein has provided further guidance on definitions. In the revised introduction to *Gender Outlaw* they wrote '[t]oday trans is the term that's inclusive of people's myriad experiences of gender. Transgender today simply means a man or a woman who has transitioned from another gender. That's what people used to call transsexual' (Bornstein 2016b: xiv–xv).

2 Halberstam writes '[t]here are no simple comparisons to be made between former slaves and sexual minorities, but I want to join Hartman's deft revelations about the continuation of slavery by other means to Leo Bersani's, Lynda Hart's and Heather Love's formulations of queer histories and subjectivities that are better described in terms of pain and failure than in terms of mastery, pleasure and heroic liberation' (Halberstam 2011: 130).

3 I will refer to Bornstein as 'they/them; she/her' in order to observe their/her chosen pronouns.

4 *Dr Who* – UK TV series 1963–1989 and 2005–ongoing. Originally created by Sydney Newman.

5 Sean F. Edgecomb notes that, 'In 2004, path-breaking trans theorist Susan Stryker eloquently argued for the politics of a post-Judith Butler trans anti-identity, suggesting that although queer theory and trans theory both stem from the same roots of feminism and sexuality studies, they have become situated as "evil twins" that drive apart notions of sexuality and gender. This rift was caused in part by a disconnection between queer and trans solidarity, with both groups grounding themselves in seemingly opposing identity politics in an effort to generate non-identitarian notions of ipseity. While I am sensitive to Stryker's position regarding the disruption of lived trans experience in contrast to performed queer experience, I hope that a union of the two might be formed through the development of performative and fluid post-identitarian notions of self.' (Edgecomb 2016: 337).

6 *The Wizard of Oz*, Metro-Goldwyn-Mayer film directed by Victor Fleming, produced by Mervyn LeRoy (1939).

7 Page Three refers to the daily feature, in UK tabloid newspapers such as *The Sun*, of topless female models on page three of the paper. *The Sun* discontinued the practice in January 2015. Lucy Holmes founded the *No More Page 3 Campaign*, which collected more than 190,000 signatures. More information at: http://nomorepage3.org/

8 Women's Institute Website: https://www.thewi.org.uk/faqs (accessed 11th June 2019).

9 Stephanie Jaworski – *Joy of Baking.com: 21 Years of Award Winning Baking & Dessert Video Recipes* - https://joyofbaking.com (accessed 10th June 2019).

Bibliography

Alabanza, Travis (2018) 'Don't Lose the Roughness of Your Bricks', in *The Outsider's Handbook*, Lu Williams (ed.) London: Live Art Development Agency, pp. 16–19.

Auslander, Philip (1997) *From Acting to Performance: Essays in Modernism and Postmodernism*, London: Routledge.

Bhabha, Homi K. (1994) *The Location of Culture*, London: Routledge.

Bornstein, Kate (1997) 'Preface', in *PomoSexuals: Challenging Assumptions about Gender and Sexuality*, Carol Queen and Lawrence Schimel (eds.), San Francisco: Cleis Press Inc., pp. 13–18.

Bornstein, Kate (2016a) *Gender Outlaw: Kate Bornstein on Men, Women and the Rest of Us*. Touring Production.

Bornstein, Kate (2016b) *Gender Outlaw: On Men, Women and the Rest of Us*, revised edition, New York: Second Vintage Books.

Balram, Dhruva (2019) 'Skin Deep meets Performance Artist, Theatre Maker, Poet and Writer Travis Alabanza', *SkindeepMag.com*, 30 November. Available at: https://skindeepmag.com/articles/skin-deep-meets-performance-artist-theatre-maker-poet-and-writer-travis-alabanza/ (accessed 3 February 2020).

Butler, Judith (1988) 'Performative Acts and Gender Constitution: An Essay in Phenomenology and Feminist Criticism', *Theatre Journal*, 40(4), 519–531.

Butler, Judith (1990) *Gender Trouble: Feminism and the Subversion of Identity*, New York: Routledge.

Butler, Judith (1993) *Bodies that Matter: on the Discursive Limits of 'Sex'*, New York: Routledge.

Case, Sue-Ellen (2009) *Feminist and Queer Performance: Critical Strategies*, Basingstoke: Palgrave Macmillan.

Chemaly, Soraya (2019) 'How Women and Minorities Are Claiming Their Right to Rage', *The Guardian*, 11 May. Available at: https://www.theguardian.com/lifeandstyle/2019/may/11/women-and-minorities-claiming-right-to-rage (accessed 9 July 2019).

Deleuze, Gilles and Felix Guattari (1987) *A Thousand Plateaus: Capitalism and Schizophrenia*, New York: Columbia University Press.

Derrida, Jacques (2002) *Writing and Difference*, translated by Alan Bass, London: Routledge.

Derrida, Jacques (1976) *Of Grammatology*, translated by Gayatri Spivak, Baltimore: Johns Hopkins University Press.

Diamond, Elin (2015) 'Lois,' in *The Only Way Home is Through the Show: Performance Work of Lois Weaver*, London: Live Art Development Agency and Intellect Live.

Doyle, Jennifer (2009) 'Blind Spots and Failed Performance: Abortion, Feminist and Queer Theory', *Qui Parle*, 18, 25–52.

Duggan, Lisa and Kathleen McHugh (1996) 'A Fem(me)inist Manifesto', *Women & Performance: A Journal of Feminist Theory*, 8(2), 153–159.

Edgecomb, Sean F. (2016) 'Queer Kinesis: Performance, Invocation, Transformation', in *Queer Dramaturgies: International Perspectives on Where Performance Leads Queer*, Alysoun Campbell and Stephen Farrier (eds.) Basingstoke: Palgrave, pp. 330–347.

Edwards, Brian (1998) *Theories of Play and Postmodern Fiction*, New York: Routledge.

Elliot, Patricia (2010) *Debates in Transgender, Queer and Feminist Theory: Contested Sites*, Burlington: Ashgate Publishing Ltd.

Farrier, Stephen (2013) 'It's about Time: Queer Utopias and Theater Performance', in *A Critical Enquiry into Queer Utopias*, Angela Jones (ed.), New York: Palgrave Macmillan.

Foucault, Michel (1995) *Discipline and Punish*, New York: Vintage Books.

Gorman, Sarah (2017) 'Femme In and Of Itself is a Failure of Femininity: Interview with Lois Weaver', *readingasawoman.wordpress.com*. Available at: https://readingasawoman.wordpress.com/2018/05/11/femme-in-and-of-itself-is-a-failure-of-femininity-interview-with-lois-weaver/ (accessed 28 August 2019).

Halberstam, Judith Jack (1998) *Female Masculinity*, Durham: Duke University Press.

Halberstam, Judith Jack (2005) *In a Queer Time and Place: Transgender Bodies, Subcultural Lives*, New York: New York University Press.

Halberstam, Judith Jack (2011) *The Queer Art of Failure*, Durham: Duke University Press.

Halberstam, Judith Jack (2012) *Gaga Feminism: Sex, Gender, and the End of Normal*, Boston: Beacon Press.

Harris, Geraldine (2002) 'Double Acts, Theatrical Couples, and Split Britches' Double Agency', *New Theatre Quarterly*, 18(3), 211–221.

Hartman, Saidiya (2008) *Lose Your Mother: A Journey along the Atlantic Slave Route*, New York: Farrah, Strauss and Giroux.

Hassan, Ihab (1987) *The Postmodern Turn: Essays in Postmodern Theory and Culture*, Ohio: Ohio State University Press.

Harvie, Jen (2015) 'Citizen Femme', in *The Only Way Home is Through the Show: Performance Work of Lois Weaver*, Jen Harvie and Lois Weaver (eds.), London: Live Art Development Agency and Intellect Live, pp. 83–89.

Harvie, Jen and Lois Weaver (eds.) (2015) *The Only Way Home is Through the Show: Performance Work of Lois Weaver*, London: Live Art Development Agency and Intellect Live.

Hutson, Lucy (2013) *If You Want Bigger Yorkshire Puddings You Need a Bigger Tin*. Touring Production.

Hutson, Lucy (2015) *Bound*. Touring Production.

Koyama, Emi (2003) 'The Transfeminist Manifesto', in *Catching a Wave: Reclaiming Feminism for the 21st Century*, Rory Dicker and Alison Piepmeier (eds.), Boston: Northeastern University Press, pp. 244–259.

Koyama, Emi (2006) 'Whose Feminism Is it Anyway? The Unspoken Racism of the Trans Inclusion Debate', in *The Transgender Studies Reader*, Susan Stryker and Stephen Whittle (eds.), New York: Routledge, pp. 698–705.

Lorde, Audre (2017) *The Master's Tools Will Never Dismantle the Master's House*, London: Penguin.

Martin, Diana Damian (2015) 'Now '15: Bound/miles and miles', *ExeuntMagazine.com*, 30 April. Available at: http://exeuntmagazine.com/reviews/now-15-bound-miles-and-miles/ (accessed 7 June 2019).

Merck, Mandy, Naomi Segal and Elizabeth Wright (1998) *Coming out of Feminism?* Oxford: Blackwell.

Muñoz, José (2009) *Cruising Utopia: The Then and There of Queer Futurity*. New York: New York University Press.

Nichols, James Michael (2017) 'Queer Icon Kate Bornstein Holds Groundbreaking Conversation with Theda Hammel', *HuffPost US*, 22 January. Available at: https://www.huffingtonpost.co.uk/entry/kate-bornstein-theda-hammel_n_587d04d9e4b0e58057ffba58 (accessed 5 June 2019).

Nirta, Caterina, (2018) *Marginal Bodies, Trans Utopias*, Abingdon: Routledge.

No More Page Three Website (2012) http://nomorepage3.org/ (accessed 3 February 2020).

Queen, Carol and Lawrence Schimel (1997) *PomoSexuals: Challenging Assumptions about Gender and Sexuality*, San Francisco: Cleis Press Inc.

Raymond, Gerard (2018) 'Interview: Kate Bornstein on Their Broadway Debut in Straight White Men', *SlantMagazine.com*, 11 July. Available at: https://www.slantmagazine.com/blog/pretty-damn-bowie-kate-bornstein-on-their-broadway-debut-in-straight-white-men/ (accessed 6 February 2018).

Reilly-Cooper, Rebecca (2016) 'Gender Is Not a Spectrum' *Aeon.co*. Available at: https://aeon.co/essays/the-idea-that-gender-is-a-spectrum-is-a-new-gender-prison (accessed 28 August 2019).

Shoemaker, Deanna (2007) 'Pink Tornados and Volcanic Desire: Lois Weaver's Resistant Femme(nini)tease in Faith and Dancing: Mapping Femininity and Other Natural Disasters', *Text and Performance Quarterly*, 27(4), 317–333.

Split Britches (1996) *Faith and Dancing*. Touring Production.

Split Britches (2001) *Miss Risqué*, collaboration with Clod Ensemble. Touring Production.

Stryker, Susan (2004) 'Transgender Studies: Queer Theory's Evil Twin', *GLQ: A Journal of Lesbian and Gay Studies*, 10(2), 212–215.

Stryker, Susan (2006) '(De) Subjugated Knowledges: An Introduction to Transgender Studies', in *The Transgender Studies Reader*, Susan Stryker and Stephen Whittle (eds.), New York: Routledge, pp. 1–17.

Stryker, Susan (2017) *Transgender History: The Roots of Today's Revolution*, revised edition, New York: Seal Press.

Van Gelder, Lawrence (2002) 'One-Acts Deal in Delicate Negotiations, in the Music Hall and Home', *New York Times*, 27 February. Available at: https://www.nytimes.com/2002/02/27/theater/theater-review-one-acts-deal-in-delicate-negotiations-in-the-music-hall-and-home.html (accessed 24 May 2019).

Weaver, Lois (2017) 'What Tammy needs to know about LGBTTQQIAAP', *Wellcome Trust*, 7 July.

6

TEMPERING ANGER: ASSERTING THE RIGHT TO DEFINE AS A COMIC *WITHOUT FURTHER CAVEAT*

In June 2019 Shazia Mirza and Isma Almas took to the tiny stage upstairs at the Retro Bar, London to try out material they would go on to show at the Edinburgh Festival Fringe. Almas introduced herself as a lesbian Muslim from Bradford, Yorkshire, who had recently adopted an Afro-Caribbean child. In an aside to her set material Almas confided that an established comedy agent had advised against citing so many different identity positions. The agent had chastised her, warning she should 'just choose one and stick to it'. Also paying lip service to the unwritten rule that comedians should claim just one identity category, Rosie Jones told a Leicester Square Theatre audience in May 2019 that: 'it took me ages to come out to myself. I thought, "I'm not gay – I'm disabled – that's *my thing* – I can't tick *two boxes* … it takes me long enough to tick one!"' In British and US stand-up successful comedy performers are expected to hone a single gimmick or onstage persona with which the audience can identify. As Jones and Almas imply, there is little room for nuance or complexity. I will argue that although female comedians are currently enjoying increased access to the comedy circuit and heightened opportunity for commercial success, they continue to experience pressure to conform to conservative racial and gender stereotypes and have a narrower range of choice than male counterparts. In this chapter I will analyse the work of Australian comedian Hannah Gadsby and UK comedians Lolly Adefope, Shazia Mirza and Bridget Christie. A review of their work suggests each has experienced a different career trajectory, honing a distinctive voice and identity over a number of years. Reference to earlier and more recent examples of work will demonstrate that despite consciously attempting to side-step stereotypical expectations of female comedians being 'feminist', 'angry' or 'political' critical reception has encouraged them to alter and adjust their personae along the way.

The high-risk nature of stand-up comedy renders it an ideal medium for the study of performance and failure. Heckling, the practice whereby audience members speak back to performers, is considered part of the performance rhetoric and comics are expected to demonstrate themselves simultaneously vulnerable *and* capable. Stand-up comedians regularly dwell upon aspects of social dysfunction and articulate a sense of how they do, or do not, conform to mainstream societal values. For Regina Barreca, 'There's hubris in humor and confidence in comedy, neither of which can be achieved without a profound sense of resilience. Failure of nerve is not an option' (Barreca 2013: 12). Sophie Quirk has observed, 'dysfunction is often presented as a way in which to triumph over life's imperfections' and Sharon Lockyer and Michael Pickering articulate their sense that 'perhaps all we can say in the end is that we laugh because we are human, flawed, frail and imperfect' (Quirk 2015: 140; Lockyer and Pickering 2005: 15). Each of my chosen artists enjoys an interesting relationship to the self-deprecatory genre expected of female stand-ups and all have spoken out against constraints imposed upon them by parochial critics and the rhetorical structure of the medium itself.

The four comedians I will discuss are all experienced stand-ups and have toured extensively in the UK and abroad. They have appeared on national and international television and two have had performances made available on Netflix streaming service. Despite this level of experience some performers feel they have to reassure audiences they know what they are doing. Trying out work-in-progress material at a recent gig, Christie went out of her way to reassure the audience, saying 'I'm very confident … if we go for forty minutes without a laugh, I'll be fine with it, so don't worry about me' (Christie 2019). What these comedians share is the experience of negotiating the contradictory terrain of the stand-up circuit and having to justify their right to be on stage as a 'female' comedian, or 'Black female' comedian, despite not necessarily setting out to make an issue of their gender or race. After critics had repeatedly misinterpreted their stage personae, reading them as the performers *being themselves* some, such as Mirza and Christie, put their characters to one side in order to actually present material as *themselves*. Several comedians reflect upon the rhetorical structure of jokes, which call for them to rely upon self-deprecation in order to win the audience's approval. Each of the performers, at some point in their career, has set out to avoid being defined by their race or gender but has found themselves drawn back to material associated with identity politics. They have felt obliged to respond to critical feedback and normative expectations imposed upon them. Despite early decisions to avoid being cast as 'angry' or to avoid discussing politics, these performers have ultimately built their sense of frustration into their acts. They can be seen to be repurposing failure by harnessing the negative emotion of anger and using it to procure counter-cultural laughter. I will examine how, often despite themselves, these artists have drawn upon anger as a generative force to galvanise change.

Much scholarly writing about women in comedy relates to their potential to be 'funny', the use of self-deprecatory humour and the incongruity of sexual attractiveness with the ability to make people laugh. Christopher Hitchens' controversial article in *Vanity Fair* acted as a catalyst for this debate back in 2007. According to

Hitchens women do not need to be funny to order to realise their evolutionary goal (which is, of course, to bear and raise children) (Hitchens 2007). In 2014 Linda Mizejewski wrote about the perceived incongruity of the attractive female comedian. She observed: 'it used to be that women were not funny, then they couldn't be funny if they were pretty. Now a female comedian has to be pretty – even sexy – to get a laugh' (Mizejewski 2014: 185). Joanne Gilbert has explored the issues informing self-deprecating comedy, observing 'whether they are writing about female comics for academic or popular audiences, critics unanimously condemn women's use of self-deprecating humour as negative, suggesting that it merely reinforces stereotypes, reinscribing patriarchy in the process (Gilbert 1997: 318). She argues that although it 'appears to reaffirm hegemonic values' it actually represents, 'a potentially subversive rhetoric' (327). Writing more recently Ellie Tomsett has articulated a personal sense of apprehension about female comedians who employ self-deprecatory humour, but stresses, 'any self-deprecatory utterance in live comedy performance will always simultaneously both reinforce and challenge hegemonic views of women and their bodies' (Tomsett 2018: 10). Eric Shouse and Patrice Oppliger have argued that US comedian Sarah Silverman can be read as 'post-gendered' because 'none of the usual generalizations about women's humour are applicable to Sarah Silverman' (Shouse and Oppliger 2012: 201). They explain how Silverman has 'broken with' the tradition of women's humour. She achieves this by:

> telling jokes rather than comic stories; by relying upon self-presentation and the demonstration of cleverness; by telling overtly hostile jokes; by eschewing traditional forms of self-deprecation in favour of ruthlessly ridiculing others; and by attacking the powerless (including the physically or mentally handicapped, those of lower socio-economic classes, the elderly and children)
>
> *(206)*

Shouse and Oppliger point to the opacity of Silverman's onstage personae as being responsible for confounding critics. They question whether it might be 'the culturally sanctioned habit of reading the "I" of women's stand-up comedy as autobiographical [which] is an important reason why the gendered norms of female humour developed in the first place' (Shouse and Oppliger 2012: 213). Christie is exhausted by, and scornful of, the topic. When asked by BBC 6 Music disc jockey Mark Radcliffe whether he could ask her what it was *like* to be a female comedian she replied:

> No! Aargh! What's it *like* being a man on the radio? It's the same as in all industries … same as engineering, aviation. We need to change the conversation. We're always coming at it from the perspective of men running everything – if we change that then we'll look at it differently.
>
> *(Christie 2018)*

Adefope has also expressed her frustration at being repeatedly asked about her ethnicity. She has said,

> it's annoying because you want those conversations to happen as there are people who would never expose themselves to those things unless you speak up about them, but at the same time, you want to focus on your own thing and be seen as a person.
>
> *(Casely-Hayford 2018)*

This chapter will interrogate how the comedians' frustrations, both with the industry and with the political status quo, emerge into their work in ways that ostensibly go against early intentions.

Quirk and Double have foregrounded the importance of a 'stage persona' for each stand-up comedian. Quirk writes,

> the theory is, to be successful you need a very clearly defined stage persona. If you look at any well-known, successful comic you can probably sum up what they do in two or three words … So if they know who you are and where you're coming from very early then it's easier … it allows [the audience] to buy into it.
>
> *(Quirk 2015: 128)*

Oliver Double has described a 'spectrum' of personae with performers ranging from 'character comedians' to 'those who perform themselves'. He writes, 'there is not so much of a clear dividing line between the two as a continuous spectrum of approaches, each example subtly shading into the next' (Double 2014: 124). Double qualifies the difficulty in identifying the position of some performers, stressing, 'just as there are elements of authenticity in exaggerated personas, so there are elements of exaggeration in comedians who apparently go on stage as a naked self' (Double 2014: 133). The crucial element here is the audiences' supposed need for a clearly recognisable persona that can be described in 'two or three words', Quirk points to the need for simplicity and an easily recognisable figure in order for the audience to 'buy into it', Several comedians have articulated their frustration with this 'one-dimensional' persona. As cited above, Almas and Jones expressed their sense of the absurdity of only being able to claim one subject-position, or 'tick one box', Similarly, Shazia Mirza has said, 'I don't want to be seen as a *Muslim comedian*, I don't want to be seen as one-dimensional as if that's all I can talk about and that's all my life is about because it's not at all' (Lockyer and Pickering 2005: 117 my emphasis). Wanda Sykes has railed against the 'stereotypes of the sassy black comic and the angry black woman', and Sofie Hagen asserts that 'these stereotypes are there to make us shut up' (Hagen 2016). Gilbert has argued that 'stereotypes are part of the currency of stand-up comedy' (Gilbert 1997: 323) and yet for Lockyer and Pickering it is context that is crucial:

> There is however nothing fixed about the fixities in which stereotypes trade. Identity and application are of direct significance. Who is comically treated by whom and with what consequences are crucial factors that can determine the outcome of a joke and whether or not it is regarded as offensive.
>
> *(Lockyer and Pickering 2005: 5)*

The artists under discussion wrangle with the proposition that their work will automatically be read as autobiographical. They battle with the expectation of an easily recognisable persona. These twin imperatives leave little room for nuance or complexity, although as Lockyer and Pickering state above, there is some scope to play with context as a way of destabilising stereotypical assumptions. Whilst setting out to avoid one-dimensional personae the artists each appear to have made an active decision, in their more recent work, to embrace anger and frame it as a way of reconciling their sense of self with that of their audiences and critics. They have embraced anger as a positive and generative emotion, observing, after Audre Lorde that 'every woman has a well-stocked arsenal of anger potentially useful against those oppressions, personal and institutional, which brought that anger into being. Focused with precision it can become a powerful source of energy serving process and change' (Lorde 2017: 27). Significantly Lorde gave this speech at a conference entitled, 'Uses of Anger: Women Responding to Racism', As part of her speech she details how white feminists have been confounded by her anger, describing her as too 'harsh', indeed so harsh so that the white feminists '[could not] hear you', Lorde states that, 'I have tried to learn my anger's usefulness to me, as well as its limitations' (31). It is possible to conceive that in taking up a persona on stage, and allowing anger to be part of a mode of self-expression, a female comedian might be heard in ways women off-stage would not. Claiming a 'right to rage' Soraya Chemaly promotes anger as a 'critically useful and positive emotion' but acknowledges biases associated with anger and race. She writes, 'in the United States, anger in white men is often portrayed as justifiable and patriotic, but in black men, as criminality; and in black women, as threat' (Chemaly 2018: xiv). She has observed that, 'anger in men confirms gender role beliefs and expectations, but anger in women confounds them' (Chemaly 2019). Rebecca Traister also acknowledges different intersectional constructions of rage:

> It's crucial to remember that women's anger has been received – and often vilified or marginalized – in ways that have reflected the very same biases that provoked it: black women's fury is treated differently from white women's rage; poor women's frustrations are heard differently from the ire of the wealthy. Yet despite the varied and unjust ways America has dismissed or derided the rages of women, those rages have often borne substantive change, alterations to the nation's rules and practices, its very fabric.
>
> *(Traister 2018: xx)*

Traister has written of her desire, as a younger woman, to distance herself from 'the angry ghosts' that 'haunted feminism's past' but goes on to acknowledge,

> it is ironic that the generation that I, in some unconscious way, worked to distance myself from is now the generation that thrills me in its bonkers rage: the women who yelled at men and gave every direct indication that they had had it with their bullshit.
>
> *(xxv)*

Celebrating the potential of anger she asserts, 'rage can be a powerful tonic. It is a communicative tool, which speakers and writers and activists not only find freeing, but which acts as a balm to listeners and readers struggling with their own sub-sumed vexations' (xxvii). Continuing the process of repurposing 'negative' emotions in earlier chapters, I will analyse the ways in which Bridget Christie, Shazia Mirza, Lolly Adefope and Hannah Gadsby draw upon reserves of anger in order to foreground the absurdity of how women in comedy are conventionally constructed. I will analyse their deployment of anger for social change.

Christie, a London-based comedian, started to develop stand-up routines alongside acting in 2003. To date she has produced 12 consecutive shows for the Edinburgh Festival Fringe including *The Cheese Roll* in 2006, in which she discussed the annual cheese rolling event held in Brockworth, Gloucestershire; *The Court of King Charles II* in 2008, in which she took on the role of King Charles and a number of other historical male figures; *A. Ant* in 2010, in which she railed against 'ant-ism' whilst dressed as an ant; *A Bic for Her* in 2013, in which she appeared as herself and spoke about the absurdity of gender specific advertising campaigns and stereotypical constructions of feminists; and 2016–2017 *Because You Demanded It*, a show about the political fallout in the aftermath of the UK's EU referendum. Christie is the recipient of a number of awards, including the Chortle Award for Best Show 2017 for *Because You Demanded It*, and three awards (Chortle, South Bank Sky Arts Award and Foster's Edinburgh Comedy Award for *A Bic for Her*) in 2013. She has written a column for *The Guardian* and recorded *Bridget Christie Minds the Gap* for BBC Radio 4. She was the first British female comedian to have her stand-up show, *Standup for Her,* streamed on Netflix (2017). Ellie Tomsett describes her as asserting her right to 'define as a comic *without further caveat*' and suggests that Christie's work has 'so far been confined to those areas sometimes referred to as "niche feminism" – the pages of *The Guardian*, and *BBC Radio 4*' (Tomsett 2017: 58 & 64 my emphasis). According to Teddy Jamieson, she 'came to prominence in 2013 when she won the Foster's Edinburgh Comedy Award (after a decade of playing to one-woman-and-her-dog size audiences) with her show about feminism entitled *A Bic for Her* (hijacking a slogan advertising female-targeted pink pens)' (Jamieson 2016). Tomsett has appropriated Kate Clinton's term 'fumerist' to describe to describe the way Christie 'clearly displays her anger at the injustices and inequalities experienced by women' (Tomsett 2017: 58).

Christie sees her job as being to 'make politics absurd', which she wryly observes means that she is 'becoming increasingly irrelevant' as UK politicians forge their own brand of absurdity in response to Brexit. *A Bic for Her* was particularly astute in its foregrounding the absurdity of sexism. Christie openly names a number of 'sexists', that is, men who have made openly misogynistic comments in the media and exaggerates the surreal by nominating an arbitrary 1980s pop star, Jimmy Somerville, as the 'Head of Women' (Christie 2015: 3). For feminist scholars Christie represents a fascinating figure; she was one of the first women in the UK to resume a conversation about feminism in the popular cultural arena. Feminism had fallen from favour in the UK in the first two decades of the 2000s, Christie explains:

> Feminism was alienating in 2010, 2011, 2012. I knew that because me and my friends were doing stuff and we were really criticised for it. People looked uncomfortable. But the following year I thought, 'Well, I'll do a whole show about it because that's what I'm interested in. I'll do this show and see what happens'.
>
> *(Jamieson 2016)*

Christie's sense of a historical antipathy towards feminism is borne out by Elaine Aston who describes an 'anti-feminist backlash' as far back as the 1980s, which made feminism a 'dirty word' and encouraged 'older generations of feminist women' to go back into the 'feminist closet' (Aston 2007: 120). Promotional material from Camden People's Theatre website gives voice to a similar observation. Reflecting upon the success of the 'Calm Down Dear' festival of feminist theatre in 2019, they write,

> [w]ho would have thought that when we took a punt in 2013 on programming our first ever festival of far-out feminist theatre – this was back when there was still some timidity around the word – that 'Calm Down Dear' would one day be an unmissable feature of CPT's annual programme?
>
> *(Camden People's Theatre 2019: venue publicity)*

Christie has charted her journey towards feminism, noting that in earlier shows such as *The Cheese Roll* she 'wasn't writing about feminism back in 2006, because a man hadn't farted yet' (Christie 2015: 160). Christie is referring to an epiphany she experienced in the Women's Studies section of a London bookstore when she had difficulty tracking down the feminist books she wanted and, upon finally identifying the relevant floor, discovered the shop assistant responsible for misdirecting her. Before departing he left an unpleasant odour, an act she interpreted as displaying contempt for feminism and womankind. Christie has stated that in her earlier work, in order to be taken more seriously, she avoided the subject of gender, even going so far as to appear in role as variety of male historical figures:

I first started doing stand-up in 2003. In my Edinburgh shows, from 2005 onwards, because I thought I'd be taken more seriously if I pretended to be a man, I had dressed as King Charles II. I wondered about wearing the robe all the time, perhaps even during childbirth as well. I thought the midwives wouldn't patronize me so much if they thought I was a man.

(Christie 2015: 167)

Sensitive to the discomfort caused by the topic of feminism for 2010 audiences Christie created a sardonic allegory in the form of an ant diatribe against 'ant-ism', Her 2010 performance was entitled *A. Ant* and featured Christie dressed in a homemade ant-costume, sporting a pink and black striped tie. The set comprised Christie, as an angry ant, railing against prejudice against ants and the lazy stereotypes bestowed upon ant comedians. Christie explains,

I remembered how clever ants were and thought that if I dressed up as an ant, and talked about what it was like being an 'ant' comedian, audiences might be more willing to buy into it … An ant talking about being an ant comedian would be far less alienating to a comedy audience than a woman talking about being a woman comedian.

(69–70)

Christie would begin the performance by playing *Antmusic* by 1980s pop group Adam and the Ants over the PR system. She would enter as if in a temper because as an ant comedian she found the intro music reductive and insulting:

What's this? '*Ant Music*'? By Adam Ant? Why has the technician played that? What, because I'm an ant? Unbelievable. If I was the black and blind comic on the bill, they wouldn't have played Stevie Wonder for me, would they? Or 'Kung Fu Fighting' for the Chinese one? Of course not. Because that would be politically incorrect.

(70)

Christie is drawing upon her personal experience of underwhelming introductions made by TV panel show hosts and comperes. When she appeared on the BBC news programme *Have I Got News for You*? she was introduced with the lines, 'Bridget Christie: a woman who collected her Foster's comedy award wearing a No More Page 3 T-shirt … but got a bigger round of applause when she took it off!' (Lawson 2014). Christie emailed the show's producers to ask them to edit the introduction because she felt the joke relied upon the audience knowing that she was a feminist comedian, which the majority did not. The producers refused and Christie asserted that she would not appear on the show again. She explains, 'have they ever introduced a male comedian with a joke about his cock?' (Lawson 2014). She satirises similar experiences in the following section of *A Book for Her*.

Ladies and gentleman, are you ready for the next act? I want you to go wild, go crazy, start stamping your feet … She's a WOMAN, but don't let that put you off. I certainly didn't the other night. Whoops! Don't tell the wife … no, no, seriously, I have not had sex with the following act … as far as I know … and even if I have, that is NOT how she got the gig. Come on now, let's get her on shall we? She's LOVELY, so go easy on her … Okay, everybody, settle down. If you wouldn't mind just waiting until the next act, who is a WOMAN, has done her set, we'll have an interval and you can get a drink and go to the toilet then.

(59)

For Christie *A. Ant* represents an interesting turning point because she gives free reign to anger about gender inequality and yet holds back from using the term 'feminism' or 'woman'. If the audience chooses not to recognise the allegorical significance of the ant the performance can be enjoyed as character comedy. The success of *A Bic for Her* in 2013 is representative of a shift in the political climate in the UK and the US, with public figures such as Emma Watson and Ed Miliband identifying as feminists, the success of Laura Bates' *Everyday Sexism* project on Twitter, Caroline Criado-Perez' campaign to put Jane Austen on the new £10 banknote, Leyla Hussein's high-profile campaign against female genital mutilation, Lucy Anne-Holmes' campaign for *No More Page 3* and the UK campaign to end taxation on sanitary products. *A Bic for Her* can be seen to be successful for its expert interweaving of serious political issues with lighter observations and the foregrounding of the absurdity of a logic that upholds a culture of double standards for women and men. Christie takes the heighted performance of anger developed in *A. Ant* and deploys it to winning effect. In common with most stand-up comedians she displays a level of self-reflexivity throughout and acknowledges that she is more than familiar with the stereotype of the angry feminist, whilst alternating between what might be perceived as 'authentic' and 'performed' anger. Tomsett has described Christie as a 'fumerist' because her work,

> both deals with feminist issues and also clearly displays her anger at the injustices and inequalities experienced by women … she manages to ensure that the show does not feel like a lecture whilst at the same time not belittling or lessening the severity of the subjects being covered.
>
> *(Tomsett 2017: 58)*

It is interesting to note that with her transition into more 'serious' material Christie jettisoned character work in favour of appearing 'as herself', Double has observed, 'just as there are elements of authenticity in exaggerated personas, so there are elements of exaggeration in comedians who apparently go on stage as a naked self' (Double 2014: 133). It would be inaccurate to say that Christie is without persona; instead she has developed an exaggerated version of herself, which knowingly acknowledges the stereotype of the 'angry feminist comedian', She scoffs at the idea that she is a 'spoof' feminist comedian and pays homage to the rich tradition of female stand-up comedy that has preceded her. She observes, 'after I did my show on feminism, everyone then started calling me "Bridget Christie the feminist comedian"', a moniker with which she was more than happy (Christie 2015: 35). Christie sends up the stereotype of the angry feminist comedian, articulating, with tongue firmly in cheek, what a feminist might be. She announces:

> I'm a feminist. All this means is that I am extremely hairy and hate all men, both as individuals and collectively, with no exceptions. Nope, not even Lawrence Llewelyn-Bowen/Paul Hollywood/Ronnie Corbett/Trevor McDonald/David Attenborough or John Nettles circa Bergerac are good enough for me … I also learned that us feminists hate being complimented, praised or having our lives improved or enhanced in any way by a man. A feminist would rather be dead than by saved by a man. Christmas is banned in the 'feminist community', along with birthdays, wallpaper, nuance, giving people the benefit of the doubt and all music. Feminists only ever listen to one song, on a loop: k.d.lang's 'Constant Craving'.
>
> *(Christie 2015: 36)*

However, alongside the apparent ridicule of feminism's humourlessness Christie builds time into her routines to explore serious topics affecting women across the world. She has discussed topics such as domestic violence, rape, labiaplasty and female genital mutilation (FGM). She couches these issues within broader personal anecdotes. She has said, 'I knew I wanted to talk about anti-rape pants and female genital mutilation and the [Müller] yoghurt commercial gave me license to do so. It's trickery, really, hiding the serious bits within the comic framework' (Lawson 2014). She has talked about the gendered associations of anger and admits she is 'very grateful' she's 'allowed to "hector" people', but resents the way that representations of her anger differ from male peers. She observes, 'when a female comic talks passionately about issues, she is perceived as "whingeing" or "moaning." A male comic doing the same thing is prin-cipled, committed and passionate. Mark Thomas, for example, didn't "bleat on" about the arms trade' (Christie 2015: 92–93). She tells a story about an audience member who approached her after a work in progress gig one eve-ning. She describes him as a 'nice friendly bloke' who said, '[t]hat was good, mate. Bit too serious for a Saturday night, but I enjoyed it. You're brave to be talking about equal pay and that sort of stuff on a weekend', In hindsight Christie reflects,

> He was right. He wouldn't have said that if the material was funny enough. He would've just said it was funny. I had to make it funnier. I reminded myself that there were no unfunny subjects, just bad material […] I had to find a way of counteracting the seriousness of the subject matter.
>
> *(193)*

After this encounter Christie concluded she needed to adjust the 'seriousness' of her onstage persona in order to make the work palatable:

> A key part of this was my on stage persona. I had to be a much more extreme version of the real me, someone a bit ridiculous, and confused, and angry about the wrong things. As well as highlighting the absurdity of misogyny, I also had to make myself absurd. If I was absurd, then I could say anything, and really have some fun with it. I also wanted to find ways of sneaking information into the show.
>
> *(193)*

Driven by the imperative to make the material 'work' and ensure future bookings, Christie realised she must temper her anger and find a way to make her indignation look absurd. Her unmediated anger is deemed too 'harsh' for a paying audience. As Chemaly has written, 'anger is a critically useful and positive emotion. Anger warns us, as humans, that something is wrong and needs to change' (Chemaly 2019). In order to meet the double imperative to both entertain and campaign for change Christie realised she must adjust her 'unfeminine' anger in order to dissipate the threat anger represents. She achieved this introducing a number of different personae, all of which roughly resemble Christie, the comedian who, in Double's terms, comes on stage as her 'naked' self. She now employs a number of different registers and at times exaggerates her anger in the role of stereotypical 'angry feminist comedian', This version of Christie figures at some distance from the more authentic 'real' Christie who self-reflexively comments upon the success of the evening's performance and delivers factual information about domestic violence or FGM. Indeed, her angry persona bears more relation to A. Ant. At times Christie adopts a conversational, yet critical stance, publicly chastising misogynistic public figures and relating anecdotes showing these celebrities to be untrustworthy and open to ridicule. At other junctures she plays the part of a comedian working with personal material, referring to her 'fictional husband' who is a 'sexist racist pig who is infuriated if he has to do a gig when he has no clean pants' and a fictional daughter who has 'a very deep voice' (Lawson 2014). As outlined above, Christie says she has to find ways of 'sneaking' facts into the show, and does this by creating a series of different personae using a range of different comedic tropes.

Christie wanted to find a way of amplifying the activist work around FGM. She contacted Leyla Hussein, one of the founders of Daughters of Eve, a non-profit organisation raising awareness of FGM, and together they created a short film entitled *What is FGM?* Christie had asked Hussein if she thought FGM was a suitable topic for a stand-up comedian and whether, as a white middle-class woman, she had a right to speak about it. Hussein explained, 'everyone brings something different to the table. We can all apply the skills we have to an issue in order to inform and educate' (Christie 2015: 236). Hussein revealed that she struggled to get people to attend conferences and talks, so felt the input of a comedian would help raise awareness. They resolved the seeming incompatibility of comedy and genital mutilation by agreeing that

FIGURE 6.1 Promotional photograph of Bridget Christie (2015)
Photograph: Idil Sukan

Christie would draw upon the angry, ignorant persona of A. Ant and interview Hussein in a 'funny, ignorant way' (240). The film begins with Christie pretending not to be able to grasp the correct order of 'FGM', repeatedly double-checking with Hussein that it's not 'FMG' because she was 'sure she heard Michael Gove say FMG' (295). In role as ignorant host, Christie refers to British misapprehensions about FGM. She identified FGM as an 'African tradition' that multicultural British people might be reluctant to criticise, then likens it to Morris dancing, a British 'tradition', Hussein and Christie participate in the following exchange:

> Christie: So, my point is that do you think that British people, because they think it's a tradition – female cutting – that it's something that they should be allowed to carry on? They tried to stop Morris dancing, you know, the government ... not the government, some people tried to stop it because it was dangerous. It's not that dangerous, they've just got some bells and hankies, but a lot of British people are like, 'No, no, no, it's a tradition; we've got to hang on to this'.
> Hussein: No, I mean, I don't think we can compare female genital mutilation to dancing, I mean, that's just violence, full stop.
>
> *(298)*

For Hussein Christie's technique of ridiculing and undermining ill-informed bigots was enormously useful. She said that the film:

isn't about dismissing the pain of FGM. I was taking the piss out of a system designed to control me. Culture gave FGM status. By laughing about it, I was lowering its status. I was taking the importance of FGM away from it, in the same way that rappers reclaimed the N-word. My response was to laugh at FGM. To take it less seriously. It has a status that it doesn't deserve.

(245)

Christie's material has been fuelled by indignation about social inequality since she started performing in 2003. Her narrative about the post 2013, post-fart, anger determines the content of the stand-up in which she ostensibly appears as 'herself' but the anger has, in fact, been present throughout her career. It is fascinating to chart the different techniques used to incorporate incendiary material into the routines. As Chemaly has pointed out, women are told that it is '"better" if women "don't seem so angry"' (Chemaly 2018: xxi). Christie has found a way to incorporate anger into her work in a way that productively undermines stereotypical configurations of female stand-ups and paves the way for social change by raising awareness of important global issues. For Christie, as for Traister, rage has been a 'powerful tonic', It is also a 'powerful communicative tool, which speakers and writers and activists not only find freeing, but which acts as a balm to listeners and readers struggling with their own subsumed vexations' (Traister 2018: xxvii).

Shazia Mirza is a London-based comedian with a strong international following, touring her show *The Kardashians Made Me Do It* (2016) to the US, Sweden, Ireland and France. Critics remark that she is 'brave' and 'uses her dead-pan delivery to great effect' (Oliver 2018; Troth 2018). She also works as a writer, producing regular articles for *The Guardian, New Statesman* and *Dawn* newspaper. She has won numerous awards including Columnist of the Year at PPA Awards in 2008 and AWA Arts and Culture Award in 2010. Mirza started performing as a stand-up in 2000. Initially drawing upon character comedy she appeared on stage wearing a hijab and made jokes about the World Trade Centre terrorist attacks in New York, 2001. At the start of her career this was the 'clearly defined stage persona' Quirk said was theoretically required in order to become a successful stand-up (Quirk 2015: 128). Mirza reflects, 'I was giving people what they expected of me' (Akbar 2006). Subsequently she took the decision to put this character to one side after only six months, experiencing frustration at its limitations. She said that she didn't 'want to be seen as a Muslim comedian'. She has said, 'no one wants to be known for being an Asian doctor, or scientist, or comedian. You want to be known as a comedian' (Akbar 2006). Further, she felt she did not 'want to be seen as one-dimensional' (Lockyer and Pickering 2005: 117). Her website features a clip from the Winnipeg Comedy Festival in 2009 in which she observes, 'the journalists in America always ask me really stupid questions, like "would you consider becoming a suicide bomber?" So I said … well, do you know what? If the comedy doesn't work out …' She counters her frustration with being seen to represent and speak for *all* Muslims with the observation that 'Muslims don't want me representing them either' (Oliver 2018). She has been 'physically and verbally attacked by Muslim men who believe Muslim women should not appear on stage' (Lockyer and Pickering 2005: 100).

Like Jones and Almas, Mirza expresses frustration at the pressure comedians face to 'tick' a single 'box' in terms of identity politics. Journalists and critics most frequently quote the line, 'My name is Shazia Mirza, at least that's what it says on my pilot's license', a line delivered soon after the 2001 terrorist attacks in New York and Washington DC. However in intervening years she has become more interested in observational comedy, which means that she comments upon her particular experience of being the child of Pakistani parents who moved to Birmingham in the 1960s and her experience of living as a Muslim woman in the UK. She speaks from an individual viewpoint in order to avoid being 'considered to be speaking about my entire race' (Baker 2015). In Double's terms she has moved from one end of the stage persona spectrum to the other, in the move away from character comedian she embraced a figure who 'appears to be an authentic human being, unaffected by the process of performance' (Double 2014: 133). She is clear that she does not intend to speak *for* a community of people, instead she states, 'I'm putting a unique perspective on being an Asian Muslim woman, and I'm trying to use that perspective to the best of my ability' (124). Part of her aim is to tackle stereotypical assumptions about Asian families and Muslim people and her hijab-sporting persona got in the way. In an article in *The Telegraph* in 2001 she said, 'The whole point of my act is to help reduce Islamophobia in Britain … there were so many stereotypes. I talked about my life and I allowed people to laugh along with me' (*Telegraph* 2001). Interviewed in 2004 Mirza asserted:

> my, routine, it's changed now […] I never ever mention anything about my religion or my culture because I think that, sometimes, like I went to see an Irish comedian the other night he's Irish, but he never once mentioned the fact that he's Irish, but you knew from what he was saying that he didn't need to mention it. So I don't, and I feel enough people know me, and they know who I am, so if I say I don't drink they know why and feel I don't need to mention that I'm a Muslim, and actually it makes it more accessible if I just mention my vulnerabilities, that I'm tempted to smoke, I'm tempted to drink, I'm tempted to take drugs and gamble and shoplift and all these things.
>
> *(117)*

Mirza has been described as a 'devout' and 'practising Muslim' (Barreca 2013: xxii; Lockyer and Pickering 2005: 100) but she points out that in the early days of her routine she wore a headscarf only because 'I was giving what they expected … I wouldn't say I'm a practising Muslim, well, only on Mondays' (Akbar 2006). Her observational comedy between 2002 and 2016 has provided more nuanced ideas about Asian and Muslim women. For example, she humorously described her methods of rebelling against, or resisting parental Muslim strictures during her student days, by deliberately looking for vices not listed in the Qur'an. She noted that taking ecstasy was not explicitly forbidden, so would get high and frequent gay bars with an easy conscience. In 2004 she asserted, 'I don't do any politics. Not like as in Margaret Thatcher, Tony Blair politics.... I don't do any of that, basically because I'm not interested in politics and I think it's very boring and I don't think even established comedians are going to change the world' (Lockyer and Pickering 2005: 199). However, in more recent work such as *The Kardashians Made Me Do It* and *Coconut* (2019) Mirza engages with the political topic of 'jihadi-brides', the actions of then Home Secretary Sajid Javid and the Conservative UK Government's policy on immigration. Talking about Donald Trump and Brexit she reveals 'I've never spoken about these things before. These themes relate to everybody' (Troth 2018). Mirza attributes this transition towards more overtly political material to her discovery in February 2015 that three schoolgirls from Britain had left the country to join ISIS. She writes:

> I wasn't planning on doing a show at The Edinburgh Festival in August 2015, but when this happened, I felt that I had to say something about it. I knew exactly what I thought. I felt angry, sad, shocked, surprised and confused. They've gone to join ISIS; they're doing this in the name of Islam? And they call themselves Muslim? [...] I am fed up of having to apologize for and dis-associate myself from the actions of deranged individuals who claim to share the same faith as me ... Blaming all Muslims for terrorism is like blaming all the Irish for *Riverdance*.
>
> *(Mirza 2016a)*

Mirza is contemptuous of the idea that the schoolgirls were making an informed political decision and argues that they were too young to fully grasp the social and political ramifications of what they were doing. She argues, 'they are teenagers so they want to rebel, so they piss their parents off by running off to Syria' (Mirza 2016b). She is critical of the drive for 'the West' to find a political motive behind the girls' decision, and contemptuous of liberal '*Guardian* readers' who accuse her of racism against her own 'people', For her the ISIS fighters have come to have the status of teenage pin-ups and have become objects of teenage obsession and lust:

> Why is it so outrageous to think that three teenage girls would not get on a plane to Syria for some cock? They do it on the Megabus all the time. EasyJet flights to Magaluf are full of cock-hungry girls. Raqqa is their equivalent of Magaluf except without the wet T-shirt contests and the giant cocktails. David Cameron needs to stand up in Parliament and say 'they're all going ... I don't know why, but I think it's cock ...'
>
> *(Mirza 2016b)*

Interestingly, her criticism of *Guardian* readers suggests that her political position is not necessarily aligned with left wing politics as is the case with most UK stand-ups

(Quirk 2018: 5). Rather than associating with left or right leaning party politics Mirza draws attention to, and ridicules, the grandiose gestures and ignorant, short-termist policies of politicians currently in office. Like Christie, Mirza foregrounds the absurdity of their lofty, white supremacist logic and lambasts their sense of exceptionalism and the ideology of meritocracy. To repeat the words of Lorde: 'every woman has a well-stocked arsenal of anger potentially useful against those oppressions, personal and institutional, which brought that anger into being' (Lorde 2017: 26). It is possible that, after Lorde, Mirza can be seen to be using anger as a way of renegotiating her position, possibly for her 'own growth' (23). As Chemaly has observed, 'anger drives us to demand accountability, a powerful force for political good… it is often what drives us to form creative, joyous and politically vibrant communities' (Chemaly 2019).

Mirza's most recent material directs her anger at the 'immigrant-on-immigrant' racism that saw Birmingham vote to leave the EU. She explains that 'Birmingham is full of immigrants – Indian, Pakistani, Afro-Caribbean, Irish, Ugandan, who all came over in the 60s' (Mirza 2019a). In a piece of writing entitled 'Oh What a Rotten Bunch of Coconuts' Mirza rails against the illusion of meritocracy promoted by 'the bootstraps brigade', public figures such as Margaret Thatcher, Alan Sugar and Sajid Javid; people from working class backgrounds who enjoyed sufficient social mobility to achieve wealth and/or public office (Mirza 2019b). Mirza is particularly critical of the Home Secretary Sajid Javid's decision to strip Shamima Begum, one of the British schoolgirls who travelled to Syria, of her British citizenship. When she fell pregnant for the third time Begum asked to return to the UK because she feared her third child would perish. In *The Kardashians Made Me Do It* Mirza ridiculed the idea that Begum and her classmates had made an informed political decision to join ISIS, arguing that they were coerced by adults and motivated by adolescent lust. In *Coconut*, she reserves particular censure for Javid who, as one of 'my lot', is stabbing another of 'my lot' in the back. She writes:

> along comes Uncle Sajid Javid, fresh off the boat from Rochdale … He looks like all of our uncles: smiley, jolly, bald, maybe had one too many curries. The only difference is, this one has the soul of Enoch Powell. It's the delusion that children of immigrant parents often have. Their ambition to succeed strips them of who they really are. By pandering to populism and hatred, what Javid fails to realise is that the people he's appealing to with these actions are never going to vote for a Tory Party led by him. These are the type of people who, once they've used him for his power, will want to deport him, and there won't be anyone left to support him, as he will have deported all his own people.
>
> *(Mirza 2019b)*

She employs the controversial term 'coconut' to criticise Javid. Explaining that, 'a coconut is a term used by brown people about other brown people if they are not seen to be helping the cause of brown people. It is a political term used about a dishonest, unethical, shameless servant of racists, the servant being from the same background as most of his victims' (Mirza 2019b). She acknowledges that this term could be racist, depending on the way it is used. She clarifies, 'when I refer to Sajid Javid as a coconut, I am not referring to his skin colour; I am referring to his lack of loyalties and patriotism towards a group of people from the same background' (Mirza 2019b). She regrets that instead of providing a positive role model as a high-profile Muslim, Javid has decided to 'pull the ladder up behind him to stop anyone that looks remotely like him getting a step up' (Mirza 2019b).

As a female Muslim on stage Mirza recognises that she occupies an unusual position, she acknowledges that 'just by standing on stage, I'm liberating women and some men clearly fear that means they'll lose the upper hand' (*Telegraph* 2001). As a Muslim woman there are additional religious and cultural expectations layered on top of mainstream patriarchal assumptions. Chemaly has stated, 'there is not a woman alive who does not understand that women's anger is openly reviled' (Chemaly 2018: xvi) and that 'gender-role expectations, often overlapping with racial-role expectations, dictate the degree to which we can use anger effectively in personal contexts and to participate in civic and political life' (xv). Mirza's ire is multifaceted, articulating anger at Islamphobic and racist assumptions, the illusion of meritocracy and the hesitant sensitivity of liberals. Chemaly points out, 'many of us are taught that our anger will be an imposition on others, making us irksome and unlikeable. That it will alienate loved ones or put off people we want to attract' (xvi). Mirza is aware that she has already risked alienating loved ones by taking to the stage, so her anger is an amplified act of subversion. Interviewed by Arifa Akbar in 2006 Mirza confessed that her early material, which covered religion and ethnicity, was 'part of a process she had to go through to find her own "voice"', that her work was 'very British and my humour is very British' (Akbar 2006) and yet in 2018 and 2019 we see a return to a discussion of religion as she rails against prominent British Muslims who have enjoyed sufficient social mobility to scale the echelons of power, and yet fail constituents by promoting an ideology of exceptionalism rather than multiculturalism. I want to argue that Mirza's relationship to identity politics, like Christie, has changed over time. She has altered her approach as a way of foregrounding the reductive and one-dimensional nature of the anticipated 'stage persona'. She rejected the stereotypical elements of Islam that critics saw in her early work, explaining that they did not correspond to her sense of an authentic self and moved towards observational comedy which gave her the opportunity to talk from the perspective of a Muslim woman with a subversive and idiosyncratic take on life. More recently, in response to her sense of outrage about the actions of so-called jihadi brides and the attitudes of the Conservative UK government, she has been prompted to denounce political figures and denigrate their shortcomings as public representatives. Mirza's anger is enormously useful in this context because it brings an informed perspective to bear upon issues about which the majority of people remain ignorant. She has created a Twitter hashtag #MuslimsAgainstIsis as a way of raising awareness of the complexity of the

issues in hand. Despite her insistence that 'hashtags don't change the world …
They're not going to stop terrorism' (Mirza 2016a) her anger can be seen to be
aligned with that of Lorde, it is a 'powerful source of energy serving process and
change', Lorde writes,

> when I speak of change, I do not mean a simple switch of positions or a
> temporary lessening of tensions, nor the ability to smile or feel good. I am
> speaking of a basic and radical alteration in those assumptions underlining our
> lives.
>
> *(Lorde 2017: 26)*

Mirza has moved away from deadpan observational humour in order to draw
attention to the complexities of racial and ethnic affiliation associated with the
2016 European referendum in the UK and call for ethnic minority figures to promote opportunities for members of their own communities rather than 'pulling up
the ladder' behind them.

Lolly Adefope is a London-based character comedian and actor. She has
appeared in numerous television programmes and films in the UK and the US,
such as *Rotters* (2015), *Shrill* (2019) and *This Time on Alan Partridge* (2019). Her first
solo stand-up comedy show was entitled *Lolly* (2015) and subsequent shows have
been called *Lolly 2* in 2016 and *Lolly 3* in 2018, although *Lolly 3* was cancelled due
to filming commitments. She has been taking shows to the Edinburgh Festival
Fringe since 2000. Tomsett has listed her as one of a number of notable female
comedians 'addressing empowerment', and remarks that in *Lolly 2* Adefope:

> directly responded to the way critics of her first solo show disproportionately
> focused on her identity as a Black woman. Many of the sketches in this show
> directly considered the reactions of people to her body and highlighted the
> continued marginalisation specific to the way race and gender intersect.
>
> *(Tomsett 2018: 14)*

Adefope is predominantly a character comedian; her sets comprise a number of
different characters played by Adefope with the occasional appearance of Lolly as
'herself'. Her first solo show, *Lolly* took the form of a community open-mic
night, with Adefope in character as compere Wendy Park. Other characters
included Gemma, a nervous amateur stand-up and an activist named 'X'.
Towards the end of the show Adefope appeared as herself, but an extremely shy,
nervous version, who could barely deliver her lines. As part of the show the
audience was treated to the 'accidental' broadcast of a conversation held backstage, in which Adefope, as Lolly, talks to the other characters about the difficulty
of being a Black stand-up comedian. It transpires that she is the only character to
experience difficulty; the others demur and insist they have not found it to be
such a challenge. Adefope's follow-up show, *Lolly 2,* took Fringe reviewers to
task because many of them insisted they would have liked to hear more about

race in the show and wanted more evidence of Adefope speaking in 'her own voice'. For example, Stephanie Merritt wrote:

> the show immediately becomes more interesting when we hear the character of 'Lolly' offstage, defending her performance by claiming how hard it is to be a black female comic – to which her characters all respond in their own voices that they are also (obviously) all black women and they didn't have any trouble. Adefope is, in reality, a strong and confident performer with a keen eye for skewering pretensions; I'd love to hear more from her in her own voice.
>
> *(Merritt 2015)*

Alice Jones echoes this sentiment, writing, 'As sparkling as her characters are, I'd like to have heard more from the real Lolly Adefope as she clearly has something fresh and interesting to say' (Jones 2015). Brian Donaldson similarly writes, 'The distinct racial make-up of this industry is touched upon with backstage chatter from all the acts seeping through to us, but it's here and gone before it can truly ignite a debate' (Donaldson 2015). Adefope was frustrated by the reviewers' focus upon her engagement/lack of engagement with race. She stated, 'I feel like a white comedian won't get told, "oh you never mentioned your race, but that's not what the show was about"' (Bromwich 2017). She clarifies:

> There's a moment in the show where I play myself and there's a tiny moment in the show where I make a joke about how hard it is to be a black comedian but I don't like dwell on it, because that's not what the show's about. And then I got some reviews that were like, 'she does talk about race a bit …' But it would have been more interesting to hear her talk about that a lot more, and there were other reviews which said, 'she doesn't even talk about race … and that is great, because you don't have to talk about race if you don't want to.' … But the point is, I should be able to do what I want in my comedy and if someone wrote a show about a parent dying – people wouldn't say, 'oh why didn't you talk about your other parent, and how they felt …?'
>
> *(Adefope 2016c)*

Adefope poured her frustration into *Lolly 2*, sharing slides of reviews that both congratulated her for playing down her racial identity and bemoaned the fact that she did not interrogate it further.

In terms of Double's spectrum of personae, Adefope would be recognised as a character comedian, with the occasional appearance of Adefope as 'herself'. Adefope told Sofie Hagen that she finds using characters reassuring and less exposing. She admits, 'I'm so desperate for people to like me' that she finds it intimidating to go on stage as herself. According to Bromwich:

> Using characters gives Adefope a way of expressing anger and addressing politically charged subjects such as Brexit and #OscarsSoWhite at one step

removed. [She states] 'If I was doing standup I would worry that someone would think I was being preachy, whereas with a character, it always tends to be the opposite of what I think. You can get away with things.'

(Bromwich 2017)

Adefope's apprehension about being perceived as 'preachy' echoes Christie's sense that she must perform 'trickery' and 'hide' serious elements within a comedic framework (Lawson 2014). Furthermore it tallies with Chemaly's assertion that anger is strictly gendered. Chemaly writes, '[a]nger in women is still considered a sign of mental or hormonal imbalance, whereas in men it is perceived as "normal" and associated with masculine control, leadership, authority and competence (Chemaly 2019). Adefope recognises the taboo of being seen to be an 'angry black woman'. She says,

> I've seen the way people look at people who are angry and black, I'm like, I'm not going to be like that. I'm going to be this funny, cool girl who doesn't do that. Now I'm more willing to be angry but I have to show that, 'yes, I'm aware of the angry black girl stereotype and I'm not doing that, I'm just angry'.

(Adefope 2016c)

For Adefope the issue of stage persona and anger dovetails because the figure of the 'angry black woman' is a readily available stereotype for critics to apply. As in the case of Christie, Jones, Mirza and Almas, Adefope expresses frustration that the cardinal rule of having an easily recognisable stage persona means that she is constructed as a one-dimensional figure and liable to be associated with misogynistic and racist stereotypes. In addition to drawing on her experience for *Lolly 2* she has worked with the BBC to create a short performance as part of BBC3's *Top Ten* online series (Adefope 2016d). The short film is entitled *Top Ten: the Conflicting Versions of Lolly Adefope*. It begins with Adefope holding a microphone and talking directly to camera as if 'naked' stand-up. She delivers a deliberate mis-fire: 'Isn't it funny how girls sit down to pee, but boys never call me back?' We subsequently see and hear from four different versions of Adefope, which I will refer to as LOLLY 1, LOLLY 2, LOLLY 3 AND LOLLY 4. We hear the voice of a male commentator off-camera. The commentator announces the different 'versions' of Adefope in a dramatic, declamatory tone and the audience is presented with a close-up of her reaction.

> COMMENTATOR: The Lolly Adefope who has just been asked why there isn't a white history month ...
> LOLLY 1: Phfft – what?
> COMMENTATOR: The Lolly Adefope who feels the need to talk about race in her stand up ...
> LOLLY 1: What?

COMMENTATOR: The Lolly Adefope who can't just see herself as a human being rather than as black?
LOLLY 1: Well, that's just ridiculous, I mean, who is writing these? Because obviously the way that society sees me is going to affect the way I see myself.
COMMENTATOR: The Lolly …
LOLLY 1: … don't interrupt me – I was going to make a really astute point and you just cut me off. Just a bit rude, that's all.
COMMENTATOR: The Lolly Adefope who learned not to see colour –
LOLLY 1: Well – no, that's not what I meant …
LOLLY 2: Well, what did you mean?
LOLLY 1: Well, I mean that you can't just ignore issues of race because …
LOLLY 3: *Enters eating a bowl of cereal*
LOLLY 2: Comedy should just be comedy
We see four different Lollys in a row. They all wear different outfits, one leans on a microphone stand
LOLLY 1: Please don't talk with your mouth full
LOLLY 2, 3 AND 4: Oooooh!
LOLLY 4: Michael McIntyre NEVER talks about race …
Voices begin to overlap
LOLLY 1: Well, I should be able to talk about it if I want, or not talk about it if I want …
LOLLY 3: *with mouth full of cereal* No – it's boring!

(Adefope 2016d)

The presence of four different versions of Adefope and the image of four Black female stand-ups on screen together works as a highly effective way of critiquing the lack of diversity in the UK stand-up scene and the need for nuance in relation to stand up personae. This works in contradiction to Quirk's observation that in 'theory … to be successful, you need a very clearly defined stage persona' (Quirk 2015: 128). In conversation Adefope has suggested that she 'ventriloquises' other people's words for comic effect, collecting accents and idiosyncrasies of people she meets. One of her popular characters is Damien Speck, a workshop leader who specialises in 'verbal sensitivity'. For this character Adefope adopts a lowered voice with a speech impediment and has Damien make ludicrous suggestions about how audience members might temper their speech in order to be politically correct:

My name is Damien Speck, specialising in verbal sensitivity … making sure you guys feel comfortable saying what you need to say. No careless whispers. Has anyone heard of 'Merry Christmas and a Happy New Year'? Has anyone heard of these words before? Has anyone heard 'brain storm'? Can anyone tell me what they have in common? … [what they have in common is] you *can't say them*. What you *can* say is 'Happy Winterval' or 'thought seizure' – instead of brain storm …

[In order to be sensitive] Get to know your foreigner friends – tell them you like their hair, clothes, etc. Ask them if they like living in London or if they prefer to go home? *Do* ask out the black girl at work that you flirted with and tell her that you're really excited because you've never had sex with a black girl before.

People say, 'what next?' You need a handbook to know what to say these days. What next? Black Hermione? They have actually hired a coloured woman to play Hermione Grainger in *Harry Potter and the Cursed Child*. Why not? If you had goblins etc … why not a black woman?

(Adefope 2019)

Speck represents an ill-informed racist who does more harm than good in his attempts to draw people's attention to the performativity of language. He stands as an excellent example of a character that gives Adefope license to cover politically sensitive material at one remove. Adefope's other characters are often equally ignorant and tend to be rather self-obsessed. At a recent fundraiser event *Comedy for Community* at the Leicester Square Theatre, she presented a character called Shelley McGirk, the CEO of Twinkle Stars talent agency. McGirk takes the form of a child-like, ebullient character who betrays her responsibility to others by taking centre stage. She asks who in the audience can sing or dance but goes on to eclipse any budding talent with a virtuoso rendition of a pop song. A similar character appears in *Carpool Share* in which Adefope apes James Cordon's well-known *Carpool Karaoke* (Adefope 2016a).[1] Adefope collects a member of a fictional boy band, who joins her in the car on the understanding that she will ask questions about his career and they will sing along to one of his songs. As the journey progresses the band member becomes frustrated because Adefope hogs the limelight, insisting that she take the solos and relegating him to harmonies. Towards the end it transpires that she has confused him with a member of a different boy band. I include these characters in order to emphasise the variety of Adefope's oeuvre. Her work is increasingly politicised as she becomes more comfortable expressing her anger (Adefope 2016c). I realise that by focusing upon Adefope's engagement with race I am potentially repeating the preoccupations of the Edinburgh Festival critics, but feel she stands as a fascinating example of a figure who is, on the one hand, dealing with her frustrations in a palatable and non-threatening way and on the other articulating frustration about limited identity positions available to stand-up comedians. Like Christie she amplifies examples of insensitive and thoughtless behaviour and renders it ridiculous. Her process of containing and managing frustration is striking, she explicitly states that she feels she must temper her anger in order not to appear 'preachy' or to fall into the archetype of 'angry Black woman'.

June 2015 saw Adefope curating an evening of comedy in North London with six female stand-ups. She borrowed Andrew Lawrence's phrase *Women Posing as Comedians* for its title. The phrase came from an online tirade by Lawrence, a comedian who posted incendiary comments about women and 'ethnic' comedians on his Facebook page in October 2014. Lawrence expressed frustration at being rejected by TV panel shows, speculating that he was not invited on to the shows because he did not help them to meet their diversity quota. As part of his tirade he expressed sympathy for UKIP policies on immigration and criticised the programmes he felt promoted anti UK sentiment. He wrote:

> Can't help but notice increasingly, a lot of 'political' comedians cracking cheap and easy gags about UKIP, to the extent that it's got hack, boring and lazy very quickly. Particularly too much moronic, back-slapping on panel shows like *Mock The Week* where aging, balding, fat men, ethnic comedians and women-posing-as-comedians, sit congratulating themselves on how enlightened they are about the fact that UKIP are ridiculous and pathetic.
>
> *(Lawrence 2014)[2]*

In her *Made of Human* podcast Hagen revealed online searches threw up a connection between Lawrence and Adefope with evidence of fans setting up a petition to arrange for Adefope to interview Lawrence. Adefope has said,

> I'd love to have a chat with him … I'm like, 'I don't get it mate? What are you on about? Let's talk about it.' Because it's so unfair to be like 'he's just crazy' because then he'll say 'oh these lefty people don't listen to me, they just say I'm crazy and dismiss it', which is a fair point to make.
>
> *(Hagen 2018)*

In 2015 Adefope incorporated Lawrence's material into stand-up routines, choosing to create a character that quoted him verbatim rather than alter his words. She revealed,

> all of the stuff I said was just quotes from him. And there wasn't anything made up, because we were going to make it a controversial character saying all these weird things and then put in some stuff that he had said, but I thought that was a bit unfair – as if you're just exaggerating it now. So I said loads of stuff that he said because I thought he can't get annoyed because I'm just quoting back what he said and he then should realise how mad it is. I thought I was being really tame!
>
> *(Hagen 2018)*

Adefope sets out to puncture the self-importance of racist misogynists and highlight their absurdity by repeating their words in a different context. This stands as an excellent example of the therapeutic potential of both humour and anger. As Barreca has written, '[h]umor can redeem a situation otherwise lost to anger, pain, frustration, or silence; making a story out of what happened to you can offer a second chance when you didn't really get a first' (Barreca 2013: 11). Adefope's anger manifests itself very differently from that of Christie and Mirza because she largely remains in character and uses the voice of the character to render offensive material absurd. She controls the context in which offensive words are uttered and by remaining in character maintains a critical distance. She deliberately puts forward a wide range of characters, even different versions of herself, in a way that highlights the desperate need for nuance, diversity and complexity in comedic personae. She resists the theory that a stand-up persona should be easy to recognise by presenting a range of characters embodying differing attitudes and ideological positions.

My final example is that of Hannah Gadsby. Gadsby is an Australian comedian born in Tasmania. In addition to working as a stand-up comedian she is a writer, actor and television presenter. She has been working in comedy since 2007 and has appeared at the Adelaide Fringe Festival, Melbourne International Comedy Festival, New York Soho Playhouse, the Soho Theatre, London and the Edinburgh Fringe Festival. She toured internationally with solo stand-up shows *Nanette* (2017–2018) and *Douglas* (2019). She played the character of 'Hannah' in *Please Like Me* between 2013 and 2016 and recorded *Hannah Gadsby: Arts Clown* for BBC Radio 4 in 2015. She has won numerous awards, including Best Emerging Comedy Award at the Adelaide Fringe Festival in 2007; the Barry Award at the Melbourne International Comedy Festival, 2017; and Edinburgh Festival Fringe Comedy Award in 2017. She appears on stage as 'herself' and her work relies on observational humour. She draws upon her experience of growing up a lesbian in Tasmania, foregrounding the fact that until 1997 homosexuality was illegal. She graduated with a BA in Art History and Curatorship in 2003 and draws upon her knowledge of art history in routines. According to Luke Buckmaster, *Nanette* represents a 'white hot, blistering performance. [It] oozes emotion, like a raw and weeping wound, but has the strength of mind and a canny comedian behind it' (Buckmaster 2018). Chris Rattan calls Nanette 'genius', explaining that 'the structure and intent of the hour-long set works so outside of what comedy does and works so well' (Rattan 2018). Aja Romano reports,

> *Nanette* has been making headlines for being difficult to watch, for making audiences uncomfortable. But what makes *Nanette* difficult to watch is what makes it hugely significant: Gadsby uses her identity – the reality of her physical presence … to deconstruct what it means to be a comedian who has been failed by comedy.
>
> *(Romano 2018)*

In *Nanette* Gadsby shares her teenage experience of realising she was gay and internalising the homophobia that was the norm in the run-up to the 1997 referendum. The first 17 minutes of *Nanette* unfold according to conventional rules of stand-up comedy. She puts herself forward as the butt of jokes and pokes fun at conservative boors. However, partway through the show she begins to deconstruct the rhetorical apparatus of stand-up comedy. She acknowledges that her career to date has depended upon self-deprecation and explains she must 'quit' comedy because she can no longer make herself the butt of the joke. The remainder of the show takes on a more serious tone. Gadsby details the comedic techniques she has historically used to temper the truth about her experience as a young lesbian. She talks about building and dissipating comedic tension, telling the audience 'that's your last joke' and becoming unashamedly emotional as she charts the toll punitive violence has taken upon her sense of wellbeing. For Sarah Balkin, Gadsby's persona creates a 'problem' for the audience because it 'both presents and truncates her traumatic experience' (Balkin 2018). Balkin suggests that 'Gadsby also casts herself as akin to Sara Ahmed's "feminist killjoy," a spoilsport figure whose unhappiness positions her as a source of tension' (Balkin 2018).

Prior to *Nanette* Gadsby customarily created material out of her experience of being a supposedly humourless lesbian art historian. However, as in the case of Mirza, Christie and Adefope she experienced frustration at the limitations of being confined to a narrow, one-dimensional persona. She stated that she needed to retire from comedy, 'because the only way I can tell my truth and put tension in the room is with anger' (Gadsby 2017). Much of Gadsby's material in *Nanette* is built upon people's expectations of how she should behave as a gay woman. Much of the pressure, she reveals, comes from the gay community itself. She defines herself as a 'quiet soul' whose 'favourite sound in the whole world is the sound of a teacup finding its place on a saucer', Her temperance is at odds with the 'busy' gay community celebrating at the Sydney Gay and Lesbian Mardi Gras. She recalls watching the celebration on television as a teenager and it being 'my first introduction to my people', She wondered at their confidence, 'flaunting their lifestyle in a parade!' After expressing surprise at the drive to 'dance and party' she sardonically observes, 'the pressure on my people to express our identity and pride through the metaphor of party is very intense' (Gadsby 2017). She mentions two other incidents with gay audience members, which make her impatient with the expectation that she will represent and speak *for* and *on behalf of* the gay community. She recalls an incident when a lesbian audience member complained her routine had not been sufficiently targeted at a gay audience, that there was 'not enough lesbian content', to which Gadsby sardonically observed, 'I was on stage the whole time!' Balkin observes that 'with this joke, Gadsby seamlessly juxtaposes two paradoxical but interrelated ideas: the centrality of her identity to her comedy, and the inability of comedy to ever fully address the complexity of that identity' (Balkin 2018). The second incident involved a message she received via Facebook, which said 'You owe it to your community to come out as transgender', She continues:

All jokes aside, I really do want to do my best by my community. I really do. But that was new information to me. I'm not … I don't identify as transgender. I don't. I mean, I'm clearly 'gender-not-normal', but … I don't think even lesbian is the right identity fit for me, I really don't. I may as well come out now. I identify … as tired. I'm just tired.

(Gadsby 2017)

Like Mirza, who expresses frustration at being labelled an 'Asian comedian', Gadsby criticises her supposed identity as 'the new gay comedian', As with the other comedians under discussion Gadsby experiences anger at the conservatism of a discipline that grooms its participants to reveal only a limited part of their personality and hone it so it clearly conforms to a narrow hegemonic worldview.

As mentioned above, 17 minutes into *Nanette* Gadsby effects a change in tone, causing the performance to shift from one of self-deprecation to one of anger. Objects of wrath include the expectation that she be self-deprecating about her sexuality and reinforce lesbianism as marginal. Within feminist comedy circles self-deprecation is a widely discussed topic, with scholars such as Tomsett and Gilbert arguing that self-deprecatory humour can be 'a potentially subversive rhetoric' and that it will 'always simultaneously both reinforce and challenge hegemonic views of women and their bodies' (Gilbert 1997: 327; Tomsett 2018: 10). Gilbert has observed that the majority of critics believe self-deprecatory humour to reinforce stereotypes and reinscribe patriarchy. She writes, 'In this sense, female comics, like so many others perform their marginality in an act simultaneously oppressive (by using demeaning stereotypes) and transgressively interrogating those very stereotypes through humourous discourse' (Gilbert 1997: 318). Gadsby directly acknowledges her use of self-deprecating humour. Her self-reflexive approach names and identifies certain comedic tropes and techniques throughout the show. She tells the audience:

> I built a career out of self-deprecating humor. That's what I've built my career on. And … I don't want to do that anymore. Because, do you understand, do you understand what self-deprecation means when it comes from somebody who already exists in the margins? It's not humility. It's humiliation. I put myself down in order to speak, in order to seek permission … to speak. And I simply will not do that anymore. Not to myself or anybody who identifies with me.
>
> *(Gadsby 2017)*

Both in the live and recorded version of *Nanette* Gadsby became visibly upset when expressing anger. Her voice became choked and she appeared to be on the verge of tears. Her frustration appears to stem from her understanding that, as a comic, she should rein in her anger and focus upon more light-hearted issues. She acknowledges that in earlier shows she fulfilled the persona of 'new gay comic' and told 'lots of cool jokes about homophobia', only to sarcastically qualify this with: 'that really solved … that problem. Tick!' (Gadsby 2017). She articulates her sense that being a female comic requires a dysfunctional attitude towards one's own identity. She says, 'I think part of my problem is comedy has suspended me in a perpetual state of adolescence. The way I've been telling that [coming out] story is through jokes.' She acknowledges her anger as doubly out of place. Firstly she should not be articulating anger as part of a comedy show and secondly, as a woman, she should avoid asserting a position of anger. She says:

Look, I am angry. I apologize. I do, I apologize. I know … I know there's a few people in the room going, 'Now, look … I think … she's lost control of the tension'. That's correct. I went on it a bit there. So, I'm not very experienced in controlling anger. It's not my place to be angry on a comedy stage. I'm meant to be doing … self-deprecating humor. People feel safer when men do the angry comedy. They're the kings of the genre. When I do it, I'm a miserable lesbian, ruining all the fun and the banter.

(Gadsby 2017)

Gadsby affirms Chemaly's sense that anger is socially regulated. For Chemaly, 'these regulations are a powerful way to enforce inequality and buttress status quo hierarchies' (Chemaly 2019). Traister is in accord when she writes, 'anger works for men in ways that it does not for women' (Traister 2018: xxii). The turning point in *Nanette* revolves around the return to an anecdote Gadsby shares at the beginning of the show. Unbeknownst to the audience she has cut the anecdote short, leaving it at a fortuitously comic moment, withholding information that would render the anecdote tragic. The story relates to her growing up in a small Tasmanian town and chatting to a woman in a café whose name was Nanette. Nanette's boyfriend had seen them chatting at a bus stop and mistaken Gadsby for a man. He had then, as the initial version of the story goes, 'almost beaten [her] up because he thought [she] was cracking on to his girlfriend', He became jealous and started to push Gadsby, shouting 'fuck off, you fucking faggot!' Nanette stepped in to explain that Gadsby was, in actual fact, a woman, causing him to stop pushing her and exclaim, 'Oh, I'm so sorry. I don't hit women!' (Gadsby 2017). Gadsby tells the audience how she would customarily leave the story there, and omit the real ending in order to maximise its comedic value. She said, 'I know how to balance that to get the laugh in the right place. But in order to balance the tension in the room with that story I couldn't tell that story as it actually happened.' What actually happened was that Nanette's boyfriend returned and said, 'Oh, I get it. You're a lady faggot. I'm allowed to beat the shit out of you.' He proceeded to violently attack her and leave her badly injured. Nobody came to help her. She did not report the attack to the police because, she confesses, 'I thought that was all I was worth' (Gadsby 2017). Gadsby congratulates herself on having constructed a strong anecdote from this story saying, 'It was very funny, I made a lot of people laugh about his ignorance, and the reason I could do this was because I'm very good at this job. I actually am pretty good at controlling the tension.' Gadsby tells the audience that she needs to retire from comedy because she can no longer bear to make herself and her sexuality the butt of the joke. Drawing upon material from her own life has proved traumatic and counter-productive because she took her story of coming out and:

froze an incredibly informative experience at its trauma point and I sealed it off into jokes. And that story became a routine, and through repetition, that joke version fused with my actual memory of what happened. But unfortunately that joke version was not nearly sophisticated enough to help me undo the damage done to me in reality.

(Gadsby 2017)

Gadsby persists in delivering the amended version of this routine because although 'the damage done to me is real and debilitating [and] I will never flourish ... I want my story ... heard.' For Gadsby,

anger is tension. It is a toxic, infectious ... tension. And it knows no other purpose than to spread blind hatred, and I want no part of it ... Stories hold our cure. Laughter is just the honey that sweetens bitter medicine.

(Gadsby 2017)

Despite Gadsby's reservations about the toxicity of anger, the process of articulating her frustration with the rhetoric of stand-up comedy can be seen to align with Lorde's notion of 'a well-stocked arsenal of anger', She explicitly calls out white men, telling them to 'pull their socks up' and reject the mainstream culture of male supremacy and homophobia. Lorde writes, 'anger is loaded with information and energy' and that learning 'anger's usefulness' can be a vital tool for 'survival' (Lorde 2017: 31). As Traister observes women's anger, although castigated, has 'often borne substantive change, alterations to the nation's rules and practices, its very fabric' (Traister 2018: xx). By commenting self-reflexively on her work Gadsby denaturalises the process of framing marginalised subjects as the butt of the joke, whilst reflecting upon the irony that her career has been founded upon just that. By embedding a treatise upon equality and mutual respect within a comedy routine she demonstrates how normative humour can work to sediment some belief systems as natural and normal and others as deviant. She plays out Gilbert's sense that 'in order to make someone the "target" or "butt" of a joke, it is necessary to make that person a thing, an object; only then is it permissible to laugh at him/her' (Gilbert 1997: 324).

In this chapter I have analysed the work of Bridget Christie, Shazia Mirza, Lolly Adefope and Hannah Gadsby in order to contemplate strategies for communicating and managing anger. These stand-ups have become drawn towards, or have drawn upon, anger for a number of different reasons. Christie spoke of her sense that she would be taken more seriously if she appeared as a male character in her early work. She ventriloquised her frustration through the voices of an ant and donkey before speaking as 'herself' in *A Bic for Her*. Mirza has long been associated with a 'deadpan' style of delivery, which indicates she deliberately forged a persona of resignation rather than one of open anger. The tone of her material changed in 2015 when she encountered news coverage of three British schoolgirls who took the decision to fly to Syria in order to join ISIS fighters. Adefope has openly talked about her apprehension at being perceived as angry and states that she uses characters in order to be able distance herself from the more incendiary parts of her material. When she does draw upon anger she states she feels compelled to do it in a self-reflexive manner that demonstrates an awareness of the stereotype of 'the angry black woman' (Adefope 2016a). In *Nanette* Gadsby explicitly talks about anger and her refusal to compound the marginalisation of lesbian culture by making it the butt of her jokes. The artists have all expressed frustration at the industry imperative to forge an easily recognisable, one-dimensional persona and worked to ensure that their characters complicate rather than reinforce stereotypical assumptions about female comedians. They each demonstrate self-awareness about modes of self-presentation and the range of behaviours they are permitted to display. Adefope has joked, 'it's exhausting, really hard being me' as outlined by her sense that if she played an angry character she had to demonstrate that she was doing so in a knowing way (Adefope 2016a). Christie has confessed that she uses 'trickery' in order to 'hide serious bits within a comic framework' (Lawson 2014) and Gadsby that she felt compelled to leave comedy because 'the only way I can tell my truth and put tension in the room is with anger' (Balkin 2018). These performers experiment with taboo behaviour in order to resist limitations imposed upon female comedians. Lorde would approve of their application of anger. They have used it as positive force and drawn upon their personal arsenal to 'grow' and campaign for 'change' (Lorde 2017: 29). They have capitalised on its positive capacity to act as a 'powerful tonic', a 'communicative tool' and a 'balm to listener and readers struggling with their own subsumed vexations' (Traister 2018: xxvii). Mirza, Gadsby, Adefope and Christie appropriate negative associations of anger and render them positive, generative and productive. To be an angry woman in a white, patriarchal, heteronormative context equates with being perceived as a failure. Angry women are castigated for being unable to retain a sense of equanimity and colloquially told to 'calm down dear', These comedians repurpose failure by railing against double standards and garnering energy and a sense of motivation from their anger. They harness anger in an imaginative, self-reflexive manner in order to draw attention to the need to adjust expectations for successful comedy and forge a supportive community. They do this whilst remaining mindful of the dangers of reinscribing reductive stereotypes. As comedians they speak to a constituency and have the potential to use anger as a catalyst for change.

As cited in my introduction to this chapter, comedy represents an ideal medium through which to explore perceptions of failure. Quirk has argued that observations about social 'dysfunction' represent a key component of stand-up comedy and Barreca has spoken of the 'profound sense of resilience' required by the stand-up comedian (Quirk 2015: 140; Barreca 2013: 12). The accepted practice of 'heckling' means that performers must acquire the ability to not only shrug off criticism, but generate an amusing riposte on the spur of the moment. Artists who use self-deprecating comedy find themselves in the unusual position of both inviting contempt and warding off criticism. The artists in this chapter can be seen to be repurposing failure in a number of ways. Firstly, they cite or 'call out' their experience of being rendered marginal or lacking in relation to the white, middle-class generic male subject. Secondly, they incorporate elements of self-deprecation into their work but use this to foreground the ludicrous standards of behaviour women are expected to meet. Thirdly, they garner negative associations of female anger and exploit them for comedic ends. They use indignation as a starting point for interrogating the double standards of advertising executives, misogynistic celebrities, racist politicians and homophobic aggressors and deploy their sense of injustice and anger to identify the problem and call for change. The artists cited in this chapter have much in common with artists cited in companion chapters. They describe the experience of being othered by hegemonic society and draw upon this experience to make comedic and subversive observations. Like the artists in Chapter two they employ irony and self-reflexivity to acknowledge and comment upon their anger. Gadsby can be seen to have much in common with the artists in Chapter three who employ performance-making as an act of self-care. In *Nanette* she states her intention to retire from stand-up in order to preserve her mental health. The comedians share several practices with artists cited in Chapters four and five, citing a profound frustration with the practice of identity labelling and ridiculing the expectation that a simplistic, one-dimensional persona will suffice. Within this chapter the negative emotion of anger and the articulation of a sense of failure can be seen to contribute to Muñoz and Bailes sense that failure is 'generative' and ultimately optimistic (Muñoz 2009; Bailes 2011). It also plays out Lorde's sense that like self-care, comedic anger can be used as a weapon against societal oppression and be used as part of 'an arsenal' of tools to be used against both 'personal and institutional' oppressions (Lorde 2017: 26). All of these artists can be understood to repurpose failure because they respond to the experience of feeling negated in a positive way: they identify and name their source of oppression; they generate powerful material out of the experience of anger and call for societal change.

Notes

1 *Carpool Karaoke*, regular feature on *The Late Late Show* with James Cordon, first broadcast 2015, based on Red Nose Day sketch in 2011 with George Michael.
2 UKIP – the UK Independence Party. A Eurosceptic, anti-immigration political party who campaigned for the UK to leave Europe in 2016.

Bibliography

Adefope, Lolly (2015) *Lolly*. Touring Production.
Adefope, Lolly (2016a) *Carpool Share*, directed and produced by Ainsley Cannon. Available at: https://vimeo.com/178524331 (accessed 10 July 2019).
Adefope, Lolly (2016b) *Lolly 2*. Touring Production.
Adefope, Lolly (2016c) 'Anger with Lolly Adefope', *The Guilty Feminist*, Episode 14. Recorded at Kings Place, London, 28 June, presented by Sofie Hagen and Deborah Frances-White. Available at: https://guiltyfeminist.libsyn.com/14-anger-with-lolly-adefope (accessed 10 July 2019).

Adefope, Lolly (2016d) 'Top Ten: The Conflicting Versions of Lolly Adefope', BBC 3 online programme in collaboration with Mixital, commissioned by Tilusha Ghelani. Available at: https://www.bbc.co.uk/bbcthree/clip/4a1c4d1e-68d1-4fa7-a1b4-dc88db9f 2c27 (accessed 28 June 2019).

Adefope, Lolly (2019) *Comedy for Community*, Leicester Square Theatre, 20 May.

Akbar, Arifa (2006) 'Why Shazia Mirza Wants to Shake Off Her "Muslim Comic Label"', *The Independent*, 28 October. Available at: https://www.independent.co.uk/arts-enterta inment/theatre-dance/news/why-shazia-mirza-wants-to-shake-off-her-muslim-comic-la bel-421942.html (accessed 4 July 2019).

Almas, Isma (2019) *Shazia Mirza and Isma Almas Work in Progress*, Retro Bar, 17 June.

Ant, Adam and Marco Pirroni (1980) *Antmusic* by Adam and the Ants, released in the UK by Epic Records. Produced by Chris Hughes.

Aston, Elaine (2007) 'A Good Night Out for the Girls', in *Cool Britannia? British Political Drama in the 1990s*, Rebecca D'Monte and Graham Saunders (eds.), Basingstoke: Palgrave Macmillan, pp. 114–132.

Bailes, Sara-Jane (2011) *Performance Theatre and the Poetics of Failure*, Abingdon: Routledge.

Baker, Vicky (2015) 'Stand Up to Taboos', *Index on Censorship*, 44(4), 8–10.

Balkin, Sarah (2018) 'The Killjoy Comedian: Hannah Gadsby's Nanette', presentation at IFTR Conference, Belgrade, 9–3 July.

Barreca, Gina (2013) *They Used to Call Me Snow White but I Drifted: Women's Strategic Humour*, Hanover: University Press of New England.

Bromwich, Kathryn (2017) 'Interview: Rising Stars of 2017: Comedian Lolly Adefope', *The Guardian*, 1 January. Available at: https://www.theguardian.com/stage/2017/jan/01/ rising-stars-2017-comedian-lolly-adefope (accessed 10 July 2019).

Buckmaster, Luke (2018) 'Nanette review: Hannah Gadsby's Brilliant Netflix Special Is Going to Set Fire to the Internet', *Daily Review*, 17 June. Available at: https://dailyre view.com.au/nanette-review-hannah-gadsbys-brilliant-netflix-special-going- set-fire-internet/75701/(accessed 10 July 2019).

Camden People's Theatre (2019) 'Calm Down, Dear 2019'. Available at: https://www.cp theatre.co.uk/wp_theatre_season/calm-down-dear-2019/ (accessed 10 July 2019).

Casely-Hayford, Alice (2018) 'Lolly Adefope On Returning To Edinburgh Fringe Festival With Her Brand New Show', *Vogue.co.uk*, 21 June. Available at: https://www.vogue.co.uk/article/ lolly-adefope-interview-2018 (accessed 28 August 2019).

Chemaly, Soraya (2018) *Rage Becomes Her: the Power of Women's Anger*, New York: Atria Books.

Chemaly, Soraya (2019) 'How Women and Minorities Are Claiming Their Right to Rage', *The Guardian*, 11 May. Available at: https://www.theguardian.com/lifeandstyle/2019/may/ 11/women-and-minorities-claiming-right-to-rage (accessed 9 July 2019).

Chortle (2014) 'Andrew Lawrence: I'm the Target of a Witch Hunt', *Chortle.co.uk*. Available at: https://www.chortle.co.uk/news/2014/10/28/21196/andrew_lawrence:_im_the_target_of_ a_witch_hunt (accessed 28 August 2019).

Christie, Bridget (2013) *A Bic for Her*. Touring Production. Netflix Special of *Bridget Christie: Stand Up for Her*. Available at: https://www.netflix.com/watch/80179907?trackId= 13752289&tctx=0%2C0%2Cb6210b976d9e2334d738f1936792b8424f7c24f0%3A0636c1 72c458ddeb0edb2cd964568d6985e10d56%2C%2C (accessed 28 August 2019).

Christie, Bridget (2014) 'Bridget Christie Interviews Leyla Hussein about FGM (Extended Edit)', *YouTube.com*, 5 July. Facial Egg Production. Available at: https://www.youtube. com/watch?v=Ja-Zu_pph0Q (accessed 29 August 2019).

Christie, Bridget (2015) *A Book for Her*, London: Penguin Random House,

Christie, Bridget (2018) 'Bridget Christie 2018-05-16 Radcliffe and Maconie [Couch-tripper]', *YouTube.com*. Available at: https://www.youtube.com/watch?v=5XiE985S6Qg (28 August 2019).

Christie, Bridget (2019) *Work in Progress*, Battersea Arts Centre, 10 July.

Dickinson, Peter, Anne Higgins, Paul Matthew St. Pierre, Diana Solomon and Sean Zwa-german (eds.) (2013) *Women and Comedy: History, Theory Practice*, Maryland: Farleigh Dickinson University Press.

Donaldson, Brian (2015) 'An Intriguing Character Show About Comedy and Race Stops Short', *The List*, 16 August. Available at: https://edinburghfestival.list.co.uk/article/73608-lolly-adefope/ (accessed 10 July 2019).

Double, Oliver (2014) *Getting the Joke: The Inner Workings of Stand-up Comedy*, Second Edition, London: Bloomsbury Methuen.

Gadsby, Hannah (2015) *Arts Clown*, BBC Radio 4 Extra, produced by Claire Jones.

Gadsby, Hannah (2017) *Nanette*, Touring Production. Netflix Special of *Nanette*. Available at: https://www.netflix.com/watch/80233611?trackId=13752289&tctx=0%2C0%2C11fa b1abfd5726fb222573e9707248605b3ebec4%3A624024d2b4d59782b1d5b0b53a045c3072 df4fe0%2C%2C (accessed 28 August 2019).

Gibbons, Neil and Rob Gibbons (dir.) (2019) *This Time with Alan Partridge*, BBC 1 Television Programme.

Gilbert, Joanne (1997) 'Performing Marginality: Comedy, Identity and Cultural Critique', *Text and Performance Quarterly*, 17, 317–330.

Hagen, Sofie (2016) 'Anger with Lolly Adefope', *The Guilty Feminist*, Episode 14. Recorded at Kings Place, London, 28 June, presented by Sofie Hagen and Deborah Frances-White. Available at: https://guiltyfeminist.libsyn.com/14-anger-with-lolly-adefope (accessed 10 July 2019).

Hagen, Sofie (2018) 'Lolly Adefope Interviewed by Sofie Hagen, February 2017', *Made of Human* podcasts. Available at: https://podtail.com/en/podcast/made-of-human-with-sofie-ha gen/76-lolly-adefope-what-if-you-don-t-like-me/ (accessed 29 June 2019).

Hitchens, Christopher (2007) 'Why Women Aren't Funny', *Vanity Fair*, January. Available at: https://www.vanityfair.com/culture/2007/01/hitchens200701 (accessed 28 August 2019).

Jamieson, Teddy (2016) 'Crisis Comedy: Fringe Star Bridget Christie on Laughing in the Face of Brexit Catastrophe', *The Herald*, 7 August. Available at: https://www.heraldscotla nd.com/arts_ents/14667006.crisis-comedy-fringe-star-bridget-christie-on-laugh ing-in-the-face-of-the-brexit-catastrophe/ (accessed 15 July 2019).

Jones, Alice (2015) 'Lolly, Edinburgh Fringe review: A Talent Show Spoof Shows Off This Rising Star's Skills', *The Independent*, 17 August. Available at: https://www.independent. co.uk/arts-entertainment/edinburgh-festival/lolly-edinburgh-fringe-review-a-talent-show-spoof-shows-off-this-rising-stars-skills-10458656.html (accessed 10 July 2019).

Jones, Rosie (2019) *Comedy for Community*, Leicester Square Theatre, 20 May.

Lansley, Oliver (2015) *Rotters*, Sky Arts Sitcom, directed by Gordon Anderson.

Lawrence, Andrew (2014) 'Andrew Lawrence 25 October 2014', *Facebook*. Available at: https://www.facebook.com/andrewlawrencecomedy/posts/cant-help-but-notice-increasingly-a-lot-political-comedians-cracking-cheap-and-e/10154749255720253/ (accessed 28 August 2019).

Lawson, Mark (2014) 'Interview: Bridget Christie: It's Trickery, Hiding Serious Bits Within A Comic Framework', *The Guardian*, 29 August. Available at: https://www.theguardian. com/culture/2014/aug/29/bridget-christie-trickery-hiding-serious-bits-comic-framework (accessed 15 July 2019).

Lockyer, Sharon and Michael Pickering (2005) 'Breaking the Mould: Conversations with Omid Djalili and Shazia Mirza', in *Beyond a Joke: The Limits of Humour*, London: Palgrave Macmillan, pp. 98–125.

Lorde, Audre (2017) 'Uses of Anger: Women Responding to Racism', in *The Master's Tools Will Never Dismantle the Master's House*, London: Penguin, pp. 22–35.

Merritt, Stephanie (2015) 'Edinburgh Festival 2015 Comedy Review – Lolly Adefope, Aisling Bea and Joseph Morpurgo Among the Highlights', *The Guardian*, 9 August. Available at: https://www.theguardian.com/stage/2015/aug/09/edinburgh-festival-2015-comedy-review-lolly-adefope-aisling-bea-joseph-morpurgo (accessed 10 July 2019).

Mirza, Shazia (2016a) 'If You Want to Know the Truth, Read the Qur'an, Not The Daily Mail', *The New Internationalist*, 25 January. Available at: https://newint.org/blog/2016/01/25/shazia-mirza-real-faith/(accessed 29 August 2019).

Mirza, Shazia (2016b) '*The Kardashians Made Me Do It* Extract', Dalkey Book Festival. Available at: http://www.dalkeybookfestival.org/podcast-shazia-mirza-kardashians-made/ (accessed 4 July 2019).

Mirza, Shazia (2019a) *Coconut*, Touring Production.

Mirza, Shazia (2019b) 'Oh What a Rotten Bunch of Coconuts', *Unbound.com*, 8 April. Available at: https://unbound.com/boundless/2019/04/08/oh-what-a-rotten-bunch-of-coconuts/(accessed 5 July 2019).

Mizejewski, Linda (2014) *Pretty/Funny: Women Comedians and Body Politics*, Austin: University of Texas Press.

Muñoz, Jose (2009) *Cruising Utopia: The Then and There of Queer Futurity*, New York: New York University Press.

Oliver, Stephen (2018) 'Review: Shazia Mirza at Newcastle Stand', *North East Theatre Guide*, 25 February. Available at: http://www.northeasttheatreguide.co.uk/2018/02/review-shazia-mirza-at-newcastle-stand.html (accessed 29 August 2019).

Quirk, Sophie (2015) *Why Stand-Up Matters: How Comedians Manipulate and Influence*, London: Bloomsbury.

Quirk, Sophie (2018) *The Politics of British Stand-Up Comedy: The New Alternative*, London: Palgrave Macmillan.

Rattan, Chris (2018) 'Gadsby's Nanette Isn't Genius - It's Something Else Entirely', *NOW*, 28 June. Available at: https://nowtoronto.com/movies/reviews/netflix-hannah-gadsby-nanette/ (accessed 17 July 2019).

Romano, Aja (2018) 'Why Hannah Gadsby's Searing Comedy Special Nanette Has Upended Comedy For Good', *Vox.com*, 5 July. Available at: https://www.vox.com/culture/2018/7/5/17527478/hannah-gadsby-nanette-comedy (accessed 10 July 2018).

Shouse, Eric and Patrice Oppliger (2012) 'Sarah Is Magic: The (Post-Gendered?) Comedy of Sarah Silverman', *Comedy Studies*, 3(2), 201–216.

Telegraph (2001) 'Muslim Makes Bin Laden a Laughing Matter', 18 October. Available at: https://www.telegraph.co.uk/news/uknews/1359751/Muslim-makes-bin-Laden-a-laughing-matter.html (accessed 10 July 2019).

Tomsett, Eleanor (2017) '21st Century Fumerist: Bridget Christie and the Backlash against Female Comedy', *Comedy Studies*, 8(1), 57–67.

Tomsett, Eleanor (2018) 'Positives and Negatives: Reclaiming the Female Body and Self-Deprecation in Stand-up Comedy', *Comedy Studies*, 9(1), 6–18.

Traister, Rebecca (2018) *Good and Mad: The Revolutionary Power of Women's Anger*, New York: Simon and Schuster.

Troth, Izzy (2018) 'Shazia Mirza: "I Don't Think About the Audience Anymore. I Just Go Ahead and Do It"', *Cherwell.org*, 28 March. Available at: https://cherwell.org/2018/03/28/shazia-mirza-i-dont-think-about-the-audience-anymore-i-just-go-ahead-and-do-it/ (accessed 16 July 2018).

West, Lindy (2016) *Shrill*, US Comedy Web Series – Broadway Video, producer Dannah Shinder, based on *Shrill: Notes from a Loud Woman*, New York: Hachette Books.

7

AFTERWORD

The artists featured within *Women in Performance: Repurposing Failure* are creating work at the cutting edge of experimental theatre and performance practice. Many have contributed to what I will call the 'rebirth' of identity politics while simultaneously querying the hegemonic drive to label and categorise. They exploit self-reflexive performance practices associated with a postmodern praxis of performing failure whilst refusing to be stymied by the postmodern tendency to '*reduce all others to the economy of the same*' (Irigaray 1985: 74 original emphasis). They borrow techniques associated with performing failure or employ a form of radical negativity, which robs the subjugated value of associated shame. After José Muñoz and Sara Jane Bailes, their exploitation of failure is 'generative' and optimistic (Muñoz 2009; Bailes 2011). For example, they: construct vulnerability as form of 'radical softness'; draw upon anger as a powerful catalyst for change; and discover a sense of joy in being 'othered'. They share a sense of euphoria in identifying as non-binary or diversely constituted 'women' and hold gendered strictures of behaviour up for ridicule. In the live moment of performance they shrug off the burden of oppression and insist upon a progressive way forward. They share stories about prejudicial and discriminatory behaviour but ultimately refuse to identify as victims. Like Amelia Jones they refuse the idea that we are 'post-identity' or 'post-race' (Jones 2012). The artists discussed have used performance-making as an act of self-care; they have created alternative, heterotopic spaces-within-spaces to draw attention to the exclusionary nature of space and plundered what Lorde has called 'a well-stocked arsenal of anger' to reconfigure stereotypes of 'angry black women' and 'angry feminists'. They have interrogated notions of gender fixity and fluidity and pushed back against constructions of trans★ people as agonised or unhappy; they have used irony as a form of satire, rendering their own ideological position inscrutable. They have borrowed postmodern form and yet identify with recognised identity categories. This presents a theoretical dilemma because, as Hill Collins and Bilge have pointed out, '[f]or those who embrace postmodern anti-categorical thinking, intersectionality's identity conceptions are essentialist and exclusionary' (Hill Collins and Bilge 2016: 100). *Women in Performance: Repurposing Failure* sets out to interrogate this tension and map contemporary theories of subjectivity on to postmodern praxis. Lavender has described subjects as being 'diversely centred' after postmodernism, and argues that in the current moment we are participating in a post-postmodern 'age of engagement' (Lavender 2016: 21). This book interrogates what it might mean to be 'diversely centred' and contemplates what the poststructuralist and postmodern turn might have leant but also taken away from feminism, gender studies and performance practice.

I want to close by sharing a series of images from performances that fell outside the parameters of the main chapters. These images chime with the main concerns of the book because they each represent a provocative attempt at an impossible task or experiment with amateurism in a creative and ingenious manner. They resist gravity, gravitas and virtuosity, hinting at an intangible and rarely articulated experience relating to the performativity of gender. As with examples from Chapters one to six, they are astute, complex and arresting. My first image is taken from Curious' *Best Before End* (2013), which I saw at Warwick Arts Centre, Warwick University. This was a sensual and meditative piece of performance about death. Helen Paris contemplated whether it was possible to 'say all the things that need to be said before it's too late'. Promotional copy revealed the performance to be about 'failing and falling with a touch of fermenting, it's about finding the right words when the words are hard to find' (Artsadmin 2013). Towards the close of the performance Paris stands immobile, centre stage. The stage is in darkness apart from the central figure illuminated under an intense white spotlight. Paris wears a floor-length, black evening gown and stares out at the audience with a sense of trepidation. Female vocals harmonise over the PA system and she begins to descend slowly towards the floor. During the blackout she has been attached to a machine, an invisible stretcher, which conveys her very gradually and barely perceptibly towards the surface of the stage. Despite the pull of gravity she remains in the same upright position as before, arms held neatly by her sides, as if already seized by rigor mortis. Paris remains composed, and yet the muscles in her arms judder with the strain of staying up. They flicker almost imperceptibly, as if resisting the challenge to play dead, insisting upon her liveness. This graceful departure acts as a reminder of the 'fall' Paris mentions at the outset of the show. She spoke of the body's instinct to survive:

> This is what happens when you fall down slowly, as you must. Your arms may fly up, they may fly out. They try and stop your fall. But you mustn't. You know you mustn't. You know you have to go – it's time.
>
> *(Curious 2013)*

The tiny, juddering muscles in Paris' arms echo her description of the instinct to survive. She draws upon her training in an attempt to remain absolutely still so that she can accurately mimic death, and yet her body betrays her and evidences its instinct to survive. This image was beautiful for its figuration of life lived on the vertical and death on the horizontal. Life represents an arduous struggle against gravity, each undertaking framed by the potential danger of the fall.

My second image is taken from Hester Chillingworth's *Shorty* (2016a), which I witnessed at Chisenhale Dance Space, London. Chillingworth identifies as non-binary, and has described Shorty as a 'deconstructed drag-child'. Promotional copy reveals that 'the solo show looks at the position of the non-binary child, and the relationship with the mind when the body is under attack. It champions the not-quite, the slight and the awkward' (Chillingworth 2016b). At the beginning of the show Chillingworth welcomes the audience as their adult self and expresses their affinity for the way children 'tell it like it is – they are unadulterated, quite literally'. They leave the stage and return a few minutes later as 'Shorty'. Shorty is dressed in a pair of white shorts, white three-quarter-length socks, black Mary Jane shoes, a black wig, large glasses and a red sports top. Shorty carries a rucksack and a lunchbox and tells the audience, 'I'm being picked up in an hour. Thanks for looking after me.' Shorty pulls a number of different props from the rucksack, including drinking bottles and a P-Buzz trumpet. They ask the audience how old they think they are and pose teasers about the terms 'in the sticks/styx' and 'status quo'. They invent point-scoring games and gratuitously gloat when they win. One of the most arresting moments for me

FIGURE 7.1 Helen Paris falls very slowly in *Best Before End* (2013), Curious
Photograph: Richard Davenport

came when Shorty performed an extended twirl accompanied by an invitation for the audience to decide whether they would identify them as a 'crunchy' or 'smooth' jar of peanut butter. After the spin Shorty demands, 'just from looking, you've got to choose one'. Audience members shout out 'smooth' and 'crunchy' and are chastised. Shorty shouts, 'don't say *different ones*, you have to *choose one*!' Shorty continues to spin, but comes to rest with their back to the audience. They mount a dialogue between Shorty and the adult carer, Chillingworth. Chillingworth asks, 'are you still talking about peanut butter? Are you sure you're not talking about something else?' to which Shorty replies 'yes'. Chillingworth repeatedly asks Shorty whether they mean to 'see which *one you are*' as being about peanut butter 'or about *something else?*' Shorty continues to insist that they are talking about peanut butter although an element of uncertainty has crept into their voice. Along with an account of being told to leave both male and female toilets, this scene offers an affecting insight into the experience of the non-binary child/adult and draws attention to the arbitrary and tyrannical nature of a binary gender system. The child-like conceit of swapping voices 'behind the backs' of the audience is amusing whilst providing a sobering insight into the mind of an unhappy child struggling to explain why they experience gender tyranny as they do.

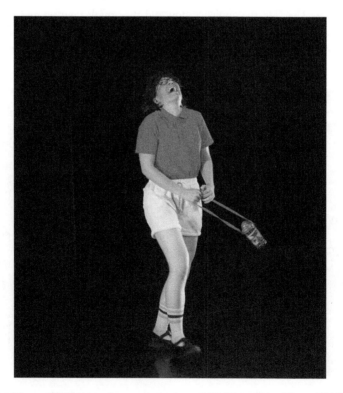

FIGURE 7.2 Hester Chillingworth appears as drag-child 'Shorty' in *Shorty* (2016) Photograph: Ivan Denia

My final image is taken from *miles & miles* by Haranczak/Navarre, a company led by Karen Christopher. This piece was created with Sophie Grodin and I caught productions at the Yard Theatre and Chisenhale Dance Space, London, in 2015 and 2016. *miles & miles* is a meditative and open performance. It presents a number of images and fragments, inviting a reading in relation to a fear of heights, falling and friendship. Promotional copy illustrates that,

> *miles & miles* is a performance positioned at the edge of a landscape. It asks the questions: How do we continue once we've lost our position? How do we accommodate ourselves on shaky ground and prepare for the uncertainty still to come? How do we become intimate with the inevitable fall?
>
> *(Christopher 2015)*

Climbing, balancing and falling feature throughout, with Christopher balancing on small blocks of wood as she mimes falling through the air; balancing precariously atop a stool and playing a scene from *Butch Cassidy and the Sundance Kid* in which the characters tremble on the lip of a precipice. I was deeply affected by the opening image, which presented multiple opportunities for analysis. Grodin and Christopher stood side by side. They were dressed in identical costumes of black trousers, sleeveless black tops and robust black Dr Marten shoes. Each had a different rope end tied around their waist. The thick rope was fed into and looped over a pulley above their heads. They stood side by side, balancing on top of a wooden shelf, which in turn is perched on top of a small wooden block. At the beginning they stand motionless, shifting weight slightly to maintain balance, straining as they attempt to correct the distribution of weight. Their first words are 'rescue is unwanted, unwarranted and will not be accepted' (Haranczak/Navarre 2016). I was taken with this image for a number of reasons. Firstly, it was fascinating to watch performers cope with the real time task of balancing. Secondly, it was arresting to see two women of different ages standing side by side tied with rope. Their appearance suggested the kind of companionship rarely seen in mainstream popular culture, a pragmatic female friendship based on positive mutual support and assistance. Thirdly, the image was freighted with narrative potential, it invited the audience to question how the two women might have come to find themselves in this scenario; it provided a tantalising image of what will come after. The performers chose to close down some narrative possibilities with their phrase: 'rescue is unwanted, unwarranted and will not be accepted' announcing self-sufficiency and even hinting the women may have consciously engineered the scenario. I found the spectacle of an uncited yet profound bond of friendship incredibly moving in the context of social and political uncertainty and existential 'shaky ground'.

These images have stayed with me and provide a valuable reminder of the potential of performance to act as a corrective to misogynistic and homophobic constructions of gender. Women, trans★ and non-binary people are particularly oppressed by the reductive binary system; when they do appear they are constructed as if their sexuality or gender identity is the most crucial aspect of their being. These images, along with the work of the other artists in the book, serve as a reminder of the joyful, generative acts of resistance to be found in countering received ideas and images. This work is situated in a climate of precarity and hostility and yet it draws upon reserves of humour, impertinence and controversy to argue for a strategic essentialism couched in a self-reflexive mode of performance.

Bibliography

Artsadmin (2013) 'Curious: Best Before End', Promotional Material. *Artsadmin Website.* Available at: https://www.artsadmin.co.uk/media/documents/promoters/Curious_BBE. pdf (accessed 4 September 2019).

Bailes, Sara Jane (2011) *Performance Theatre and the Poetics of Failure: Forced Entertainment, Goat Island and Elevator Repair Service*, London and New York: Routledge.

Chillingworth, Hester (2016a) *Shorty*. Touring Production.

Chillingworth, Hester (2016b) 'Shorty', *Chillingworth Website.* Available at: https://www. hesterchillingworth.com/index.php/projects/shorty/ (accessed 4 September 2019).

Christopher, Karen (2015) 'miles & miles', Karen Christopher website. Available at: http:// www.karenchristopher.co.uk/performance.1.10.html (accessed 4 September 2019).

Curious (2013) *Best Before End.* Touring Production. Available at: https://www.youtube. com/watch?v=orMdLrXM230 (accessed 4 September 2019).

Haranczak/Navarre (2016) *miles & miles.* Touring production.

Hill Collins, Patricia and Sirma Bilge (2016) *Intersectionality*, Cambridge: Polity Press.

Irigaray, Luce (1985) *This Sex Which is Not One*, translated by Catherine Porter with Carolyn Burke, New York: Cornell University Press.

Jones, Amelia (2012) *Seeing Differently: A History and Theory of Identification and the Visual Arts*, Abingdon: Routledge.

Lavender, Andy (2016) *Performing in the 21st Century: Theatres of Engagement*, Abingdon: Routledge.

Muñoz, José (2009) *Cruising Utopia: the Then and There of Queer Futurity*, New York: New York University Press.

INDEX

Note: Page numbers in italic denote images. Page numbers in the format 73n5 refer to endnotes.